GODWIN-HILL

and

RELATED FAMILIES

by

Ruth Godwin Gadbury

sketches

Mary Word Hood

Preface

When my father, Enoch Godwin, was about 75 years old, he expressed his desire that the family information that he had be duplicated so that all of his children could have copies of the known facts of their ancestry. This we did, but that basic information aroused a desire to know more about the ancestors and also to preserve all the records in a more permanent form.

Searches have been made in several states, including Arkansas, Mississippi, Tennessee, North Carolina, and Virginia, plus many trips within Texas, where records were gleaned in courthouses, cemeteries, archives, libraries, and family Bibles. Members of the family have willingly contributed information and photographs. Several researchers have abstracted records for me and other genealogists working on related lines have been generous in sharing information. For all of this help I am deeply grateful.

The primary purpose has been to trace the family lines from the oldest ancestors on whom records could be obtained through the present generations of the Enoch and Nollie Godwin family, including some collateral lines.

Most enjoyable have been the visits with lovely relatives, many of whom I was meeting for the first time. Friendships have grown and correspondences have continued over the years.

I am impressed that we have an ancestry to be proud of. Our forebearers, like the present families, were a freedom-loving, self-reliant, and independent people.

My greatest regret is not being able to extend the family lines farther back in time, though considerable effort was made to do so. Hopefully, someone in the future will use this work as a springboard to further trace the ancestors.

Sincere thanks go to all who have made this book possible, those who provided information, pictures, and other support. Especially do I appreciate Mary Hood's delightful sketches and Betty Poe's capable typing of the manuscript.

The fulfillment that comes of associating with the authors of our past and the satisfaction of preserving this family knowledge for our descendants and relatives will be the reward of our labors.

Ruth Gadbury

June 1980

Numeration:
    Roman numerals indicate the generations in order, beginning with our first known ancestor of each family line discussed. Arabic numerals indicate the order of children in each family, if known.

iii

Ancestor Chart

Enoch Godwin
B 2 Mar. 1886 Hunt Co., TX
M 16 Aug. 1908
D 22 Oct. 1971 Lometa, TX

John Allen Godwin
B 27 Jan. 1854 Clark Co., Ark.
M 15 Oct. 1874
D 23 Oct. 1932 Lometa, TX

Liva Ann Smith
B 11 Oct. 1856 Calhoun Co., Ala.
D 28 Apr. 1935 Lometa, TX

John Allen Godwin, Sr.
B 1812-1815 NC
M by 1835
D 1 Jun. 1853 Clark Co., Ark.

Aletha Spencer
B 18 Oct. 1814 Montgomery Co., NC
D 10 Feb. 1899 Mills, Co., TX

Enoch Smith
B 19 May 1806 SC
M 22 Dec. 1835
D 10 Jun. 1885 Hopkins Co., TX

Jane Moore
B 23 Dec. 1814 SC
D 29 Oct. 1885 Hopkins Co., TX

Allen Godwin
B 11 Mar. 1783 NC
D 28 Aug. 1872, MS

Polly Green

Seymore Spencer
B 1778-82 NC
D 1847 MS

Tabitha Bennett

James Smith
B 9 Jun. 1751 VA
D 11 Sep. 1840 SC

Elizabeth
D 11 Dec. 1810 SC

Aaron Moore

Bettie

William Spencer
Hannah (Suggs?)
Solomon Bennett
Thomas Smith
Elizabeth Fleming

Nollie Bell Hill
B 10 Feb. 1885 Coleman Co., TX
D 13 Jan. 1974 Ozona, TX

Pleasant G. Hill
B 28 Aug. 1859 Tippah Co., Miss
M 16 Aug. 1883
D 20 Jul. 1948 Brownwood, TX

Kitty Bell Bishop
B 11 Mar. 1866 Hardeman Co., TN
D 21 Jun. 1889 Ft. Davis, TX

James Hill
B 26 Aug. 1825 Jefferson Co., TN
M by 1852
D 16 Apr. 1918 Mills Co., TX

L. Parolee Godwin
B 25 Dec. 1836 McNairy Co., TN
D 10 Mar. 1909 Comanche, TX

Alvin Bishop
B 20 Sep. 1821 NC
M 21 Oct. 1841
D 14 Sep. 1888

Mary Jane Cox
B 13 Sep. 1826 TN
D 8 Jan. 1880 Comanche Co., TX

Elijah Hill
B 1895 Jefferson Co.,TN
D 1857 McNairy Co., TN

Rebecca Koffman
B 1793
D 1897 McNairy Co.,TN

Allen Godwin
B 11 Mar. 1788 NC
D 28 Aug. 1872 MS

Martha

Asa Bishop
B 1790, VA
D 1864 Hardeman Co., TN

Susan Stevens
D by 1850

Eli Cox
B 1786
D 1860

Sarah Brown
D by 1836

Daniel Hill
Ellen Nodding
Daniel Koffman
Elizabeth
Allen Godwin
Fanney

Contents

GODWIN CHART

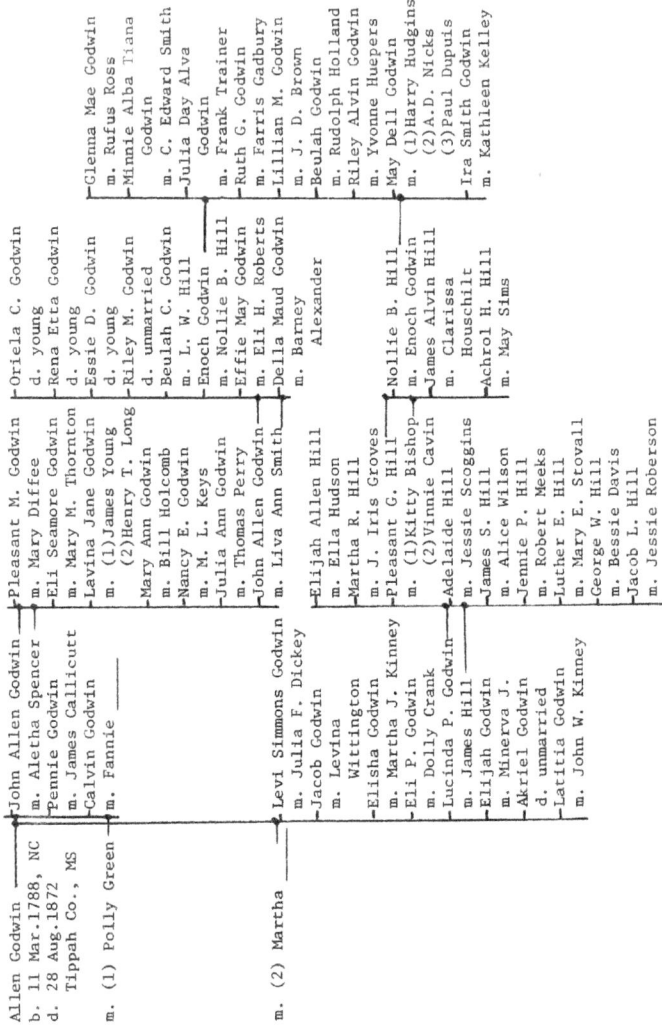

I

Allen Godwin
b. 11 Mar.1788, NC
d. 28 Aug.1872
Tippah Co., MS
m. (1) Polly Green

m. (2) Martha

II

John Allen Godwin
m. Aletha Spencer
Pennie Godwin
m. James Callicutt
Calvin Godwin
m. Fannie

Levi Simmons Godwin
m. Julia F. Dickey
Jacob Godwin
m. Levina Wittington
Elisha Godwin
Martha J. Kinney
Eli P. Godwin
m. Dolly Crank
Lucinda P. Godwin
m. James Hill
Elijah Godwin
Minerva J.
d. unmarried
Latitia Godwin
m. John W. Kinney

III

Pleasant M. Godwin
m. Mary Diffee
Eli Seamore Godwin
m. Mary M. Thornton
Lavina Jane Godwin
m. (1)James Young
   (2)Henry T. Long
Mary Ann Godwin
m. Bill Holcomb
Nancy E. Godwin
m. M. L. Keys
Julia Ann Godwin
m. Thomas Perry
John Allen Godwin
m. Liva Ann Smith

Elijah Allen Hill
m. Ella Hudson
Martha R. Hill
m. J. Iris Groves
Pleasant G. Hill
m. (1)Kitty Bishop
   (2)Vinnie Cavin
Adelaide Hill
m. Jessie Scoggins
James S. Hill
m. Alice Wilson
Jennie P. Hill
m. Robert Meeks
Luther E. Hill
m. Mary E. Stovall
George W. Hill
m. Bessie Davis
Jacob L. Hill
m. Jessie Roberson

IV

Oriela C. Godwin
d. young
Rena Etta Godwin
d. young
Essie D. Godwin
d. young
d. unmarried
Beulah C. Godwin
m. L. W. Hill
Enoch Godwin
m. Nollie B. Hill
Effie May Godwin
m. Eli H. Roberts
Della Maud Godwin
m. Barney Alexander

Nollie B. Hill
m. Enoch Godwin
James Alvin Hill
m. Clarissa Houschilt
Achrol H. Hill
m. May Sims

V

Glenna Mae Godwin
m. Rufus Ross
Minnie Alba Tiana Godwin
m. C. Edward Smith
Julia Day Alva Godwin
m. Frank Trainer
Ruth G. Godwin
m. Farris Gadbury
Lillian M. Godwin
m. J. D. Brown
Beulah Godwin
m. Rudolph Holland
Riley Alvin Godwin
m. Yvonne Huepers
May Dell Godwin
m. (1)Harry Hudgins
   (2)A.D. Nicks
   (3)Paul Dupuis
Ira Smith Godwin
m. Kathleen Kelley

I

Allen Godwin

The earliest known Godwin ancestor of our line was Rev. Allen Godwin, a Baptist minister in his later life, born 11 March 1788, North Carolina, a year before that territory became a state. He died 28 Aug. 1872 near Blue Mountain, Tippah Co., Miss.

Allen was married to Polly Green in February 1809, the application for bond dated 15 Feb. 1809 in Cumberland Co., N.C., but Allen gave Johnston Co., N.C., as his home on a deed soon thereafter. David Beaman who had married Silvy Godwin 12 Nov. 1800, in Johnston County, went on Allen's marriage bond.

In Cumberland Co., N.C. Deed Bk. 26, P. 387 there is a record of Allen Goddin of Johnston Co., N.C. buying a tract of land from David Beaman on 18 Oct. 1809. This land was "near Green's line" with one testator being Edward Green, possibly of Polly's family.

In the 1810 census of Cumberland Co., N.C. Allen and Polly are given as between 16 and 26 with one girl under 10. At this time nearly all the people in the state worked at agriculture with tobacco being the leading crop as well as the commodity most used for money. Cotton was second in importance. North Carolina had fewer slaves and more small farms than any other southern state. Tools were primitive and transportation poor.

Allen enlisted in the War of 1812 on 1 Oct. 1814 in Co. G. of the 5th Reg. of N.C. Militia, Infantry. This was soon after the British had occupied Washington, D.C., burning the Capitol and other public buildings. But the British fleet had been driven back from Baltimore in September, 1814, the engagement that inspired Frances Scott Key to write the words to "The Star-Spangled Banner." Allen's enlistment lasted for only 7 days, so near was the end of the war.

He is listed in the Cumberland Co., N.C. Tax List for 1815 as a land owner, but no poll is listed, so he probably did not live there.

A Land Grant, #2157 for 150A., from the State of North Carolina to Allen Godwin in March 1816 in the County of Johnston, N.C. describes the borders of the land as by "his own land" and bordering James Godwin on the county line. This was on the south side of Black Creek on Colours Branch in southwestern Johnston County.

Other Godwins owning land in this vicinity were

William, Wilie, and Elizabeth, plus James mentioned above.
Allen and William Godwin witnessed a James Godwin deed in
1817. Wilie was the son of James, as shown by James' will
in 1855, Johnston Co., N.C.
   Many Godwins lived in N.C. in the 1800's and the name
is still prominent there, with one village being named
Godwin.
   In 1820 census of Washington Co., Ga., p. 136, Alan
Godwin is listed with he and his wife 26-45, 2 boys under
10 and 3 girls under 10, also 3 slaves. Soon after this
he must have lost his wife and 2 of the girls. In Washington County, he was beside, or with, Elias Godwin and
his wife, an older couple over 45 with one boy under 10,
6 girls under 10 and one girl 10-16, also 5 slaves. Elias
appears to be the son of Thomas Godwin of Johnston Co.,
N.C. whose will was probated Nov. 1807, naming, among
other children, Elias and Ely, names that Allen also gave
his children. The relation to Allen, however, is not
known.
   Allen Godwin is listed as a fortunate drawer in the
1821 Land Lottery of Georgia. He was of O'Neil's Militia
Dist., Wayne Co., Ga. and drew Land Lot No. 148, Sec. 1,
Dooley Co., Ga. This lottery was for lands acquired from
the Creek Indians, laid off in May 1821.
   The lottery record shows Allen living in Wayne Co.,
Ga. where a Jacob Godwin is listed in the 1820 census.
Allen named a son born in 1827--Jacob.
   By 1830 Allen is in Montgomery Co., N.C. census, p.62,
East of Pee Dee and Yadkin Rivers and has remarried. He
is now 40-50 with his wife 20-30, 3 boys under 5, 2 boys
10-15 and one girl 10-15. The three children 10-15 were
by his first wife Polly.
   Living nearby in Montgomery Co., N.C. is Pleasant
Callicutt and in adjoining Moore County is James Callicutt.
Allen's oldest daughter Pennie later married a James Callicutt, but Montgomery County records were destroyed in a
courthouse fire.
   Come 1840 and Allen Godwin lives in McNairy Co., Tenn.
still listed in the census as 40-50 with his wife 30-40,
with seven children. The children's birthplaces show that
they made the move to Tenn. between 1834 and 1836.
   They were in Tippah Co., Miss. by 1848 and are listed
there in the census of 1850, their nearest neighbor being
James Callicutt and Pennie his wife. Pleasant Callicutt
lived nearby also.
   Many land transactions are recorded in Tippah County,
Miss. for Allen Godwin. He first bought land there 10 Nov.
1842 and added to his holdings from time to time. There
are several gift deeds "for love and affection" from Allen

and his wife Martha to their married children.

Up to this time Allen had listed his occupation as a farmer, but in 1860, still in Tippah Co., Miss., he is listed as a Baptist Minister, age 62 (actually 72). He is said to have been the first moderator of the Tippah-Benton Baptist Association when it was organized in 1860. He performed the marriage ceremonies for some of his grandchildren.

Among the rolling hills and fertile bottoms a few miles west of Blue Mountain, Mississippi, Allen Godwin lived out his life in a community surrounded by the families of Deen, Hill, Callicutt, Spencer, and his own married children. So many Deens lived there that the community was at one time called the Deentown Community. The country church where Allen may have preached is Macedonia Church, though sometimes called Deentown Church also.

Allen Godwin died apparently without a valid will and Daniel Hunt was appointed administrator 1 Aug. 1873, Tippah Co., Miss. Minute Bk., Chancery Court, p. 464, confirmed p. 471. The cemetery where Allen's stone still stands is now abandoned on a wooded vine-choked hillside beside a logging road on land leased to a lumber company. The stone reads:

Allen Godwin
Born Mar. 11, 1788
Died Aug. 28, 1872

A light from our household is gone
A voice we loved is still
A place is vacant in our heart
That never can be filled

I.   Allen Godwin m. (1) Polly Green, Feb. 1809, Cumberland Co., N.C.
     Children: (first marriage)
     II-1.   John Allen Godwin, b. ca. 1815, N.C.
     II-2.   Pennie Godwin, b. ca. 1818, Ga.
     II-3.   Calvin Godwin, b. 1815-20, Ga.

             m. (2) Martha_____ by 1825, N.C.
     Children: (second marriage)
     II-4.   Levi Simmons Godwin, b. ca. 1825, N.C.
     II-5.   Jacob G. Godwin, b. ca. 1827, N.C.
     II-6.   Elisha H. Godwin, b. 1832, N.C. or Ala.
     II-7.   Eli P. Godwin, b. ca. 1834, N.C. or Tenn.

3

II-8. Lucinda Parolee Godwin, b. 1836, Tenn.
II-9. Elijah Godwin, b. ca. 1840, Tenn.
II-10. Akrial (Achrol) H. Godwin, b. ca. 1842, Tenn.
II-11. Latitia F. Godwin, b. ca. 1849, Miss.
        (The boys in the last family were called twin
        names: Levi-Eli, Jake-Ake, Elisha-Elijah.)
JOHN ALLEN GODWIN, SR.
II-1. John Allen Godwin, Sr., son of Allen Godwin and
        Polly Green, b. 1815-1820, N.C., d. 1 June 1853,
        Clark Co., Ark., m. Aletha Spencer around 1835.
        Children:
  III-1. Pleasant Marion Godwin
  III-2. Eli Seamore Godwin
  III-3. Lavina Jane Godwin
  III-4. Mary Ann Godwin
  III-5. Nancy Elizabeth Godwin
  III-6. Margret Pennah Godwin
  III-7. Catherine Godwin
  III-8. Ellen Godwin
  III-9. Julia Ann Godwin
  III-10. John Allen Godwin

        This family comprises the next chapter.
PENNIE GODWIN
II-2. Pennie Godwin, b. about 1818 in Georgia or N.C. the
        daughter of Allen Godwin and Polly Green, both of
        North Carolina., m. James Callicutt about 1833 and
        lived in Tippah Co., Miss. James was b. about 1810-
        1820 in N.C. James and Pennie are listed in the
        1840 through 1870 census of Tippah County. In 1860
        they had amassed a tidy fortune but by 1870 this
        had been drastically reduced by the ravages of the
        War. Also they had moved from the Ripley area to
        Salem in northwest Tippah County by 1870. Censuses
        show them to have these children:
  III-1. Jane Callicutt, b. ca. 1834, Miss.
  III-2. Pleasant Callicutt, b. ca. 1839, Miss.
  III-3. Thomas Callicutt, b. ca. 1842, Miss.
  III-4. Sarah Callicutt, b. ca. 1845, Miss.
  III-5. Ezekiel T. Callicutt, b. ca. 1847, Miss.
  III-6. Bird A. Callicutt, b. ca. 1852, Miss.
  III-7. Calvin J. Callicutt, b. ca. 1855, Miss.

  III-3. Thomas Callicutt, son of James Callicutt and
        Pennie Godwin, b. ca. 1842, Miss., d. 7 July
        1899, buried Blue Mountain Cemetery, Miss.,
        m. Mollie _____, b. ca. 1852, Miss.
    IV-1. Minnie Callicutt
    IV-2. Willie Callicutt, b. 30 Dec. 1872, d. 27
          June 1947, m. Emma Swain 15 Dec. 1895.
4

V-1. Haywood Callicutt
V-2. Lawrence Callicutt m. Edwina Hardin.
V-3. Edwin Callicutt
IV-3. Thomas J. Callicutt, 1876-1948, m. Lula
 Alvis, 1876-1960, on 25 April 1900.
 V-1. Thomas Alvis Callicutt, 1901-1969, m. Ella
  Lorene Ellis.
 V-2. Lee Callicutt, 1903-1974.
 V-3. Josephene Callicutt

III-4. Sarah E. Callicutt, b. ca. 1845 Miss., m. William Downs 21 Sept. 1860.

III-5. Ezekiel (Zeke) Callicutt, b. ca. 1847, Miss.,
 m. Isabell Gibson 15 Oct. 1873. Isabell d. by
 1879.
IV-1. Rosa Lee Callicutt
IV-2. George T. Callicutt
IV-3. Martha B. Callicutt

III-6. Bird A. Callicutt, b. 19 Apr. 1852, Miss., d.
 5 Jan 1894, m. Jennie Smith 21 Nov. 1872,
 Tippah Co., Miss. Jennie b. 20 Dec. 1850, d.
 11 Jan. 1938. Lived in Tippah Co., Miss.
IV-1. Belle Callicutt, b. 6 Oct. 1873, d. 3 Feb.
 1894, unmarried.
IV-2. Viola Callicutt, 1876-1968, m. Joe A. Goudy
 1 Dec. 1895.
 V-1. H. D. Goudy
 V-2. Claud Goudy
IV-3. Mary Laura Callicutt, b. 28 July 1877, d.
 13 May 1966, m. James T. (Jim) Godwin 18
 Feb. 1896. Jim b. 6 Sept. 1878, d. 9 June
 1945.
 V-1. Mamie Lee Godwin
 V-2. Mattie Bell Godwin
 V-3. Birdie Lou Godwin
 V-4. Lottie Fay Godwin
 V-5. Ine Mae Godwin
 V-6. Iva Mae Godwin
 V-7. James F. Godwin
 V-8. Robert P. Godwin
IV-4. Lura Callicutt m. Bruce Goudy 25 Jan. 1899.
 V-1. Ernest Goudy
 V-2. Rayburn Goudy
 V-3. Leona Goudy
 V-4. R. V. Goudy
 V-5. Roy Goudy
 V-6. Lester Goudy
 V-7. Bertie Goudy

IV-5. Sallie C. Callicutt, 1883-1951, m. Charlie
    Birdsong 23 Aug 1902. Charlie, 1881-1938.
  V-1. Wardie Birdsong
  V-2. Ruby Birdsong
  V-3. Jennie Birdsong
  V-4. Manning Birdsong
  V-5. Charles Birdsong
  V-6. Sallie Birdsong
  V-7. Robert Birdsong
  V-8. Margret Birdsong
IV-6. Calvin E. Callicutt, b. 27 Sept. 1893, d. 13
    July 1898, 4 yrs.
IV-7. David Callicutt m. Ethel Vanhoozer 18 July
    1907.
  V-1. Vinson Callicutt
IV-8. Docie Callicutt m. J. Oscar Reeves 18 June
    1908.
  V-1. Harold Reeves
  V-2. Ralph Reeves
  V-3. Mary Ruth Reeves
  V-4. Oscar Perry Reeves
  V-5. Annie R. Reeves
IV-9. Jennie Callicutt m. J. Oscar Reeves after
    Docie's death and raised her sisters children,
    no children of her own.

CALVIN G. GODWIN

II-3. Calvin G. Godwin, b. 1815-1820, Georgia or N.C.,
son of Allen Godwin and Polly Green of N.C. Calvin
was a cripple who lived with his father until in
his 20's, was with his sister Lucinda Parolee Hill
and family in 1870, spent some time with his nephew, Bird A. Callicutt, in the 1870's, and by 1880
at 62+ years of age had married Fannie_____. The
census takers caught them twice that year. In June
Calvin is listed as a farm laborer with wife Fannie,
then later as a basket maker, 62, b. Ga. and wife
Fannie, 48, b. N.C. Fannie is keeping house, both
living with a young man, William R. Riley, and his
son, John B. Riley.

After Allen Godwin died in 1872, Calvin wrote
letters to Texas in July of 1878 to children of his
full brother, John Allen Godwin, asking them to come
back to Mississippi and put in for their part of
Allen Godwin's estate. Calvin had not received his
part and hoped they would file a law suit and he
could testify. We found no record of a contest of
any will, but the letters that Calvin wrote have
been carefully preserved now over 100 years.

In his letter to Lavina Jane Godwin Long he said,

"Your father was my own brother and his children feels near to me. . . I have fondled you on my knees when you was a baby and so I have Marion and Eli and I wish very much to see you all. . . May the Lord ever bless you and yours,"
(signed) C. G. Godwin

To John Allen Godwin, Jr. he writes his plan for them to "brake" his father's will and gives directions for getting to Ripley, Miss., "When you get to Ripley enquire the way to Bird A. Calicotts. He lives near the Oxford Road due west from Ripley about five miles. If you are a good walker you can walk it in an hour or a little more. . . James Callicott is well.
Farewell, C. G. Godwin"

LEVI SIMMONS GODWIN

II-4. Levi Simmons Godwin, b. ca. 1825, N.C., son of Allen Godwin and his second wife, Martha, d. 1886, m. Julia Frances Dickey who was b. ca. 1833, Georgia, daughter of Joseph and Sarah Dickey of near Montgomery, Ala., where Levi and Julia resided until about 1858, removing then to Tippah Co., Miss. near Salem.
Levi Godwin enlisted in the Confederate cause 9 Aug. 1862 at Orizaba, Miss. as a Pvt. in Co. D, 7th Miss. Cavalry. He is listed as a courier and appears on a report of Prisoners of War surrendered May 29, 1865 at La Grange, Tenn. to Brig. Gen. J. P. C. Shanks and was parolled the same date. (This was over six weeks after Lee had surrendered to Grant on 9 April 1865.)

III-1. Amanda Godwin, 1848-1923, m. Asa Yopp.
III-2. Samuel Allen Godwin, 1850-1929, m. (1) Fannie A. Dugger, 1846-1900, and (2) Cora Cobb Dickerson.
III-3. William Franklin (Bill) Godwin, 1852-1923, b. Ala., m. (1) Elizabeth Whittington, m. (2) Mary Clark Moore Dean.
III-4. Sarah Elizabeth (Sally) Godwin, 1854-1944, b. Ala., m. James Allen Godwin, 1853-1893, son of Elisha H. Godwin and therefore a cousin. (More details in Elisha Godwin family.)
III-5. Mary Jane Godwin, b. 1856-58, Ala., m. Thomas Jackson Deen.
III-6. Jacob Willis (Jake) Godwin, b. 20 Sept. 1860, Miss., d. 2 Mar. 1927, m. Olive (Ollie) Smith 20 Dec. 1893. Ollie b. 22 May 1871, d. 3 May 1951. (Children not especially in order)

Godwin-Hill and Related Families

IV-1. Jacob Willis Godwin, Jr.
IV-2. Mabel Godwin
IV-3. Katie Sue Godwin, b. ca. 1895.
IV-4. Julia Godwin, b. ca. 1896.
IV-5. Harvey L. Godwin, b. ca. 1898.

III-7. Lucinda Parolee Godwin, b. 23 Sept. 1864, Miss.,
d. 16 June 1943, m. George Washington Deen, li.
Blue Mountain, Miss.
IV-1. William Pearl Deen, 1881-1967, m. Myrtie L.
Hill, li. Kress, Texas. (Treated further in
Elijah A. Hill family.)
IV-2. Lucy Deen, 1883-1955, m. Will Hill, son of
Samuel Hill, li. Ripley, Miss.
IV-3. Leondras Ray Deen, 1887-1967, li. Blue Moun-
tain, Miss.
IV-4. Otho W. Deen, 1888-1968, li. Corinth, Miss.
IV-5. Luther Baars Deen, 1890-1935.
IV-6. Julia Deen, b. 1891, m. Henry Megginson, li.
Myrtle, Miss.
IV-7. Effie Watson Deen, 1893-1975, m. Lester
Jones, li. Chalybeate and Ripley, Miss.
IV-8. Joe L. Deen, 1895, li. Kress, Texas, later
Tuckerman, Ark.
IV-9. Avie Lee Deen, 1898-1899.
IV-10. Elizabeth Deen, 1901- , m. Oliver Mattox.
IV-11. Ellis Dickey Deen, 1903- , li. Memphis,
Tenn.
IV-12. Mattie Lou Deen, 1907-1960, m. Eugene Ray.
IV-13. George Hubert Deen, 1909- , li. Memphis,
Tenn.
This family information furnished by Effie
Watson Deen Jones in 1967.

III-8. Levi (Lee) Godwin, b. 5 Oct. 1868, d. 12 June
1929, m. (1) Alice P. Goudy 14 Sept. 1890, Alice
1868-1914. m. (2) Bessie McKnight Scott.
Children of Lee and Alice:
IV-1. Annie Lee Godwin, b. May 1892, Miss.
IV-2. Jennie Ruth Godwin, b. 14 Oct. 1894, d. 26
Oct. 1965, unmarried.
IV-3. Thelma Godwin, b. 22 June 1898, d. 13 Dec.
1953, m. R. V. Pierce.
IV-4. William Joseph Godwin, b. 21 June 1902, d.
18 Nov. 1950, m. Ruth Henley 20 July 1929.
V-1. Betty Jo Godwin, m. William H. Mitchell 7
Sept. 1955, li. Winston-Salem, N.C.

III-9. Carrie Godwin, 1873-1942, m. Will M. Winborn,
li. New Albany, Miss.

8

These nine children of Levi and Julia all lived to be over
50 years of age before the circle was broken by death.

Children of Levi and Julia Godwin

1st Row, L to R:
Mary Jane Godwin Deen, William F. (Bill) Godwin, Samuel L.
Godwin, and Amanda Godwin Yopp

2nd Row:
Lucinda Parolee Godwin Deen, Carrie Godwin Winborn and
Sarah Elizabeth Godwin Godwin

3rd Row:
Lee Godwin and Jacob Willis Godwin

JACOB G. GODWIN

II-5. Jacob G. Godwin, b. ca. 1827, N.C., son of Allen
       Godwin and his second wife Martha. He served in
       the Confederate cause from March 18, 1862 until af-
       ter the Appomattox surrender April 9, 1865, leaving
       his command at Selma, Ala. He had enlisted at Ori-
       zaba, Miss. under Capt. G. A. Woods when a company
       of Tippah County farmers was formed. The company
       became Co. D. 7th Miss. Cavalry, later changed to
       Co. H, 37th Regiment of Mississippi Infantry.
         He m. Levina C. Whittington in 1850. Levina b.
       1831, Ala. They lived in Tippah Co., Miss. from
       1850 until in the 1870's when they moved to Grayson
       County, Texas. All of their children were born in
       Miss.
         A deed in Tippah Co. Miss. shows that Allen Godwin
       gave Jacob Godwin land in January 1869.
   III-1. Allen A. Godwin, b. 1851, Miss. li. Hereford,
           Texas, m. Lucy C. _____.
       IV-1. Andrew D. Godwin.
       IV-2. Dora A. Godwin.

   III-2. Wilbur T. Godwin, b. 1853, Miss., li. Whites-
           boro, Texas.

   III-3. Eli. L. Godwin, b. 25 July 1858, Tippah Co.,
           Miss, d. 23 Aug. 1922. Located in Grayson Co.,
           Tex. at Gordonville as a farmer in 1879.
           m. (1) Siotha P. Rodgers 25 Nov. 1880. Siotha
           b. 2 Oct. 1855, d. 31 Oct. 1890, a native of
           Ark.
       IV-1. Burl Newton Godwin, b. 12 Sept. 1881, Tex.,
              d. 3 July 1964, m. (1) Lottie Cook 16 Jan.
              1901. Burl was a barber and "dealer in fine
              stocks." (Grayson Co. Plat Book)
           V-1. Lillis V. Godwin
           V-2. Willis E. Godwin, twin to Lillis.
           V-3. Margaret B. Godwin
           V-4. Eunice Godwin
              Burl N. m. (2) Mary Barber
           V-5. Burl Newton Godwin, Jr., b. 20 May 1925,
                 m. Frances Flowers.
               VI-1. Hazel Godwin m. _____ Camp.
               VI-2. Katie Godwin m. _____ Court.
               VI-3. Burl Newton Godwin, III
               VI-4. Gracie Godwin
               The B. N. Godwin, Jr. family lives at Sherman,
               Texas. We visited with them and copied mater-
               ial from Eli L. Godwin's Bible 13 July 1971.

IV-2. Henry M. Godwin, b. 4 Feb. 1884, Grayson Co.,
Tex.
IV-3. Willie F. Godwin, dau., b. 7 Sept. 1886, d.
6 Aug. 1944, m. _____ Hamilton.
Eli L. Godwin m. (2) Virena Ellen Draper 26 Jul.
1891. Virena b. 4 June 1872, Grayson Co., Tex.
d. 25 May 1950.
IV-4. Dow B. Godwin, b. 19 July 1892.
IV-5. App Z. Godwin, b. 23 Aug. 1894.
IV-6. Rue M. Godwin, b. 29 Dec. 1896, d. young.
IV-7. Maud E. Godwin, b. 12 Jan. 1897, d. 4 Oct.
1915.
IV-8,9 Twin baby Godwins, b. 6 Feb. 1900, d. 6 and
7 Feb. 1900.
IV-10. J. Y. Godwin, b. 16 Dec. 1900, d. 16 Nov.
1913.
IV-11. Gladys Godwin, b. 1 Sept. 1903, d. 28 July
1965.
IV-12. Mets Godwin, b. 30 June 1906.
IV-13. Everee Godwin, b. 30 Nov. 1909.
IV-14. Marius Inez Godwin, b. 29 Feb. 1910.

III-4. Elijah M. (Lige) Godwin, b. 1862, Miss., li.
Nebraska.
III-5. D. Godwin, b. 1863, Miss.
III-6. Willis L. Godwin, b. 1866, Miss.

III-7. Cornelia Etta Godwin, b. 5 Jan. 1870, Tippah Co.,
Miss., d. 31 May 1933, m. William Franklin (Bud-
dy) Hudson 1883. Buddy, son of George Hudson
and wife Susan, was b. 1 Oct. 1862, d. 17 May
1928, both buried in Democrat Cemetery, Mills
Co., Tex.
Etta and Buddy came to Comanche from Whitesboro,
Texas in the early 1890's at the insistance of
his sister Ella, who had married Lige Hill and
had found central Texas a good place to live.
IV-1. Mollie Abilene Hudson, b. 3 Feb. 1885, d. 19
Apr. 1960, m. Buckmaster, 8 children.
IV-2. Lula B. (Lu) Hudson, b. 25 Sept. 1887, d. 3
December 1970, m. A. B. (Art) Simpson, 3
boys, 1 girl.
IV-3. Lessie L. Hudson, b. 6 Apr. 1890, m. (1)
Gilbert Tomlinson, (2) Fred Schulz, 2 boys.
IV-4. George Oliver Hudson, b. 22 June 1893, d. 22
Sept. 1948, m. Ruth Hanes, 1 boy, 1 girl.
IV-5. Jacob Ralph Hudson, b. 4 Feb. 1895, d. 30
Mar. 1968, m. (1) Marie Jones, (2) Stella ___.
IV-6. Cleo Virena Hudson, b. 1 Aug. 1897, m. A. P.
(Pierce) Hodges. Pierce d. 11 Nov. 1967.

> Cleo now lives with her son Hudson in the
> Democrat Community, Mills Co., Tex., very
> active on the farm and as a seamstress (1979).
> V-1. Norman Hodges
> V-2. Hudson Hodges
> V-3. June Hodges
> V-4. Connie Hodges
> V-5. Lou Hodges
> V-6. Naidago Hodges
>
> Lessie Schulz and Cleo Hodges have furnished in-
> formation on these families.

ELISHA H. GODWIN

II-6. Elisha H. Godwin, son of Allen Godwin and his second
wife, Martha, b. ca. 1832, Montgomery Co., N.C. (or
Ala.), d. 5 Feb. 1863, Chattanooga, Tenn. Hospital,
m. Martha Lucinda Jane Kinney about 1852, Lucinda
Jane was daughter of James Kinney, Sr.
    Elisha enlisted in the Confederate Army at Orizaba,
Miss. March 18, 1862 in Co. H, 37th Regiment of the
Miss. Infantry under Capt. G. A. Woods. He died of
disease in the hospital at Chattanooga while he was
in the service and is presumably buried there. He
left a young wife and four small children. When his
wife, Lucinda Jane, made application for back pay
due her husband after his death, she stated that he
was born in Montgomery Co., Ala. In the account of
the Quartermaster, he was described as 30 years old,
6 ft. 1 in. tall, with fair complexion, blue eyes,
light hair, and by occupation a farmer. Since his
parents were in Montgomery Co., N.C. in 1830, there
is some question about the state of his birth.
    In the 1860 census of Tippah Co., Miss. he is
given as a farmer, 28 years of age, born in N.C.
Lucinda Jane is 27, born in Tenn.
III-1. James A. Godwin, 1853-1899.
III-2. Margret L. Godwin, 1856, d. young.
III-3. Susanne J. Godwin, 1858-1925.
III-4. Sarah D. Godwin, b. 1860, d. young.
III-5. Joseph Elisha Godwin, 1862-1895.

> Elisha's widow, Martha Lucinda Jane, married Samuel
> Hill, brother to James Hill, in Sept. 1860 and had
> children Marcus (Mark), Tom, Dave, Will, Emma, Carrie
> and Sallie. Will, the last one alive, passed away
> in 1970.
>   We had the privilege of meeting Mr. Will Hill in
> the summer of 1968. He recalled coming with his

Allen Godwin

Elisha H. Godwin,
son of Allen Godwin

Joseph Elisha Godwin,
son of Elisha H.
Godwin

Sarah Catherine Deen
Godwin, wife of
Joseph Elisha Godwin

Children of Joseph and Sarah Godwin

Deborrah Godwin Paine

Joe Ella Godwin Martin

Mary Godwin
Janie Godwin Clemmer

Samuel Houston Godwin and wife
Martha E. Rushing Godwin

13

father on the train to Comanche, Tex. when he was just a boy to visit the James Hill family.

III-1.   James Allen Godwin, son of Elisha H. and Lucinda Jane Kinney Godwin, b. 12 June 1853, d. 1 Nov. 1893, m. Sarah Elizabeth Godwin, a cousin, dau. of Levi Godwin. Rev. Allen Godwin, Baptist minister and grandfather of both parties, performed the ceremony. Sarah E. Godwin b. 30 Dec. 1854, Ala., d. 13 Nov. 1944. Sarah was widowed at 38 years of age with 8 children, having lost 3 while young.
   IV-1.   Mary Susan Godwin m. (1) William P. Sanders, (2) John W. Carnal, (3) Jess Tisdale.
   IV-2.   Elisha L. Godwin m. Agnes Johnson.
   IV-3.   Eliza Godwin, d. young.
   IV-4.   Infant son, d. at birth.
   IV-5.   Infant son, d. at birth.
   IV-6.   Maggie Alnora Godwin, b. Aug 1880, Miss., m. John H. Coombs.
   IV-7.   Lillian Godwin, b. May 1883, Miss., m. James Edgar Coombs, bro. to John.
   IV-8.   Belle Godwin, b. Mar. 1885, Miss., unmarried.
   IV-9.   Samuel Leonard Godwin, b. Jan. 1887, Miss., m. Falitia May Nance.
   IV-10. Willie Godwin, b. July 1892, Miss., m. Lee Omar Martin, bro. to Joe Martin.
   IV-11. Ruby Cynthia Godwin, b. Oct. 1897, m. Luther McMillin Deen.

III-3.   Susanne J. Godwin, dau. of Elisha H. Godwin and Lucinda Jane Kinney, 1858-1925, m. William Henry Goolsby.
   IV-1.   James Thomas Goolsby, m. (1) Fannie Coley
   IV-2.   Nando Goolsby, m. Dolphus F. Collins.
   IV-3.   Ben R. Goolsby, m. Annie R. Renick.
   IV-4.   Effie Lee Goolsby, m. (1) Henry A. Rooker, (2) John Henry Traynum, (3) Cavinor Virgil Rowland.
   IV-5.   Delia Goolsby m. A. E. Renick.
   IV-6.   Ophelia Goolsby m. Joe Perkins.
   IV-7.   Modenia Goolsby m. Jessie Miller.
   IV-8.   Mattie Goolsby m. Lee Roy Miller.
   IV-9.   Josie Goolsby m. Cleo Hensley.
   IV-10. William D. Goolsby m. Sallie Irene Chism.

III-5.   Joseph Elisha Godwin, 1862-1895, born soon after his father left for Civil War duty, died at 34 leaving a young wife and five children, m.

Allen Godwin

Left: Joe Ella Godwin
Martin, Joe Martin
Parents of Howard, Mildred,
and Joe Godwin Martin

Right: Mildred Martin

Below: Dr. Joe Godwin Martin Family
Front: Millie, Leslie, Edith
Hines Martin
Back: Melanie, Joe Hines, Dr. Joe
Godwin Martin

Far Right: Denise and Joe Hines
Martin

15

The Howard P. Martin Family

Lee A. Walker Martin,
Howard P. Martin,
Parents of Mary Watson

Mary Watson Martin Harrell
Robert Roy Harrell, Jr.

Children of Mary Watson and Bob
Amanda Leigh Harrell
b. 1 Feb. 1976

Right: Martin Todd and
Robert Brant Harrell,
b. 11 July 1979

Sarah Catherine (Sally) Deen, 1860-1943, b. Miss.
IV-1. Mary E. Godwin, b. ca. 1882, Miss., unmarried.
IV-2. Deborrah Franklin Godwin, b. ca. 1884, Miss.,
m. Thomas Richard Paine.
IV-3. Samuel Houston Godwin, b. ca. 1886, Miss., m.
Mary Elizabeth Rushing.
IV-4. Martha Jane (Janie) Godwin, b. ca. 1888,
Miss., m. Samuel E. Clemmer.
IV-5. Joe Ella Godwin, b. 28 Apr. 1892, d. 22 Feb.
1972, buried Tippah County Memorial Garden,
m. Joe Martin who was b. 4 Jan. 1890, d. 30
Dec. 1960, buried Blue Mountain, Miss. Joe
was a well known cattle dealer and land own-
er in Tippah Co., Miss.
V-1. Howard Perry Martin, b. 13 Oct. 1911, lives
Ripley, Miss., employed by State Livestock
Board, m. Lee Alhin Walker 4 Jan. 1948. Lee
b. 21 April 1915, teaches Homemaking.
Vl-1. Mary Watson Martin, b. 27 Nov. 1949, m.
Robert R. Harrell, li. Houston, Texas.

V-2. Daphen Mildred Martin, b. 17 Oct. 1912, li.
Ripley, Miss., now retired after many years
employment in the office of a medical
clinic.
Mildred has helped immensely gathering
information for this compilation.

V-3. Joe Godwin Martin, D. V. M., b. 29 July
1926. He has a veterinary clinic in Ripley
where he also raises registered dogs.
Married Edith Christine Hines 28 Aug. 1954.
Edith b. 21 Aug, 1927, teaches math.
VI-1. Joe Hines Martin, b. 29 Sept. 1955.
VI-2. Mildred Ruth Martin, b. 21 Dec. 1958.
VI-3. Melanie Erlyne Martin, b. 29 Apr. 1962.
VI-4. Leslie Marie Martin, b. 21 Dec. 1966.

ELI P. GODWIN

II-7. Eli P. Godwin, son of Allen Godwin and his second
wife Martha, b. ca. 1834, N.C., d. 1898 during a
typhoid epidemic in Tippah Co., Miss. Pearl Deen,
grandson of Levi G. Godwin, remembers sitting up with
Eli the night he died. There were hardly enough well
people to care for the ill.
Eli m. Dolly Crank. He was a cripple, unable to
walk, but he supervised his farm work and did all
the jobs he could riding a jennet, using a lady's
side saddle.

Children of Eli P. Godwin and Dolly Crank:

III-1.	Jeff Godwin	III-4.	Cindy Godwin
III-2.	John Godwin	III-5.	Joe Godwin
III-3.	Julia Godwin	III-6.	James T. (Jim) Godwin

III-1. Jeff Godwin, m. twice, lost his first wife and five children, only one daughter, Blanch, living to be grown.

IV-1.	Blanche Godwin	IV-4.	Jessie Godwin
IV-2.	Fred Godwin	IV-5.	Essie Godwin
IV-3.	Carl Godwin	IV-6.	Catherine Godwin

These children live in and around Memphis, Tenn.

III-2. John Godwin, moved to Texas.
    IV-1. Tim Godwin, li. near Ennis, Texas.

III-3. Julia Godwin m. ____ Robbins
    IV-1. Freddie Robbins, dau.
    IV-2. Minnie Robbins
    IV-3. Pearl Robbins

III-4. Cindy Godwin, m. ____ Jackson.
    IV-1, 2, Twins, moved to Texas.

III-5. Joe Godwin, li. Dequeen, Ark.

III-6. James Thomas (Jim) Godwin, b. 6 Sept. 1878, d. 9. June 1945, m. Mary Laura Callicutt 18 Feb. 1896. Mary b. 28 July 1877, d. 13 May 1966, dau of Bird A. Callicutt.
    IV-1. Mamie Lee Godwin m. Herman Gunn.
    IV-2. Mattie Bell Godwin m. Homer Reaves.
    IV-3. Birdie Lou Godwin m. Homer Hill, son of Will Hill
    IV-4. Lottie Fay Godwin m. W. A. Stafford.
    IV-5. Ina Mae Godwin m. Ruffin Mitchell.
    IV-6. Iva Mae Godwin, twin to Ina Mae, m. Earl Means.
    IV-7. James Franklin Godwin m. Arola Green.
    IV-8. Robert Payne Godwin, unmarried.

Information on Eli P. Godwin family supplied by Birdie Godwin Hill of Blue Mountain, Miss. When I met Birdie and two of her sisters in 1968, I felt a close affinity with them. They were another family of Godwin girls with two brothers, double related to Allen Godwin, so like my own family.

LUCINDA PAROLEE GODWIN

II-8. Lucinda Parolee Godwin, dau. of Allen Godwin and his second wife, Martha, b. 25 Dec. 1836, McNairy Co., Tenn., d. 10 March 1909, age 73, Comanche, Tex., m. James Hill by 1852. James, son of Elijah Hill and Rebecca Koffman (Coffman), b. 26 Aug. 1825, Jefferson Co., Tenn., d. 16 April 1918, Mills Co., Tex. Both buried at Comanche, Tex.

III-1. Elijah Allen Hill (Lige)
III-2. Martha Rebecca Hill (Mattie)
III-3. Pleasant Gideon Hill (P.G.)
III-4. Elanor Adelaide Hill (Addie)
III-5. James S. Hill (Jimmy)
III-6. Jennie P. Hill (Janie)
III-7. Luther Ernest Hill
III-8. George W. Hill
III-9. Jacob Leslie Hill (Jake)

This family treated in more detail in the James Hill family section.

ELIJAH A. GODWIN

II-9. Elijah A. Godwin, son of Allen Godwin and his second wife, Martha, b. ca. 1840, Tenn., m. Minerva J. ____ by 1860. Minerva b. ca. 1840, Tenn.
Elijah enlisted in the Confederacy at Orizaba, Miss. 18 Mar. 1862, in Co. H, 34th Miss. He was captured at Chattanooga, Tenn. 24 Nov. 1863 and imprisoned at Rock Island, Ill., was exchanged 27 Mar. 1865 at ____ Wharf, James River, Va., and paroled 27 May 1865 at Holly Springs, Miss.
Elijah and Minerva are listed in the Tippah Co., Miss. census of 1860 living near his father, Allen Godwin, and a brother, Jacob. In 1870 they are still there with five children. By 1880 they have relocated in Grayson Co., Texas, having left Miss. after their last child was born there in 1876.

III-1. James A. Godwin, b. ca. 1862, Miss.
III-2. John L. Godwin, b. ca. 1866, Miss.
III-3. Martha L. Godwin, b. ca. 1868, Miss.
III-4. Elizabeth H. Godwin, b. ca. 1869, Miss.
III-5. Mary E. Godwin, b. ca. 1870, Miss.
III-6. Leota Godwin, b. ca. 1872, Miss.
III-7. Latitia F. Godwin, b. ca. 1874, Miss.
III-8. Jacob O. Godwin, b. ca. 1876, Miss.

ACHROL H. GODWIN

II-10.   Achrol (Akriel) H. Godwin, son of Allen Godwin and
his second wife, Martha, b. ca. 1842, Tenn., d. 6
Nov. 1861 in Hopkinsville, Ky. of measles contrac-
ted while in the service of the Confederacy.
He had enlisted at age 20 on July 31, 1861 at
Orizaba, Miss. as a Pvt. in Co. B. of the 23rd
Regiment of Mississippi Volunteers and died within
the year.

LATITIA F. GODWIN

II-11.   Latitia F. Godwin (Aunt Tish), b. ca. 1848, Miss.,
m. John W. Kinney and was living in Tippah Co.,
Miss. in 1880. Latitia's mother, Martha Godwin,
age 74, was with her when the census was enumerat-
ed that year. John Kinney was b. ca. 1840.
Latitia's father, Allen Godwin, gave her and her
husband 130 acres of land in Sept. of 1867, land
bordering Elijah Godwin, James Godwin, and James
Callicutt. Then in Oct. 1872, just 2 weeks before
Allen Godwin died, he deeded 82 acres to his wife
Martha for $500.00 and she in turn deeded it to
J. W. Kinney for $500.00, both deeds recorded the
same day. In December of that same year Martha
deeded 88 acres to John W. Kinney for $700.00, all
land in Tippah County, Miss.
III-1.   George Allen Kinney, b. ca. 1867, Miss.
III-2.   Annie Kinney, b. ca. 1868, Miss.
III-3.   Henry A. Kinney, b. ca. 1870, Miss.
III-4.   William H. Kinney, b. ca. 1877, Miss.
III-5.   Rosa Lee Kinney, b. ca. 1880, Miss.
There may have been more children after 1880.
This family is said to have moved to Tenn.

* * * * * * * * * *

In retrospect we see Allen Godwin as our pioneering
patriarchal ancestor who in his travels, migrated from his
home in Johnston Co., N.C. to Georgia, back to Montgomery
Co., N.C., on to McNairy Co., Tenn, then settled in Tippah
Co., Miss. for his maturing years.
He married twice, both North Carolina girls, had a
total of 15 children, but lost his first wife and three of
their daughters and later a son of the second marriage
early in his life. Three of his sons were said to be
cripples.
Allen was primarily a farmer, later a Baptist minister. He had five sons and two grandsons to serve on the
Confederate side of the Civil War. Two sons did not return.

His influence on the principals of this book was more extensive than usual, since at least four of the early families can trace their ancestry back to him on both paternal and maternal sides.

Allen Godwin lived near Blue Mountain, Tippah Co., Miss. 1842-1872.

Blue Mountain's old business district

Macedonia Church, Deentown Community, where Allen Godwin lived.

FAMILY CENSUS OF ALLEN GODWIN

Married: (1) Polly Green   Date: Feb. 1809   Place: Cumberland Co., N.C.   Recorded: Cumberland Co. Marriages
        (2) Martha   ca. 1825

Census Year:		1810	1820	1830	1840	1850	1860
County, State, Pg.	Sex	Cumberland, NC p. 261-595	Washington, GA p. 136	Montgomery, NC	McNairy, TN	Tippah, MS p. 478-1188	Tippah, MS p. 130-894
Allen b. 1788 N.C.	M	16-26	26-45	40-50	40-50	60	62
Polly/Martha	F	Polly 16-26	Polly 26-45	Martha 20-30	Martha 30-40	45	50
b. 1810	F	-10					
b. 1810-1820	F		-10				
John Allen b. 1815-1820, NC	M		-10	10-15			
Pennie b. 1815-1820, GA	F		-10	10-15			
Calvin b. 1815-1820, GA	M		-10	10-15	20-30		
Levi Simmons b. 1825, N.C.	M			-5	15-20		
Jacob b. 1828, N.C.	M			-5	10-15		

Family Census of Allen Godwin (Continued)

Census Year:	1810	1820	1830	1840	1850	1860
County, State, Pg.	Cumberland, NC p. 261-595	Washington, GA p. 136	Montgomery, NC	McNairy, TN	Tippah, MS p.478-1188	Tippah, MS p.130-894
	Sex					
Alexander (?) b. 1825-1830	M		-5			
Elisha b. 1832, N.C.	M				Elisha 18	
Eli P. b. 1834, N.C.	M				Eli 16	
L. Parolee b. 1836, TN	F				Parolee 13	
Elijah b. 1840, TN	M				Elijah 10	
Akriel H. b. 1842, TN	M				A. H. 8	Arseal 17
Latitia b. 1848, MS	F				Frances L. 2	Latitia 11

23

FAMILY CENSUS OF JAMES CALLICUTT

Married Pennie Godwin   Date: ca. 1833   Place: Recorded:

Census Year County, State, Pg.	Sex	1840 Tippah, MS	1850 Tippah, MS	1860 Tippah, MS	1870 Tippah, MS
James b. N.C.	M	20-30	James b. N.C.	48 James b. N.C.	52 James b. N.C.	60 James b. N.C.
Pennie b. ca. 1818	F	20-30	Manna b. N.C.	32 Fanina b. N.C.	42 P. b. GA	45
Jane b. 1834	F	5-10	Li. Shedrick Downs Jane b. MS	16		
Pleasant b. 1839	M	-5	Pleasant b. MS	11		
Thomas b. 1842	M		Thomas b. MS	8 Thomas b. MS	18	
Sarah b. 1845	F		Sarah b. MS	5 Sarah b. MS	15	
Ezekiel b. 1847	M		Ezekial b. MS	3 Ezekeal b. MS	12 A. b. MS	23
Bird A. b. 1852	M			Bird A. b. MS	8 B. A. b. MS	20
Calvin J. b. 1855	M			Calvin J. b. MS	5 A. G. b. MS	14

24

II

John Allen Godwin, Sr.

John Allen Godwin, son of Allen Godwin and his first wife, Polly Green, was born in North Carolina about 1812-1815 and died in Clark Co., Ark. 1 June 1853. His father had received a Land Grant from the State of North Carolina in 1816 for 150 acres in the southwestern part of Johnston County where John Allen probably was born.

He was married about 1836 to Aletha Spencer, who was born in Montgomery Co., N.C. 18 Oct. 1814 and died in Mills County., Tex. 10 Feb. 1899. She is buried in Big Valley Cemetery. Aletha was the daughter of Seymore Spencer and his wife Tabitha Bennett. Tabitha was the dau. of Solomon Bennett, Rev. Sol.

John and Aletha had 10 children, the last one, John Allen Jr., being born nearly 8 months after John and three of the young daughters had died during a fever epidemic in the summer of 1853 near Arkadelphia, Ark.

From the children's birthplaces on census and other records, the travels of this family can be traced. In 1837 soon after they married they were in Tippah Co., Miss. John Allen was one of the original land owners in that county with a Grant to former Chickasaw Indian lands which were sold in 1836 as Tippah County was being formed. The grant was in Township 4, Range 2 east of Ripley and Blue Mountain.

They moved to McNairy Co., Tenn. in 1839, were back in Tippah County from 1842 to 1846 when they sold three-fourth section of land to Hiram C. Spencer, brother of Aletha, before moving to Clark Co., Ark. John Allen's travels seem to have paralleled his father's until he made this break in 1846 by moving to Arkansas. Levi Spencer, brother of Aletha, is also found in the census of Clark County in 1850.

In Arkansas they bought land in a wild country heavily timbered with pine, oak, cottonwood, and willow. When they cleared the land, they raised cotton in the fertile rolling sandy soil. Aletha's grandchildren remember her stories of how she kept a fire going in the fireplace all night to keep the wild animals from coming down the chimney.

To settle John Godwin's estate in Clark Co., Ark. in 1853 Thomas D. Kingsbury was appointed administrator and the final settlement shows the balance against the estate to be $208.47 plus costs of $12.97 with the credits to be

2 bales of cotton for $120.00 and income from land sold
$80.00. The estate was insolvent and the administrator
asked that it be closed, Clark Co., Ark. Probate Records.
    After losing her husband, Aletha continued to farm
with the help of her children, the older boys being 14
and 15. These two boys both married in Arkansas, enlisted in the Confederate cause and both died of disease as
young men in 1865.
    When a granddaughter, Beulah Hill, was asked about
her grandparents, she produced from her trunk a receipt
made to her grandfather John Godwin, payment for a barrel
of whiskey. And the most outstanding thing she remembered
about Grandmother Aletha was that she wore a size 2 shoe.

    John Goalin (Godwin)
    Bot of J. Miller
    1 barrell of whiskey 35½ gal. at 20½ a g. $7.30
    20 lbs. of coffee at 9 cts. per lb.   1.80
        Rec'd paymen   9.10
        Nov. 19th 1845   J. Miller

    Several letters written to Aletha were in the posses-
sion of a grandson, Enoch Godwin. They tell of the homes
and health of her sisters, brothers, and their children.
J. M. Ingraham, who married her sister Elizabeth, writes
"Dear Sister" from Myers Landing, Arkansas on June 28,
1878 in answer to the first letter they had received from
Aletha since the War. He gives a description of a flour-
ishing country, gardens, and orchards, with wheat 90¢ a
bushel and bacon from 7 to 8 cents.
    Elizabeth Spencer Ingraham writes from Sebastian Co.,
Ark. that her husband and son had enlarged their stock in
their store which was in a good country to make a living,
but they had a lot of sickness like colds and pneumonia.
Her son Lee was a doctor there. She pleas, "O do let me
hear from you. . . We haven't long to stay here. Let us
all meet in heaven."
    L. H. Ingraham writes for his mother (Ma) in 1888 and
again in 1889 from Lavaca, Ark. He states that his parents are looking quite old. L. H. may be Lee, the doctor.
    Aletha Godwin m. (2) J. D. Cain of Saline Co., Ark.
on 16 Jan. 1861 when she was 46. The marriage did not
last long, but she was known thereafter as "Grandma Cain"
to her grandchildren.
    She moved to Upshur Co., Tex. in Dec. 1865 and on to
Hopkins Co. in 1866. When her youngest son, also named
John Allen, married in 1874, she lived with him, or he
with her, in Como for several years before moving to Mills
County, Tex. to the Big Valley Community in late 1890.

It was here that she died during the terrible blizzard of 1899 at age 84. (The Weather Bureau at Waco, Tex. recorded -5° on Feb. 12, 1899, the coldest ever recorded there.) Aletha's grandson, Enoch Godwin, told of taking the news of her death to the aunts and uncles in the community. At each house he was so near frozen he had to be helped off his horse. Aletha was carried in a wagon to the cemetery and buried without ceremony.

Children of John Allen Godwin and Aletha Spencer:
- III-1. Pleasant Marion Godwin
- III-2. Eli Seamore Godwin
- III-3. Lavina Jane Godwin
- III-4. Mary Ann Godwin
- III-5. Nancy Elizabeth Godwin
- III-6. Margret Pennah Godwin
- III-7. Catherine Godwin
- III-8. Ellen Godwin
- III-9. Julia Ann Godwin
- III-10. John Allen Godwin, Jr.

Aletha Spencer Godwin Cain

Big Valley Cemetery,
Mills Co., Tex.

Mrs. Aletha Cain
Born
Oct. 18, 1814
Died
Feb. 10, 1899

Children of John A. Godwin and Aletha Spencer

Seated: John A. Godwin, Jr.
Liva A. Godwin.
Standing: Jane Godwin Long,
Mary Godwin Holcomb, Julia
Godwin Perry.

Maston L. (Bob) Keys
Elizabeth Godwin Keys

III-1. Pleasant Marion Godwin, son of John Allen Godwin and Aletha Spencer, b. 20 Aug. 1837, Tippah
Co., Miss., d. 1865, Ark., m. Mary Diffee 28
Oct. 1858, both of Clark Co., Ark.
Marion and Mary were living at Monticello,
Ark. when he enlisted as a Confederate soldier
in 1862 in Co. L, 1st Regiment, Arkansas Cavalry. Service comments on his record were "with
horse gun." He is said to have died of going
in swimming too soon after having the measles.

III-2. Eli Seamore Godwin, son of John Allen Godwin
and Aletha Spencer, b. 12 Feb. 1839, McNairy
Co., Tenn., d. 1865, Ark., m. Mary Melvina
Thornton 21 Oct. 1860, Hot Springs Co., Ark.
Eli enlisted in the Confederate Army in Clark
Co., Ark. at age 23 in May 1862, was discharged
24 July 1862 from the hospital at Camp Rush at
Little Rock with a pulmonary illness. He was
in the 37th Regiment of Trans-Mississippi Infantry. He was paid $11 per month and was given
$10 traveling allowance to go home to Clark Co.,
a distance of one hundred miles. He was described as five feet, eleven inches tall, blue-eyed,

28

with light hair and complexion.

LAVINA JANE GODWIN LONG

III-3. Lavina Jane Godwin, oldest daughter of John
Allen Godwin and Aletha Spencer, b. 9 Dec.
1840, McNairy Co., Tenn., d. 1937, going on 97,
buried Big Valley Cemetery, Mills Co., Tex.
Jane moved with her parents from McNairy Co.,
Tenn. to Blue Mountain, Tippah Co., Miss. in
the 1840's, then on to Clark Co., Ark. near
Arkadelphia in 1846, where she grew up and
married. She was widowed with three small children during the Civil War. Later she remarried
and was in Hopkins Co., Tex. in 1870. She was
again widowed in 1877 with 9 children under 20
and another on the way. About 1892 she, with
her unmarried children, moved to the Cole
Springs Community, Brown Co., Tex. southwest
of Mullin on the Pecan Bayou, later locating in
the Big Valley Community, Mills Co.
Jane m. (1) James Anderson Young about 1858.
James Young enlisted in the Confederate cause
on 21 June 1862 for a period of 3 years and was
soon a corporal. He was issued a gun and horse
in Co. K, 1st Regiment, Arkansas Cavalry, enlisting in the same regiment and on the same
date as his brother-in-law, Marion Godwin.
James died while in service.
Lavina Jane m. (2) Henry Travis Long about
1865. Henry Long b. ca. 1826, d. 1877.

1870 Census Hopkins Co., Tex. Prec. 3, P.O. Black Oak

	Age		Born
Long, Henry	44	Farmer	Tenn.
Levina	28		Tenn.
Henry	4		Tex.
Robert	3		Tex.
John	1		Tex.
Young, Araminta	10		Ark.
Mary	7		Ark.
James	6		Tex.

They lived near Aletha Cain, Lavina Jane's
mother, who had moved to Hopkins County in 1866.
The Longs were in Hunt County in 1873.
Jane Long was a remarkable woman. She was
widowed twice, both times with small children,
remained a widow for 60 years the second time

and raised her 10 children to be grown. She
broke a hip while in her 90's, but recovered
and was again active until her death at near
97.

Children of Jane Godwin and James A. Young:
IV-1. Araminta (Minnie) Young, b. 29 Mar. 1859,
Ark., d. 12 May 1908, m. Robert Hashaw.
V-1. Dovie Hashaw m. Bob Molar.
V-2. Lula Hashaw

IV-2. Mary Young, b. 17 Jan. 1859, d. 2 Oct.
1946; m. James H. Johnson who was b. 6 May
1863, d. 23 Apr. 1933.
V-1. Cloy Johnson m. Roscoe Bolder.
V-2. Mattie Johnson m. Jake Cockrell.
V-3. Bob Johnson m. LuAva _____.
V-4. Molar Johnson m. Mattie (Leonard).
V-5. Ernest Johnson m.
V-6. Joe Johnson m. Minnie Weathers.
V-7. Willie Johnson, d. young.
V-8. Grace Johnson m. Carl M. Wood.
V-9. Fred Johnson

IV-3. James W. (Bud) Young, b. ca. 1864, Tex.,
m. Mattie Sheets.
V-1. Will Young
V-2. Frank Young, d. young.
V-3. Oliver Johnson Young, d. 1979.

Children of Jane Godwin and Henry T. Long:
IV-4. Henry Thomas (Tommy) Long
IV-5. Robert W. Long
IV-6. John W. (Johnny) Long
IV-7. Riley Franklin Long
IV-8. Benjamin (Ben) Long
IV-9. Marion Dan Long
IV-10. Catherine Travis (T) Long

IV-4. Henry Thomas (Tommy) Long, b. 7 Mar. 1865,
Hopkins Co., Tex. d. 17 Apr. 1921, m. Nan-
nie Walker who was b. 23 June 1866, d. 23
Sept. 1941. Both buried in North Brown
Cemetery, Mills Co., Tex.
V-1. Nora Long m. Ed Randles
V-2. Ethel Long m. Joe Dennis
V-3. John Long m. Nola Randles
V-4. Charlie (Bunk) Long, d. young.

Sons of Lavina Jane Godwin Long and Henry Travis Long

Front: Dan Long
Back: Robert, Riley, and Ben Long

IV-5. Robert W. Long, b. 9 Jan. 1867, d. 16 Nov.
1953, m. Sarah E. Ritchie, who was b. 1 Sept.
1874, d. 24 July 1955, buried Big Valley Cemetery.
  V-1. Dan Long m. Arkie Hartman
  V-2. Lillie Long m. Jack Attaway
  V-3. Adrian Long m. (1) Louise Grant, (2) Pearl
Hale Long.
  V-4. Lois Long m. Edgar Barrington.
  V-5. Myrtle Long m. John Jackson
  V-6. Ishmael Long m. Pearl Hale.

IV-6. Johnny William Long, b. 20 Jan. 1869, d. 2
Feb. 1933, m. Sarah Alice Bull, who was b.
27 Oct. 1872, d. 14 May 1968. Both buried
North Brown Cemetery, Mills Co., Tex.
  V-1. Delia Long m. J. Elbe Burdette.
  V-2. Dovie Long m. (1) Jeremiah Roberts, (2)
Manly Hill.
  V-3. Travis Long m. Willie Featherston.

V-4.   James Bowie Long m. Erah (Tommie) Alexander.

V-5.   Elvie Long m. Carl Edgar Moreland.

V-6.   Thelma Long m. Charlie Booker.

Thelma furnished the Johnny Long family information.

IV-7.   Riley Franklin Long, b. 6 Jan. 1871, d. 13 Aug. 1915, m. Fannie R. Harper of Star 25 June 1896.   Both are buried in Big Valley Cemetery.

V-1.   Maude Long m. Hugh Dennard.

V-2.   Zada (Zay) Long m. Watson Miller.

V-3.   Jack Long m. Melvina Fox.

V-4.   Tiny Inez Long m. Virgil Reed.

IV-8.   Benjamin (Ben) Long, b. 10 May 1873, Hunt Co., Tex., d. 25 Jan. 1962, m. Annie Belle Burdette of San Saba Co.   Annie b. 15 Feb. 1881, d. 14 Sept. 1963.   Both buried in Big Valley Cemetery, Mills Co., Tex.

V-1.   Ruby Pearl Long, b. 18 May 1899, m. Dee Hartman 2 Oct. 1919, Mills Co., Tex.

VI-1.   Dorothy Hartman m. J. D. McKenzie 1 Sept. 1940.

V-2.   Robert Lee Long, b. 4 Oct. 1901, m. Lucille Moore.

V-3.   Dera Francis Long, b. 30 May 1904, m. Floyd Sykes 6 Feb. 1926, Mills Co.

V-4.   Loy Benjamin Long, b. 7 Aug. 1906, m. Ruth Ellis.

V-5.   J. C. (Jake) Long, b. 29 Feb. 1908, m. Athelyn Garrett.

V-6.   Pauline (Polly) Long, b. 1 Sept. 1911, m. (1) Gordon Miller, dec'd, m. (2) Herman Johnson.

V-7.   Woodrow Wilson (Woody) Long, b. 27 Aug. 1913, m. Neppie Bird.

V-8.   Annie Bell Long, b. 7 July 1915, m. R. T. Padgett 23 Oct. 1934, Mills Co., Tex.

V-9.   Virginia Elizabeth Long, b. 4 Sept. 1917, m. J. A. Stark, Jr., 8 Dec. 1937, Mills Co., Tex.

IV-9.   Marion Dan Long, b. 1875, d. 1941, m. Annie Louise Weaver 30 June 1904, Mills Co., Tex. Annie b. 1887, d. 1978.   They lived at Midland, Tex., buried at Big Valley Cemetery.

John Allen Godwin, Sr.

V-1. Roy Long
V-2. Rex Long
V-3. Glenn Long
V-4. Katie Belle Long m. (2) M. D. Floyd

IV-10. Catherine Travis (Aunt T.) Long, b. 1877, m.
Charles W. Law, lived in Arlington, buried in
Eastern Star Cemetery, Arlington, Texas.
V-1. Janie Law, b. 27 Sept. 1910, d. 1 Oct. 1910.
V-2. Morris Law (Adopted), lives Georgetown, Tex.

Ruby Hartman has been helpful with information
on the Long families.

MARY ANN GODWIN HOLCOMB

III-4. Mary Ann Godwin, daughter of John Allen Godwin and
Aletha Spencer, was b. 26 Dec. 1842, Tippah Co.,
Miss., d. 20 April 1946 at age 103. Married Bill
Holcomb who was b. 1842, d. 1929. They lived at
Ladonia, Fannin County, and Kentucky Town, Grayson
Co., Texas.
    In a letter to her mother, Aletha Cain, written
Aug. 18, 1895, Mary says, "O! Mother, how I wish I
could be with you just one time more! I still
have that hope though of us meeting again sometime
. . . I don't want you to be bothering about us
children. We will all do the best we can." Mary
was 53 and Aletha was 81 and since Aletha was in
Montague County that year, they were probably no
more than 100 miles apart.
    After Mary was widowed in 1929, she lived with
her daughter Janie in Ft. Worth. She had begun to
lose her eyesight in her 40's and was totally
blind for many years. After she was quite elderly
she spent her days rocking in a rocking chair,
taking a pinch of snuff every little while, all
the time wearing her favorite black bonnet, which
she wore to the table also. When Janie passed
away, Mary lived with another daughter, Callie
Lawson, at Greenville.
    In December 1945 she was living with her daugh-
ter, Hettie Carr, at Tyler when she celebrated her
103rd birthday the day after Christmas.
    She had 9 children; these 4 may not be in order:
IV-1. Janie Holcomb m. _____ Payne, li. Ft. Worth, Tex.
V-1. Lexie Payne m. _____ Williams.
IV-2. Callie Holcomb, m. _____ Lawson, li. at Greenville and Bonham, Tex.

33

IV-3. Hettie A. Holcomb, b. 1871, m. A. L. Carr, li.
      Tyler, Tex.
IV-4. Truman A. Holcomb, 1876-1956, li. near White-
      wright, Tex.
  V-1. Marvin Holcomb
  V-2. Ocie Holcomb
  V-3. R. B. Holcomb
  V-4. Travis Holcomb
  V-5. Myrtle Holcomb m. _____ Mitchell.

Five generations in Mary Ann
Godwin Holcomb family

Seated: Janie Payne, Mary
Ann Holcomb holding great-
great-grandchild.

Standing: Great-granddaughter,
Lexie Payne Williams, dau. of
Janie Payne.

NANCY ELIZABETH GODWIN KEYS

III-5. Nancy Elizabeth (Lizzie) Godwin, daughter of John
       Allen Godwin and Aletha Spencer, b. 19 Aug. 1844,
       Tippah Co., Miss., d. 1916, age 72. m. Maston
       Lindsey (Bob) Keys 19 Aug. 1860, Clark Co., Ark.
       She was 16, he 19. Maston L. Keys, 1841-1936, d.
       age 95.
         Lizzie was under 2 years of age when her family
       made the move from Tippah Co., Miss. to Clark Co.,
       Ark. where she grew up and married. She and her
       husband moved to Texas, living at Lenore and
       Lockney. Children not especially in order.
  IV-1. Mary Jane Keys m. Josh _____. Mary d. 27 Oct.
        1892 of a mysterious illness, leaving children.
  IV-2. Alice B. Keys m. Louis Lackey, Baptist preacher.

Alice and Louis lived at Tacitus, Haskell Co.,
Texas in 1897 when Alice wrote her grandmother
Aletha Spencer Godwin Cain. She spoke of the
improbability of their ever meeting again ex-
cept in the next world. Alice d. at age 100.
- V-1. Anna Lackey, maybe others.
- IV-3. Quency Keys m. Florence.
  - V-1. Lindsey Keys and others
- IV-4. Henry Keys m. Sally ____, at least one daugh-
  ter, lived Mills Co., Texas.
- IV-5. Liva Ann Keys, b. 26 Sept. 1877. d. 10 Mar.
  1966, m. Isaac M. Weaver, who was b. 13 Sept.
  1877, d. 19 June 1931. Liva and family lived
  at Big Valley, Mills Co., Texas.
  - V-1. Myra Weaver m. Elmo Smith, li. at Lockhart.
    Texas.
  - V-2. Homer Weaver m. Mary Cockerll.
  - V-3. Floyd B. Weaver m. Evelyn Nelson, li. Goldth-
    waite. Texas.
  - V-4. Robert Weaver m. Gene ____.
  - V-5. Howard Weaver, unmarried.
  - V-6. Flora Weaver m. Joe Lynch.
- IV-6. Kenyon Keys m. Alma (or Amma) Huckabee. Sever-
  al children, one set of twins.
- IV-7. Minnie Keys m. Elery Lackey.
  - V-1. Eunice Lackey

Floyd B. Weaver of Goldthwaite and Myra Weaver
Smith of Lockhart provided information on this
family.

This letter from Aunt Lizzie exemplifies their faith,
patience and endurance.

Lenore, Tex Nov. the 27 92
Mrs. L. J. Long and Mother and Brother and Sisters
Greetings to you all.
We air all well and hope you all the same our wheat
is looking fine we have 45 acres sode we aim to break
some more new land this winter if we can I wanted to
have come to see you all last summer but I could not
on account of Mary Janes sickness she dide the 27 of
last month. She was taken sick last April and her pa
went out thair to see her and she got a little better
and come home with him tha got hear about the 2 of
Jul and she never set up but verry little after she
got hear and thair was 15 weeks that she was not up
only as we hope her up no one cant begin to tell how
she suffered I never have saw no sutch case thair
was 6 doctors saw her first and last but nun of them
did not no what was the matter with her but thanks

be to the Lord as she had to die she dide in his hands we talked all about ding to her and she told us that she had no fears of death she was made to rejois several times during her sickness she wood laugh and tell us her way was clear her misery was mostly in her head and rite leg we had the best neighbors you most ever saw tha hope lift her all most day and night for 15 weeks tha nour faild to come and help us. Josh has gon back to hunt Co with the children I want you all to rite to us as soon as you get this tell Henry and Sally that we air all well and that his pa will rite to them soon Ma if we live till next summer I want to come to see you if I can I want you all to remember us in your prairs

rite soon and dont fail yours as ever

N. E. Keys

III-6.   Margret Pennah Godwin, b. Apr. 1846, Clark Co., Ark., d. 1853, age 7.

III-7.   Catherine Godwin, b. 5 Feb. 1848, Clark Co., Ark. d. 1853, age 5.

III-8.   Ellen Godwin, b. 12 Feb. 1850, Clark Co., Ark., d. 1853, age 3.

The above three girls died during a fever epidemic that also took the life of their father.

JULIA ANN GODWIN PERRY

III-9.   Julia Ann Godwin, daughter of John Allen Godwin and Aletha Spencer, b. 4 Jan. 1852, Clark Co., Ark., d. 25 Dec. 1933, age 81. She m. Thomas D. Perry 8 June 1871, Clark Co., Ark.

Tom Perry b. 10 April 1850, d. 27 Feb. 1914, both buried in Big Valley Cemetery, Mills Co., Tex.

Julia and Tom lived in the Bismarck Community in Clark Co., Ark. and attended the De Roche Church. They moved to Mills Co., Tex. in early 1889 when their youngest son Garland was six weeks old.

They were married in 1871; in 1971 six of their seven children were still alive, all except Rosa.

IV-1.	Mary Ellen Perry	IV-5.	Ollie May Perry
IV-2.	Rosa A. Perry	IV-6.	Grover Cleveland
IV-3.	Essie Pearl Perry		Perry
IV-4.	Edith Percy Perry	IV-7.	Garland T. Perry

John Allen Godwin, Sr.

Children of Julia and Tom Perry
Seated: Mary Ellen Faulkner
        Grover Cleveland Perry
        Garland T. Perry
Standing: Essie Pearl Daily
          Edith Percy McWhorter
          Ollie Mae White

Julia Godwin Perry
Tom Perry

IV-1.   Mary Ellen Perry, b. 2 Sept. 1872, Clark Co.,
        Ark., m. Thomas Faulkner, d. 30 July 1975, age
        nearly 103, in Heritage Home at Goldthwaite,
        Tex. She had outlived all her children except
        one.
   V-1.   Lorena Faulkner m. Virgil Mahan.
   V-2.   Boyd Allen Faulkner, li. Vernal, Utah.
   V-3.   Luther Faulkner m. Elsie Simpson.
   V-4.   Vida Faulkner m. Claud Laird.

IV-2.   Rosa A. Perry, b. 6 July 1874, d. 12 Dec. 1901,
        buried Big Valley. Rosa fell off a rail fence
        as a child, breaking her back, which caused her
        to be humped and dwarfed, unable to walk.

IV-3.   Essie Pearl Perry, b. 18 Aug. 1878, Clark Co.,
        Ark., m. Jim Daily 4 Dec. 1898, Mills Co., Tex.,
        li. Big Springs, Tex.
   V-1.   Era May Daily, b. 5 Mar. 1900, Taylor Co.,
        Tex., m. Earl J. Davis 23 Aug. 1918.
   VI-1.   Grover T. Davis, b. 5 Sept. 1919.
   VI-2.   Darrell James Davis, b. 15 May 1925.
   VI-3.   Arless Waymon Davis, b. 14 May 1930, d. 14
        Nov. 1952, Korean War, plane missing.

VI-4. Nelda Lauell Davis, b. 8 Apr. 1933.
V-2. Grady Erma Daily, b. 26 Sept. 1904, Borden Co.,
Tex.; m. Roscoe Hardwick.
VI-1. Noma Lee Hardwick, b. 3 Feb. 1920.
VI-2. Alta Blanche Hardwick, b. 22 July 1927.
V-3. Claudie Velma Daily, b. 26 Sept. 1906, Borden Co.,
Tex., m. Clarence Mercer 1925.
VI-1. Albert Douglass Mercer, b. 1926
VI-2. Elda Mae Mercer, b. 1929.
V-4. Perry Stevon Daily, b. 25 April 1907, Howard Co.,
Tex., m. Tech Knappe 1935.
VI-1. Perry Lee Daily, b. 10 March 1943.
V-5. Orbin Homer Daily, b. 25 Nov. 1910, Runnels Co.,
Tex., m. Barbara Hasten 1937.
VI-1. Orbin Homer Daily, Jr., b. 1938.
VI-2. Barbara Ann Daily, b. 4 Jan. 1944.

Era May Daily Davis of Big Springs, Texas kindly
furnished this Daily information.

IV-4. Edith Percy Perry, b. 15 April 1881, d. Sept. 1971,
m. A. Parks McWhorter of Upshur Co., Tex., 11 Oct.
1898, Mills Co., Tex. Parks b. 18 Aug. 1879, d.
23 Feb. 1925.
V-1. Audrey Pearl McWhorter, b. 2 Nov. 1899, m. Char-
ley O. Stark 16 Feb. 1919, Mills Co., Tex.; m.
by W. R. White (later Dr. White), li. in Goldth-
waite, Tex. Charley d. 19 Aug. 1949.
VI-1. Merlene Stark m. Dee Hammond. Ch.: Gary
Frances, Jean, Johnny Wayne, Jo Nell.
VI-2. Oran Stark m. Oveldo Norman, no children.
VI-3. Charlene Stark m. C. D. McLean. Ch.: Paula,
Scott, Terry.
VI-4. Billy Stark m. _____. Ch.: Stephen and
David.
VI-5. John Dean Stark, d. 30 Apr. 1960, unmarried.
V-2. Bessie Marie McWhorter, b. 13 Oct. 1901, d. 1969,
m. Milton C. Collier.
VI-1. James Harland Collier.
VI-2. Allen Collier
VI-3. Louise Collier
V-3. Ruth McWhorter, b. 14 Oct. 1903, d. 1965, m. (1)
_____ Lawson, (2) _____Churchill, no children.
V-4. Clyde McWhorter, b. 6 Aug. 1905, d. age 6.
V-5. Vernon McWhorter, b. 14 June 1911, m. Rose Wolfe.
V-6. Norman (Red) McWhorter, b. 23 May 1913.

John Allen Godwin, Sr.

VI-1. Norma Lee McWhorter
VI-2. Verna Mae McWhorter

Audrey McWhorter Stark gave above information.

IV-5. Ollie May Perry, b. 8 May 1883, m. Elijah F. (Lige)
       White 8 Dec. 1901, Mills Co., Tex.
       V-1. Ila White   V-6. Lois White
       V-2. Dan Perry White   V-7. Millie Ann White
       V-3. Elliot White   V-8. Floyd White
       V-4. Alba White   V-9. Gene White
       V-5. Tommy White   V-10. Dean White, twins

IV-6. Grover Cleveland Perry, b. 26 Jan. 1886, d. 14 Feb.
       1971, m. (1) Fannie Brown 14 July 1907. Fannie b.
       17 Dec. 1888, d. 14 Feb. 1932, Cleveland m. (2)
       Nettie Russel. Children of Cleveland and Fannie:
       V-1. Townsend C. Perry m. Maud Montgomery 28 Nov. 1928.
       VI-1. Harold Perry   VI-3. Brenda Perry
       VI-2. Don Perry   VI-4. J. C. Perry
       V-2. Bernard Perry m. Vida Montgomery 1932.
       VI-1. Larry Perry
       V-3. Bernice Perry m. Jack Montgomery 1932.
       VI-1. Janice Montgomery
       VI-2. Glyndon Dale Montgomery
       V-4. Ralph Perry m. Bertha Wilder.
       V-5. Nelma Rea Perry m. Billie H. Richardson
       VI-1. Linda Richardson   VI-2. Karen Richardson.

Information from Mrs. Maud Perry of Goldthwaite.

IV-7. Garland T. Perry, b. 17 Dec. 1888, d. 24 Nov. 1979,
       Goldthwaite, Tex., m. Betty McGowan 5 Aug. 1913,
       Mills Co., Tex. Betty b. 11 June 1896, Mills Co.,
       d. 25 Feb. 1980, Goldthwaite, Mills Co., Tex.
       V-1. Ellis Glee Perry m. Amos Shelton.
       V-2. Gorman Perry m.
       V-3. Rose Ellen (Posey) Perry m. O. P. Shelton.
       V-4. Gladys E. Perry m. Steve Singleton.
       V-5. Eammon Perry, unmarried, li. San Saba, Tex.
       V-6. Sherman Perry unmarried, li, Goldthwaite, Tex.
       V-7. Zona L. Perry m. Woody Shanks.
       V-8. Ralph Charles Perry, d. 1955, unmarried.
       V-9. Wayne Perry m. Nan Fletcher.
       V-10. Willie M. Perry m. E. J. Curtis.
       V-11. Bulah Ann Perry m. J. D. Wright.
       V-12. Jearlene Perry, unmarried, li. Goldthwaite.

III-10. John Allen Godwin, b. 27 Jan. 1854, Clark Co., Ark.
         d. 23 Oct. 1932, age 78, m. Liva Ann Smith 15 Oct.
         1874, Hopkins, Co., Tex. (Chapter 3).

39

JOHN ALLEN GODWIN, SR. m. ALETHA SPENCER ca. 1835 CENSUS

Name / Birth	Sex	1840 McNairy Co., TN	1850 Clark Co., Ark.	1860 P.1, Hse.4, Cedar Township, Arkadelphia Clark Co., Ark.	1870 P.54, Prec. 3, P.O. Black Oak Hopkins Co., Tex.
John A. b. 1815-20	M	John A. 20-30	John farmer 30 NC		
Aletha b. 18 Oct. 1814	F	20-30	Eletha 30 NC	Aletha 46 NC	Alethia Cain 56 TN
Marion b. 20 Aug. 1837	M	-5	Marion 12 MS		
Eli b. 12 Feb. 1839	M	-5	Eli 10 MS	Eli C. 20 MS	
Jane b. 9 Dec. 1840	F		Lavina J. 8 TN		
Mary Ann b. 26 Dec. 1842	F		Mary Ann 6 MS	Mary Ann 16 MS	
Elizabeth b. 19 Aug. 1844	F		Elizabeth 5 MS	Nancy E. 15 MS	
Margaret b. Apr. 1846	F		Margaret 4 Ark.		
Catherine b. 5 Feb. 1848	F		Catherine 3 Ark.		
Ellen b. 12 Feb. 1850	F		Ellen 2/12 Ark.		
Julia Ann b. 4 Jan..1852	F			Julia Ann 7 Ark.	Julia 17
John Allen, Jr. b. 27 Jan. 1854	M			John A. 5 Ark.	John 16

40

III

John Allen
Godwin, Jr.

John Allen Godwin, Jr., son of John Allen Godwin, Sr. and Aletha Spencer, was b. 27 Jan. 1854, Clark Co., Ar., south of Hot Springs. He died 23 Oct. 1932 at age 78 at his home in Mills Co., Tex. near Lometa. He m. Liva Ann Smith 15 Oct. 1874, Hopkins Co., Tex. in the home of her parents.

Liva Ann was b. 11 Oct. 1850, Calhoun Co., Ala., the daughter of Enoch Smith and Jane Moore. She d. 28 Apr. 1935 at 8 O'clock Sunday evening at the home of her daughter, Beulah Hill.

John Allen Godwin and Liva Ann Smith Godwin

John Allen's father had died before John Allen, Jr. was born and his two older brothers died in 1865 when he was eleven. His mother then moved her family from Arkansas to Upshur Co., Tex. in December of that year, then on to Hopkins Co. in 1866. When he was about 14 or 15 years old, being the only boy left in the family, he was sent back to Arkansas horseback to collect a debt owed to his mother. He accomplished his mission and on the way back he rode along with a stranger who suggested a short cut through the woods. After they were well into the woods and night had come, the boy feared the stranger meant to

41

rob him. Though he kept his hand on his gun back of his saddle all the way through the woods, he met no trouble.

He joined the Baptist Church in 1872 at age 18.

Liva Ann had come with her parents, Enoch and Jane Smith, three brothers, and four sisters from Calhoun Co., Ala. to Hopkins Co., Texas in 1870 at age 20. Here she and John Allen met and married. Husking bees and country socials were popular in their younger days. Liva Ann was a quiet, pleasant woman with freckles and light very wavy hair which she wore in a bun at the back of her head. She was a neat housekeeper, proud of her feather beds and pillows and her beautiful parlor which was rarely used after her younger daughters married. She was also a good cook, but very frugal.

She lost her first three babies when they were 9 to 15 months old, two of them she thought died because she became pregnant again so soon and her milk no longer agreed with them. They raised five children to adulthood. And her mother-in-law lived with the family for most of 25 years.

After John and Liva Ann married in 1874, they made their home in Hopkins County, moved to Hunt County in 1883 but back to Hopkins County in 1886. There at Como, Texas with John F. Smith, a brother-in-law, he operated a General Merchandise Store for a few years. The wooden frame house with a porch across the front that John Allen built still stands in Como facing the railroad track just as Enoch Godwin remembered it from his early childhood there.

Their first five children were born in Hopkins County, Enoch in Hunt County, Effie back in Hopkins County, and Della, the youngest, in Mills County. Besides the three children who died in infancy, Riley, their next son, died at 27. John and Liva and their other four children all lived to be between 75 and 85 years of age.

John Allen was primarily a farmer, so in 1889 he sold his interest in the store and bought three new wagons and three teams of mules, loaded the wagons and started for Mills County, Texas near Goldthwaite. It began to rain a real East Texas rain and being December, they soon were very cold and bogging in the deep mud. At Greenville he chartered a box car, loaded everything and everybody in it and came on to Goldthwaite, settling in Big Valley Community.

They made a move to north central Texas in 1895 to Montague County near the Red River. John Allen plowed there with six yoke of oxen in the red farm land. When the dust storms came, he would keep plowing until he could not see the first yoke of oxen. They fished in the Red River that year.

42

The John Allen Godwin Home--about 1897
Big Valley Community, Mills Co., Texas

Seated: Mrs. Godwin, no relation, Aletha Spencer Godwin Cain.
Standing: Effie Godwin, Beulah Godwin, Della Godwin, Liva Ann Godwin, John Allen
          Godwin, Enoch Godwin.

The J. A. Godwin Family--about 1912--Long Cove

Adults: Liva Ann and J. A. Godwin, Effie Godwin, Della Godwin, Beulah Godwin Hill,
          L. W. Hill, Nollie and Enoch Godwin
Children: Zella T. Hill, Allen Hill, Glenna Mae Godwin, Tiana Godwin, held by
          Enoch Godwin

But during the cold winter John Allen maintained that his mules always stood facing Mills County, which was south, so the next year they moved back to Big Valley Community, then on to the Long Cove Community near Lometa on July 28, 1901. Here he bought 640 acres of land between two of the hills that enclose Long Cove.

He later sold 160 acres each to his son Enoch and Beulah's husband, Lonnie Hill, and retained 320 acres to retire on, which is what he did when his children all married. He ran beef cattle on the pasture land and rented the farm land out on "thirds and fourths," which meant that he got one-third of the feedstuff for his animals and one-fourth of the cotton for cash.

J. A., as he became known, made his occasional trips to town in a buggy, carrying for sale the extra eggs and butter, and bringing back their grocery needs. He bought Cream of Wheat and Saltine crackers which they ate for breakfast, the crackers crumbled in the hot Cream of Wheat. He kept peppermint sticks of candy to delight the grandchildren or reward those who brought his mail to him. His favorite pasttime was sitting on his wide front porch in his rocking chair with his feet propped up on the banister smoking his pipe of home-cured tobacco. And thus he lived out his life.

His sons were farmers and his daughters married farmers. All were Baptist, with Beulah, Enoch, Effie and their families involved in the Long Cove Baptist Church.

As the children married, John Allen helped each of them secure land nearby and as they died each child and spouse were buried near the parents in the Long Cove Cemetery north of Lometa, Texas, being clustered close in death as in life.

John Allen Godwin and Liva Ann Smith Children:
IV-1.   Orilla C. Godwin
IV-2.   Rena E. Godwin
IV-3.   Essie D. Godwin
IV-4.   Riley Marion Godwin
IV-5.   Beulah Clementine Godwin
IV-6.   Enoch Godwin
IV-7.   Effie Mae Godwin
IV-8.   Della Maud Godwin

IV-1.   Orilla Cordelia Godwin, b. 6 Nov. 1875, d. 25 Aug.
        1876.
IV-2.   Rena Etta Godwin, b. 14 Sept. 1877, d. 16 Sept.
        1878.
IV-3.   Essie Demayes Godwin, b. 21 Jan. 1879, d. 9 May
        1880.
IV-4.   Riley Marion Godwin, b. 19 Apr. 1880, d. 12 Apr.
        1907.

Riley never married, was a farmer who owned his own farm when he became ill and died at 27 years of age. His obituary said the cause of death was peritonitis; the family thought his death was caused by eating too many mulberries, but the description of the symptoms could fit appendicitis and eventual rupturing. His death was such a tragic occurrence that it overshadowed the family happenings for many years. When his brother Enoch died 64 years later, he still had Riley's trunk with his clothes and possessions in it.

Preserved in Enoch's handwriting on a yellowed sheet of paper is this note which could have been part of a letter:

He is only sleeping, awaiting for the judgment day when we shall meet again. It was so hard to give him up but as he said before he died, "The Lord's will be done, not mine."

T. and Robert, Aunt Jane and Dan Long and Aunt Julie Miller came down and was at the burying.

Riley was in his right mind up until about an hour before death and he then was unconscious.

Anybody never had any better neighbors than we have. The night he died nearly every family in the Cove was represented here by some of the family.

Two obituaries have been preserved and both tell of his deathbed conversion. One relates:

Being perfectly conscious and realizing that he must soon pass to the Great Beyond, he, in the presence of several devoted Christians, gave his heart to Jesus, and passed from this life, leaving this blessed assurance which shall ever comfort our hearts that he is not dead but gone to live with his Savior.

How our sad hearts were made to rejoice as we looked upon his peaceful and smiling face as he repeated the words of our blessed Savior, "Come unto me all ye that labor and are heavy laden and I will give you rest." Matt: 11:28.

He is described as "highly respected. . . a dutiful son, a loving brother, and was noble, generous, kind, and true."

46

A neighbor, Bessie Shuler, remembered Riley as a tall, large man with blond hair like Beulah's, the rest of the children being black-headed. He had eaten too many mulberries, she said, and died of locked bowels. She recalled that he had told the family just before he died what he wanted each of them to have of his possessions. Effie and Ely were to have his place where they were living at the time. Enoch was to have his stereo viewer and pictures that went with it, Della his horse and buggy. His father was to have his money, about $200.00, using part of it to erect for him a gravestone as tall as he was, 6 ft., 1 in. This stone is the tallest in the Long Cove Cemetery.

IV-5.   Beulah Clementine Godwin, dau. of John Allen Godwin and Liva Ann Smith, b. 8 May 1883, Hopkins Co., Tex., d. 30 Aug. 1963, Lampasas Co., Tex., m. Lonnie Walker Hill 24 Nov. 1901, Goldthwaite, Mills Co., Tex. Lonnie b. 23 Jan. 1881, Grayson Co., Tex., son of Elijah Hill and Ella Hudson. He d. 6 June 1964, San Antonio, Tex.
V-1.   Allen Walker Hill
V-2.   Zella T. Hill
V-3.   Mattie Estell Hill (adopted)

This family treated in detail in Elijah Hill Chapter.

IV-6.   Enoch Godwin, son of John Allen Godwin and Liva Ann Smith, b. 2 March 1886, Hunt Co., m. Nollie Bell Hill 16 Aug. 1908, Brownwood, Tex. Nollie b. 10 Feb. 1885, Santa Anna, Coleman Co., Tex., d. 13 Jan. 1974, dau. of Pleasant Gideon Hill and Kitty Bell Bishop.
V-1.   Glenna Mae Godwin
V-2.   Minnie Alba Tiana Godwin
V-3.   Julia Day Alva Godwin
V-4.   Ruth Geraldean Godwin
V-5.   Lillian Merle Godwin
V-6.   Beulah Merline Godwin
V-7.   Riley Alvin Godwin
V-8.   May Dell Godwin
V-9.   Ira Smith Godwin

This family is the subject of the next chapter.

EFFIE MAE GODWIN ROBERTS

IV-7.   Effie Mae Godwin, daughter of J. A. Godwin and Liva Ann Smith, b. 7 June 1888, Hopkins Co., Tex., d.

Ely Hood Roberts and
Effie Godwin Roberts,
about 1912

Below: Mayme O'Neal Roberts,
Leonard Roberts, Effie
Godwin Roberts, Erma Lois
Roberts Ballem, and Jimmy
Ballem, about 1972

48

2 June 1973, Ft. Worth, Tarrant Co., Tex., m. Ely
Hood Roberts 4 Feb. 1906, Mills Co., Tex. Ely
b. 9 Feb. 1885, Hood Co., Tex., d. 15 Oct. 1937,
Lometa, Tex., son of A. R. Roberts and Dora Stephen-
son. Effie and Ely are buried in Long Cove Cemetery, Lometa, Tex.

They lived their married life in Center and Long
Cove Communities near Lometa where Ely farmed.
They were a fun-loving couple with many friends.
They often gave parties for the young people, mov-
ing much of the furniture out of their three-room
house to accommodate the group. Both were Baptist.

V-1. Ruby Mae Roberts
V-2. Alvin Enoch Roberts
V-3. Leonard Albert Roberts
V-4. Erma Lois Roberts
V-5. John Allen Roberts

V-1. Ruby Mae Roberts, b. 17 Aug. 1909, li. one day.
V-2. Alvin Enoch Roberts, b. 12 Aug. 1910, d. 27 Sept.
      1910.
V-3. Leonard Albert Roberts, b. 12 April 1913, Center
      Community, Lampasas, Co., Tex., d. 18 May 1979,
      Arlington, Tex., buried in Mt. Olivet Cemetery,
      Ft. Worth, Tex., m. Mayme Belle O'Neal 8 Oct.
      1936, Lampasas Co., Tex. Mayme b. 2 Aug. 1908
      at Moline, Lampasas Co., Tex., dau. of David
      Thomas O'Neal and Susanna Baker.

Mayme had taught school 6 years and also operated a beauty shop in Lometa before she married.
Leonard and Mayme spent most of their married
life in Ft. Worth and Arlington. Leonard worked
on a dairy and in a packing house, then he and
Mayme operated a family grocery store for about
15 years before Leonard began work as store manager for Southland Corp., retiring in 1978 after
19 years with Southland. They were affiliated
with the Bible Church.

After Leonard's death this touching witness to
his faith was found in the family safety deposit
box:

Thank You Lord

Thank you first of all for saving a sinner
like me.
Thank you for answered prayer.
Thank you for walking by my side and guid-
ing my footsteps along the way these many
years.
Thank you for the many happy years thou hast

spared me.

Thank you for an earthly home to enjoy while on this earth. I am ready to leave it, when you are ready for me to occupy that home you have gone to prepare for all your children.

Thank you for a wife who has brought me many, many happy hours, not only as a wife, but as a lover, a business partner, a companion and mother to a son who has brought us many years of happiness, along with a lovely daughter-in-law and into their union you brought us a beautiful and loving granddaughter.

Thank you for the sunshine.

Thank you for the rain.

Thank you for the beautiful clouds that you use to decorate a beautiful blue sky.

Thank you Lord for thy word which you have promised will never be destroyed, by daily reading can help lighten many of our human problems.

Thank you Lord for saving my life. Even tho I have walked through the Valley of the shadow of death more than once, I knew you were by my side.

Thank you Lord for having been my light and my salvation during my life time. I had no fear. You have been my strength. I have no fear of death for I know you are by my side as well as the side of my loved ones.

May the love of God and the Communion of the Holy Spirit be with us all til we meet again.

(Signed on the envelope) L. A. Roberts.

VI-1.   Leonard Darwin Roberts, son of Leonard A. Roberts and Mayme O'Neal, b. 12 Feb. 1939, Ft. Worth, Tarrant Co., Tex., m. Doris Jean Moody 28 June 1957, Tarrant Co., Tex. Doris b. 27 Dec. 1938, Wolfe City, Hunt Co., Tex., dau. of Claude Andrew Moody and Abbie Mae Forston.

        Doris is PBX operator and Darwin works for Containers Corp. They live in Ft. Worth and are both Baptist.

VII-1.   Darla Denise Roberts, b. 14 July 1960, Ft. Worth, Tarrant Co., Tex.

V-4. Erma Lois Roberts, dau. of Effie Godwin and Ely
      Roberts, b. 16 Aug. 1918, Long Cove Community, Mills
      Co., Texas. m. James J. Ballem 3 May 1947, Ft.
      Worth, Texas. Jimmy was b. 26 April 1912 in Tarrant
      Co., Texas, the son of James Joseph Ballem and wife,
      Sarah Ella Shotwell.
      Erma Lois lived her girlhood years in Long Cove,
      but she and Jimmy have lived in Ft. Worth since
      marriage. Jimmy spent some years in the paint busi-
      ness but his occupation of longer standing was with
      the wholesale drug business until two heart opera-
      tions caused him to be unable to work. At the last
      surgery in 1966, a "Star Edward" valve was placed in
      his heart.
      Erma Lois has worked as a clerk in a packing house,
      at Cake Box Bakery, and for the last several years
      at R. E. Cox Department Store. They are both Bap-
      tists.
      No children.

V-5. John Allen Roberts (J.A.), son of Effie Godwin and
      Ely Roberts, b. 21 April 1924, Long Cove, Mills Co.,
      Texas, m. Mary Kathryn York 21 Aug. 1943. Kathryn
      b. 6 Oct. 1925, dau. of R. M. York and Bernice Belle
      Wallace.
      John served in the Navy on the west coast during
      World War II, while Kathryn lived in Seattle to be
      near. The rest of their married life has been spent
      in Lometa where they have been associated for many
      years with the Locker Plant. Kathryn was a beauty
      operator for 16 years. They also ranch and John
      carpenters.
  VI-1. Patricia Ann Roberts
  VI-2. John Lynn Roberts
  VI-3. Debbie Lynn Roberts (adopted)

Kathryn
John Lynn
Patricia
Debbie
John (J.A.)

VI-1.   Patricia Ann Roberts, b. 13 July 1946, m. (1)
        Jackie Hamrick, (2) Robert Milton, (3) Gean
        Ditmore.

VI-2.   John Lynn Roberts, b. 26 Dec. 1948, m. (1)
        Linda Varette, (2) Jane Tobar, (3) Ann Carson
        Heniger, (4) Diedra Woods, 22 Sept. 1978,
        Abilene, Texas.
   VII-1.   Michael Keith Roberts, b. Mar. 1966, son
            of Linda and John Lynn.
   VII-2.   James Allen Roberts, b. 1971, son of Jane
            and John Lynn.
   VII-3.   Tony (Heniger) Roberts
   VII-4.   Kevin (Heniger) Roberts, sons of Ann, adop-
            ted by John Lynn.

VI-3.   Debbie Lynn Roberts, adopted, b. 1 Dec. 1966,
        student at Lometa School.

DELLA MAUD GODWIN ALEXANDER

IV-8.   Della Maud Godwin, dau. of John Allen Godwin and
        Liva Ann Smith, b. 21 Sept. 1891, Mills Co., Tex.,
        Big Valley Community, d. 14 Dec. 1966, Lampasas Co.,
        Tex., buried in Long Cove Cemetery north of Lometa,
        m. Barney Pickens Alexander 26 Oct. 1909, at the
        home of her parents in the Long Cove Community.
        Barney b. 2 Sept. 1888, d. 19 July 1967, son of
        Thomas Livingston and Harriet Alexander.
          Della and Barney lived near Lometa for a few
        years then at Santa Anna, Tex. Barney was a farmer
        and Della was a great cook. They divorced, remar-
        ried, then divorced again, living their latter
        years alone.
   V-1.   Marion Lester Alexander, b. 27 Dec. 1911, li. 3
          days.
   V-2.   Norma Velma Alexander
   V-3.   Liva Juanita Alexander
   V-4.   Roland Ray Alexander, b. 25 Oct. 1929, stillborn.

   V-2.   Norma Velma Alexander, b. 2 Aug. 1913, Long Cove,
          Lampasas Co., Tex., m. Willie Andrew (Bill) Price
          26 Dec. 1936 in the Baptist Parsonage, Santa
          Anna, Coleman Co., Tex. Bill was b. 18 Sept.
          1906, Prentiss Co., Miss. near Boonsville, son of
          Willie Andrew Price, Sr. and Mary Price.
            Velma and Bill have lived most of their married
          life in Evant, Tex. except for short periods in
          Odessa, Tex. and Tucson, Ariz. Velma has worked
          as a telephone operator and as a secretary, but

Velma and Bill Price
Fortieth Wedding
    Anniversary 1976

Della and Barney Alexander   Juanita and Otha Stephens
Wedding Picture 1909   1964

spends much of her time now making handiwork items,
from painting to quilting. Her hobby of collecting
pitchers has become a collection of well over 600.
   Bill served two periods of enlistment in the
army, his last discharge being 30 Sept. 1945. He
opened Bill's Warehouse in Evant in 1946 and operated it until 1968, buying wool and mohair.
   They are spending their retirement years at
Evant and at their cabin on Lake Buchanan.
VI-1. Glen Doyle Price
VI-2. Albert Ray Price
       Both adopted 6 Dec. 1956.

VI-1. Glen Doyle Price, b. 20 Nov. 1944, m. Brenda
       Massingill Aug. 1964, Evant Methodist Church.
       Glen and Brenda lived at Ft. Worth and Austin.
                        53

Glen is now a furniture salesman in Austin. Divorced.

VII-1. Ricky Glen Price, b. 22 Dec. 1965.
VII-2. Darren Dewayne Price, b. 21 Jan. 1968.
VII-3. Gina Michelle Price, b. 24 Mar. 1973.
VI-2. Albert Ray Price, b. 21 Aug. 1947, m. Cindy Hill 19 Dec. 1968, Baptist Church, Austin, Tex. Albert and Cindy lived at Austin where Albert is manager of Data Processing at Seaton Hospital. Divorced.
VII-1. Clayton Ray Price, b. 25 Aug. 1972, Austin.

V-3. Liva Juanita Alexander, dau. of Della Godwin and Barney Alexander, b. 12 Oct. 1923, Santa Anna, Coleman Co., Tex.; m. Louie Darrell Whitley 15 Apr. 1939. Louie b. 1920, Weir, Tex. He was 18 she 15, when they married. They lived at Austin and Santa Anna, Tex.
VI-1. Janice Kay Whitley
VI-2. Jackie Wayne Whitley

VI-1. Janice Kay Whitley, b. 25 July 1940, Santa Anna, Coleman Co., Tex.; m. Jimmie Wayne Meeks 4 Sept. 1959, lived Amarillo and Denver, Colo. Children both adopted, b. Amarillo, Tex.
VII-1. Treon Kay Meeks, b. 30 Dec. 1965.
VII-2. Regina Ann Meeks, b. 11 Jan. 1970.

VI-2. Jackie Wayne Whitley, b. 25 Sept. 1941, Santa Anna, Coleman Co., Tex.; m. (1) Wanda Bourn 22 Nov. 1962, lived Amarillo and Canyon, Tex.
VII-1. Joy Dawn Whitley, b. July 1965.
VII-2. Jamie Dwaine Whitley, b. 6 Feb. 1970. Both children b. Amarillo, Tex. Jackie m. (2) Lamuang Dillard, native of Thailand, live at Grand Junction, Colo.
VII-3. Linda (Dillard) Whitley, b. Jan. 1971, adopted by Jackie.

Juanita m. (2) J. H. Bullard, lived at Lampasas 8 years where they operated a taxi service. m. (3) Otha Poma Stephens 30 Oct. 1963. Otha b. 19 Aug. 1910, Moline, Lampasas Co., Tex., son of Theodore Harrison Stephens and Mary Hanna (Mayme) Stubbs, both formerly of Ripley, Miss.

Juanita and Otha live at Lometa. He operates heavy machinery and she is a practical nurse.

IV

Enoch Godwin

Enoch Godwin was born 2 March 1886, Hunt County, Texas, second son of John A. and Liva Ann Smith Godwin. He died 22 Oct. 1971 at home in the Long Cove Community north of Lometa, Tex. He married Nollie Bell Hill 16 Aug. 1908, Brownwood, Tex. in the parsonage of the First Baptist Church by the pastor, Bro. George McCall.

Nollie Bell Hill was born 10 Feb. 1885 near the present town of Santa Anna, Coleman Co., Tex. Her father was Pleasant Gideon Hill, son of James Hill and Parolee Godwin. Her mother was Kitty Bell Bishop, daughter of Alvin Bishop and Mary Jane Cox. Children:

V-1. Glenna Mae Godwin
V-2. Minnie Alba Tiana Godwin
V-3. Julia Day Alva Godwin
V-4. Ruth Geraldine Godwin

55

Godwin-Hill and Related Families

V-5. Lillian Merle Godwin
V-6. Beulah Merline Godwin
V-7. Riley Alvin Godwin
V-8. May Dell Godwin
V-9. Ira Smith Godwin
V-10. Jeanette Boatwright, foster child.

    Enoch's parents had moved from Hopkins County in
northeast Texas to Mills County when he was 4 years old.
It was in the Big Valley School out of Goldthwaite that
he started to school at age 7. He attended the second
year in Montague County, then back in Big Valley until
1901, two years at Long Cove, and 1903-04 in Lometa, where
he boarded with Supt. S. J. Enochs, a man he admired very
much.
    Lometa School at that time was a two-story frame
building with 4 rooms, 2 upstairs and 2 down. Grade
school was on the lower floor. Miss Fannie Rugley taught
the Junior High age group and Professor Enochs the highest
classes. There was no strict grade division; the students
moved on by finishing one book and getting another a little
harder. The readers were McGuffeys from first grade
through sixth readers, then they read the Texas History
book as a reader before studying it for a history.
    Two teachers at Big Valley who left a lasting impres-
sion with Enoch were Mr. Arthur Oliver and Miss Ella Peck.
Miss Peck carried out her rules with "switch power." The
only spanking Enoch ever got in school, however, was when
he and a cousin, Cleveland Perry, got Miss Ella's switches
from behind the blackboard and built a fire with them at
Sunday School which was held in the school building. The
"bad guys" told on these two "good boys" and Professor
Oliver spanked them both.
    Nollie's mother died when she was 4 years old so she
and her brothers Alvin and Achrol were raised by their
grandparents, James and Parolee Hill, in the Democrat Community in southwest Comanche County on the Mills County
border.
    Nollie attended the Rocksprings School north of Mullin,
then took the teachers' tests and taught there one year.
With some money saved, she attended a business school in
Ft. Worth for a while before her marriage.
    Enoch and Nollie met when they were children when
Nollie's grandmother Parolee Hill went to visit Enoch's
grandmother Cain who had first married John Godwin, Parolee's half-brother.
    In September of 1900 when the great rains came, Big
Valley was under water the 24th, 25th and 26th and Galveston had her disaster. Enoch's Uncle Bob Keys had everything washed away. The Hills sent word that they would
56

Rocksprings School--Larger Students and Teachers--about 1906.

Front: Zackie Johnson, Lee Stephens, Carrie Williams, Minnie Scoggins, Olga Thompson, Mary Johnson, Philip Hill, Olga Hill, _____ Hickman, Achrol Hill.

Back: Johnny Douglas (Teacher), Laura Hickson, Amos Dunlap, Nollie Hill (Teacher), Pearl Aldredge, _____ Hickman, Emmitt Bolden, Lessie Hudson, George Henry, Laurence McKinney.

give him cottonseed to feed that winter and when Enoch
took a wagon to get a load of it, he met Nollie again, now
a very attractive teenager, but they were both very shy.

The families visited occasionally and Enoch and Nollie
began corresponding in 1906, became engaged in 1907, and
married in 1908. Transportation was too slow for many
dates, since they lived about 35 miles apart. When Enoch
did go to visit Nollie, he stayed overnight.

By the time they married, Nollie lived with her grandparents at Comanche where she worked as a telephone operator. She made her wedding dress in a sewing class she was
taking. Then she and Enoch both rode the train, meeting
in Blanket, and came to Brownwood where Enoch hired a hack
to take them to the church parsonage. Dr. McCall insisted
he had never married anyone in a hack, so they went into
the parlor where Mrs. McCall was witness to their wedding.

Enoch had been pressing Nollie to set a wedding date
since they became engaged. He had purchased 160 acres
from, and adjoining, his father and had built a house with
three rooms, two halls, and a rounded porth in front.

Enoch Godwin Home--1908.

Then one week in August of 1908, Nollie called Enoch
and said they could be married on Saturday. This was going to be August 16, Nollie's parents' wedding anniversary
date. They planned the meeting in Blanket, but Nollie did
not tell her grandparents out of fear of the reaction of
an uncle who still lived at home.

The first letter to them from Nollie's Grandmother
Hill was very formal and frank. She addressed them as

"Mr. and Mrs. Godwin" and told Nollie that she did not do right by not telling her that she was going to get married. She then invited them to come get Nollie's "things" any time they could. (Signed) Mrs. L. P. Hill.

They spent the first day of wedded life in a hotel in Brownwood and returned to Antelope Gap that night by train where they were met by Lonnie Hill in a hack. They remained with Enoch's parents until Tuesday when they took a wagon to Goldthwaite to get their household goods. Spent less than $100.00 for furniture and groceries and all.

On Sunday they had looked their new house over and while sitting on the porch Nollie had said, "One thing I'm going to have is a sewing machine!" and soon she got that too--a treadle Singer that she used most of the rest of her life.

Enoch and Nollie made a bargain that she would dress all the girls they had and he would dress the boys. Nollie couldn't know that they would have seven girls and only two boys, but with her sewing machine, she kept her bargain.

Enoch was a farmer, raising cotton, corn, maize, and fodder, usually hygier, or kaffir corn as it was then called. This was cut with a reaper or row-binder making bundles that were shocked in the field to dry. He always had an assortment of cows for meat and milk. For several years he raised registered Poland China hogs and Nollie raised and sold chicks or settings of eggs from Brown Leghorn chickens. At one time she had six incubators in continuous operation through the spring months. Enoch always raised some sheep and at times kept goats if the brush became a problem.

Enoch managed the cotton gin in Lometa from 1916 through 1919, even buying his first Model T Ford in July of 1916 to make the 9-mile trip into town. He purchased his next Model T in 1924 and before that one wore out children bulged over the doors when the whole family went to church.

He was also director and stockholder in the Lometa State Bank, which had to close its doors in the late 1920's--a crushing blow to customers and especially so to stockholders, who not only lost their investment, but had to repay their part of the shares. The bank's failure, with the Depression years that followed, made life quite difficult. They were do-without-it years, but from the garden, chickens, and pigs there was plenty to eat.

The family went through a calamitous time in late 1928 and early 1929 when the oldest daughter, Glenna Mae, had ruptured appendix and spent several weeks in King Daughters Hospital at Temple. The night Enoch brought her home, the youngest child, Smitty, was born and Day

Alva had a bad case of the flu. Eventually most of the
family, with the exception of the mother and new baby and
Glenna Mae, took the flu. Glenna Mae had stayed with Aunt
Beulah Hill who, with Uncle Lonnie, was ever so helpful
during the two weeks that the family was ill. And the
sheep were lambing too. A nurse and companion came to
stay at the house. She nursed the family and he nursed
the sheep.

The nine Godwin children were born at home about 9
miles out in the country with Dr. W. D. Biggs attending
all except the last. He was ill during the flu epidemic
also, so the family depended on Dr. Wittenburg, also of
Lometa.

Enoch was a Director of the Rural Telephone Company
of Lometa and was often trustee of the Long Cove School
where all the children attended.

The children were always encouraged to learn but it
was Nollie who instilled in her children the desire for
an education beyond the local school. They all graduated
from high school and attended college, eight of them attending John Tarleton Agricultural College, now Tarleton
University, at Stephenville, Texas.

Much of the family life was church oriented. They
were faithful attenders of the Long Cove Baptist Church,
with the children being baptized and joining the church
early in life. Enoch often taught a class or was Sunday
School Supt. He was church treasurer for nearly 22 years
and a deacon since 1925. At home, Bible reading and prayer was the custom at the breakfast table, Enoch and Nollie
taking turns. They continued this practice into their
mid-80's as long as they could go to the table.

For over 63 years Enoch and Nollie lived on the farm
where they settled and worked hard to raise their large
family of healthy children.

They also made room in their home for the orphaned
daughter of a cousin, Jeanette Boatwright, who was 16
when she came to live with them. Jeanette graduated from
high school and went through nurses' training at Brecken-
ridge Hospital, Austin. She was often helpful and very
appreciative of their care of her.

As their infirmities warned them of the impending de-
parture from this life, the faith of Nollie and Enoch in
a afterlife--a heavenly home--was strong. They looked
forward to the riches of their glorious inheritance (Eph.
1:18). Both were aware that they would never be well
again. Nollie's mental faculties were clear at times and
she would speak of her desire to go to her "heavenly reward." Enoch's mind was clear. He had less desire to
leave this earth and his wife, but never any anxiety over
the certainty of a better life ahead.

Summarization

Enoch and Nollie Godwin married in Brownwood in 1908, lived on their farm near Lometa for 63 years and raised nine healthy children, eight of whom are still alive in 1980. The oldest daughter passed away at 45; the others are all past 50. Enoch and Nollie lived to be 85 and 88 respectively. They possessed little beside the land on which they lived, yet they sent all of their children to college, with six of them earning degrees.

The Long Cove Baptist Church was the center of their religious life with Bible reading and prayer at the breakfast table every day.

Hard work with close management was a way of life; chores were assigned at the breakfast table where appearance was mandatory.

Their generosity toward their kin and neighbors was well-known.

Enoch and Nollie Godwin Family

Seated: Riley, Enoch, Nollie, Smitty
Standing: Jeanette Boatwright, Glenna Mae, Day Alva, Lillian, May Dell, Beulah, Tiana, Ruth

Enoch Godwin

Enoch and Nollie Godwin's Golden Wedding Anniversary, Aug. 16, 1958

Little ones in front: Paul Hudgins, Francene Hudgins, Jeanene Holland, Ricky Hudgins, Judy Godwin
First Row: Anita Brown, May Dell Hudgins, Enoch and Nollie Godwin, Judy Brown, Joe Godwin, Gary
        Holland, Kay Godwin, Day Alva Trainer, Jeanette Brown, Lillian Brown
Back: Frank Trainer, Edward Smith, Tiana Smith, Beulah Holland, Rudolph Holland, Dixie Trainer,
        J. D. Brown, Peggy Smith, Yvonne Godwin, Bonita Gadbury, Farris Gadbury, Ruth Gadbury,
        Farrisa Gadbury, Smitty Godwin, Riley Godwin holding Riley Lee Brown.

63

Godwin-Hill and Related Families

GLENNA MAE GODWIN ROSS

V-1. Glenna Mae Godwin, dau. of Enoch Godwin and Nollie
Hill, b. 20 Oct. 1909, Mills Co., Tex., d. 24 Sept.
1955, Del Rio, Tex., m. Rufus Joe Ross 18 June 1930,
Lometa, Lampasas Co., Tex.
Rufus b. 8 Jan. 1904 Edwards Co., Tex. about 20
miles south of Rock Springs, son of Dan L. Ross and
Nancy Elizabeth Burleson, both born in Llano Co.,
Tex.
Glenna Mae attended school at Long Cove, a two-
teacher school, until her junior year in high school
when her parents sent her to Mary Hardin Academy at
Belton. She then graduated from Lometa High School
in 1928.
She attended Draughans Business College at Abilene
in the fall, becoming very ill in November. She was
brought home, did not improve, then was taken to
King Daughters Hospital at Temple where she was operated on for ruptured appendix. Her recovery was
slow, she did not return home until Jan. 2, 1929,
the day Smitty was born and the family began taking
the flu.
The next fall she went as governess to the two
children of Mr. and Mrs. Violin Ross on a ranch out
of Pumpville in West Texas. There she met Rufus Joe
Ross, Violin's brother, and they were married the
following June. Rufus was ranching in Terrell County about 25 miles north of Pumpville, raising sheep
and goats.
Their married life was spent mostly in Terrell
County, however they were at Iraan, Texas in 1933-34
and at Ft. Davis in 1935 and for some years thereafter.
They drove their stock from Ft. Davis to Dryden
during the depression, camping along the way. When
they started out they had 1300 goats and $13.00.
They lived on a ranch about 5 miles out of Dryden
for several years, then bought a home in Dryden and
continued to ranch until the drouth of the early
1950's when there was no grass and they sold their
stock.
Their great disappointment was that they had no
children so they were overjoyed when an adoption
agency in San Antonio granted them a week-old boy
in January of 1947. Bennie Ray, they called him.
Glenna Mae was a Baptist, but joined the Methodist
Church in Dryden since there was no Baptist church
there. She was a capable leader in church and community activities.

64

Glenna Mae Godwin Ross Family

Rufus and Glenna Mae Godwin Ross
1909-1955

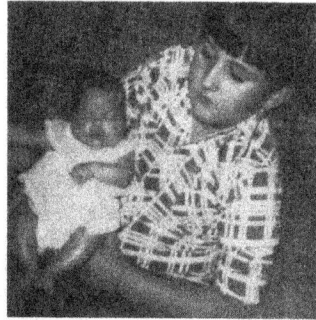

Glenna Mae Ross
Joe Charles Ross

Children of

Bennie Ray and
Andra Ross

She became ill of an indefinite malady in late summer of 1955, spent some time in the hospital at Del Rio, then passed away September 24. She was buried in the Ross plot in Sanderson Cemetery.

VI-1.   Bennie Ray Ross, b. 23 Dec. 1946, San Antonio, Texas. Adopted. Ben m. Andra Myrtle Welch 22 Aug. 1968.

Andra b. 2 Feb. 1950 Camp Wood, Real Co., Tex. dau. of Linton Wiley Welch and Nell Marie O'Bryant Welch (Hyde), who were m. 26 June 1942 in San Antonio, Texas.

Bennie Ray was 8 years old when his mother passed away; he remained with Rufus until he was 12, then his Aunt Lillian and Uncle J. D. Brown took him to live with them and go to school in Grand Prairie, where he graduated from high school after spending one year at Lometa High School and one year at Allen Academy in Bryan, Texas. He served in the army in Viet Nam and is now working in Brown Furniture in Ozona, Texas.

VII-1.   Joe Charles Ross, b. 1 Aug. 1971, Alpine, Tex.
VII-2.   Lisa Ann Ross, b. 9 May 1973, Ft. Stockton, Tex., li. one day.
VII-3.   Glenna Mae Ross, b. 17 July 1979, San Angelo, Tex.

MINNIE ALBA TIANA GODWIN SMITH

V-2.   Minnie Alba Tiana Godwin, dau. of Enoch Godwin and Nollie Hill, b. 15 April 1912, Lometa, Mills Co., Tex., m. Charlie Edward Smith 19 Jan. 1939, Goldthwaite, Tex. by Bro. J. D. Long.

Edward b. 24 June 1908, Bertram, Burnet Co., Tex. son of Charlie W. and Lizzie Klose Smith.

When Tiana was five days old, a blustery April hail storm beat out the window panes to the bedroom where she and her mother were, but she was safely covered with a pillow.

Tiana attended the two-teacher Long Cove School through the eighth grade, went to Lometa in the ninth, to Long Cove in the tenth, then back to Lometa to graduate in 1931. Attendance at Baylor, Belton was cut short by illness, but she later was in Tarleton State College at Stephenville for a year.

After a year of teaching at Democrat north of Mullin, she went to Memphis, Tenn. to enter nurses training, but when she found her college credits would not count, she returned to Tarleton for another year, then to Hobbs, N.M. where she worked in a sewing shop with Mrs. McChristian for two years.

Tiana and Edward had known each other since childhood, had dated occasionally, and sought advice of each other on important questions during their dating years.

After marriage, they lived on the Smith farm and ranch north of Lometa for 12 years, then bought a home northeast of Lampasas where they have built up their herd of milk cows and operated a dairy for nearly 30 years.

VI-1. Peggy Jean Smith
VI-2. Jerry Ronnie Smith

Tiana Godwin Smith Family

Front: Cindy Wolfe, Charley Wolfe, Jeffrey Smith
Back: Peggy Smith Wolfe, Julie Wolfe, Richard Wolfe,
        Tiana Godwin Smith, Edward Smith, Jean Wolfe,
        Jerry Smith

VI-1. Peggy Jean Smith, b. 28 Sept. 1943, San Saba, Tex.,
       m. Richard Earl Wolfe 28 Sept. 1961 at the home of
       her parents near Lampasas, Tex. Richard b. 8 Aug.
       1942, Lampasas, son of Wayne J. Wolfe and Ruby
       Greer.

       Peggy and Richard have farmed and dairied, but
       at present Richard is combining farming and opera-
       ting a feed and seed store at Adamsville, Tex.

       After the arrival of their four children, Peggy
       acquired an incredible 28 hours of college credit

67

through the College Level Examination Board and continued college work at Tarleton State University,
Stephenville to earn her degree in 1976 and is now
teaching in Lampasas.

VII-1.   Jean Earlene Wolfe, b. 24 Nov. 1962, Lampasas,
         Tex.
VII-2.   Julie Dianna Wolfe, b. 1 Apr. 1964, Lampasas,
         Tex.
VII-3.   Cindy Susanne Wolfe, b. 9 July 1969, Lampasas,
         Tex.
VII-4.   Charlie Richard Wolfe, b. 21 Dec. 1970,
         Lampasas, Tex.

VI-2.   Jerry Ronnie Smith, b. 7 Jan. 1950, Comanche, Tex.,
        m. Nelda Sue Mears 1 Dec. 1970, Kempner Baptist
        Church. Nelda is the adopted daughter of M. E. and
        Effie Landry Mears of Lampasas, Tex., b. 28 Aug.
        1952, San Angelo, Tex.
            Jerry and Nelda lived on the dairy farm and assis-
        ted in the operation. Now divorced, but both still
        reside in or near Lampasas.
VII-1.   Jeffrey Ray Smith, b. 1 Apr. 1974, Lampasas, Tex.

         * * * * * * * * * * * * * * * * * * *

Edward Smith had m. (1) Stella Mosier 25 Nov. 1931,
Mills Co., Tex. Stella was b. 1907 and d. 1938, the
daughter of Thomas Jefferson Mosier and Emma Lee
Ila Absher of Mullin, Tex. Stella is buried at
Lometa, Tex.
1.   James Edward Smith
2.   Noreta Jeanette Smith

1.   James E. Smith, b. 15 Feb. 1934, Goldthwaite,
     Tex., m. Nancy Ann Edwards, who was b. 27 Jan.
     1939, Detroit, Mich., daughter of Tom and Ber-
     nice Edwards, later Bernice Meeks (Mrs. Joe
     Meeks).
         Jimmy received his B.S. degree from Southwest
     Texas State Teachers College in San Marcos in
     May 1955, then a M. Ed. degree in El Paso in
     1965, has taught 18 years in Van Horn and 7
     years in El Paso, is presently teaching at Van
     Horn, Texas.
         Nancy has been employed by Holiday Inn of Van
     Horn for the last nine years. working evenings,
     has been promoted from Restaurant Cashier to
     Front Desk Manager.
         When Nancy's mother passed away, her sister

Karen Meeks came to live with them, then after
their grandfather passed away, their grandmother
also came to live with them, has been with them
five years now.
1. Marianne Smith, b. 16 July 1957, El Paso,
    Tex., attended Hardin Simmons University
    at Abilene 3 years, m. Jim Angell 13 May
    1978.
2. Steven E. Smith, b. 23 Oct. 1959, El Paso,
    is attending Hardin Simmons.
3. Marguerite (Margie) Smith, b. 13 Aug. 1962,
    El Paso.
4. Joe E. Smith, b. 3 April 1967, El Paso.
5. Paul E. Smith, b. 3 April 1967, twin to Joe E.

2. Noreta Jeanette Smith, b. 6 March 1938, Lampasas,
    Tex., m. Robert James Henderson, Jr. 23 Dec. 1957
    at Kempner, Tex. Bobby b. 4 Nov. 1935, Copperas
    Cove, Tex., son of Robert James Henderson, Sr.
    and wife Opal Herring.
    Noreta graduated from Lampasas High School and
    earned her B.S. Degree in Elementary Education at
    Texas Woman's University at Denton, Texas in the
    summer of 1959. She has been teaching in the
    Lampasas Elementary School for 14 years.
    Bobby has done mechanic work, but is now in
    partnership in the Smith Dairy and farming opera-
    tions. They live near Lampasas.
    1. Shari Lynn Henderson, b. 13 June 1960,
        Lampasas, Tex.
    2. Sheila Diane Henderson, b. 30 Aug. 1962, Lam-
        pasas, Tex.

JULIA DAY ALVA GODWIN TRAINER

V-3. Julia Day Alva Godwin, third daughter of Enoch Godwin
      and Nollie Hill, b. 24 Nov. 1913, near Lometa, Mills
      Co., Tex., m. Frank Brock Trainer 24 July 1936 at
      the home of her parents near Lometa by Rev. Forrester,
      Baptist minister.
      Frank b. 16 April 1907, Chillicothe, Ohio, d. 11
      Nov. 1965, Chillicothe, the son of James H. and
      Arminta Brock Trainer of Ohio.
      Day Alva attended grade school at Long Cove and
      graduated from Lometa High School in 1931. After
      attending John Tarleton Agricultural College in
      1931-32, a junior college at the time, she was
      governess to the two children of Mr. and Mrs. Lee
      Martin on the Old McNutt Ranch near Comstock, Tex.

for a year. She spent the next two winters teaching at Juno, Tex., a grade school with about 20 pupils in grades 1 through 6 in Val Verde County, where she received $75.00 per month.

In 1951 she returned to teaching and continued her education at Ohio University where she received her B.S. Degree in the summer of 1957, cum laude. That year she began teaching in Central School in Chillicothe where she remained for nine years. She taught a total of 27 years, retiring in 1975 to become a happy gardener and traveler.

Day Alva and Frank had met on a train trip to California in Sept. of 1935. Frank had been visiting relatives in Albuquerque, N.M. and Day Alva and her mother were on their way to visit Alvin and Clarissa Hill and their new baby in Calif. They later corresponded, then Frank visited her in Juno, where she was teaching. They became engaged and were married the following July.

Their first home was Toledo, Ohio, then for short periods in several towns where Frank was transferred by the railroad for which he worked. There were stays in Willard, Ohio, Painesville, Ohio, then New Castle, PA. where their first baby was born. In 1939 they were moved to Chillicothe, Ohio where they have lived since.

Frank had graduated from high school in Chillicothe and was a machinest apprentice at the Baltimore and Ohio (B&O) Railroad shops there for four years. In all he worked for the B&O about 20 years.

In Oct. of 1942 he enlisted as a Seabee in WW II, serving in the Solomon Islands in the South Pacific. While in the service he received a Presidential Commendation for making a great number of aluminum pens for setting broken bones of war casualties.

After the War, Frank was promoted to Shop Foreman on the B&O RR at Chillicothe and later to night supervisor of the shops. In 1953 he accepted a job with the Atomic Energy Commission Plant in Piketon, Ohio, a happy change for Frank.

Day Alva, a Baptist from age 13, became a Methodist to be with Frank in his church. Frank sang in the Trinity Methodist Church choir and took part in the Atomic Operetta Guild for 3 years.

VI-1. Frank Emlyn Trainer
VI-2. Dixie Lee Trainer

VI-1. Frank Emlyn Trainer, b. 25 Dec. 1937, New Castle, PA., m. Marva Rose (Liz) Huxtable 29 Aug. 1959, Cleveland, Ohio.

Day Alva Godwin Trainer Family

Day Alva
Godwin
Trainer

Frank B.
Trainer
1907-1965

Frank E.   Liz   Dixie   Bob
     Trainer   Lauer

Sarah   Frank   Anita   Bobby

Paul   Laura   Julia   Daniel

71

Liz, b. 8 Aug. 1938, Cleveland, Ohio, dau. of
Marvin Earl and Dorothy Margaret Fisher Huxtable.
Frank graduated from Chillicothe High School in
1956, received his degree in Electrical Engineer-
ing from Case Institute in Cleveland in 1960, and
his Masters Degree in the same field from Purdue
U., Lafayette, Ind. He worked for IBM as Project
Manager for most of 15 years but now has a busi-
ness of his own, Trainer and Associates, Computer
Consulting, Program Development, Hinsdale, Ill.
Liz is a Registered Nurse.

VII-1. Sarah Kathleen Trainer, b. 10 Nov. 1962, Ft.
Wayne, Ind.

VII-2. Frank William Trainer, b. 19 Sept. 1964,
Cincinnati, Ohio.

VII-3. Paul Godwin Trainer, b. 18 Oct. 1968, Cincinnati, Ohio. Adopted.

VII-4. Laura Margaret Trainer, b. 18 June 1970,
Columbus, Ohio. Adopted.

VI-2. Dixie Lee Trainer, b. 1 Oct. 1942, Chillicothe,
Ohio, Ross Co., m. Robert F. Lauer, Jr. 24 Feb.
1964, Chillicothe, Ohio.
Robert (Bob) Lauer, b. 10 Nov. 1942, Columbus,
Ohio, son of Robert F. and Marie Messerschmitt
Lauer of Ohio. Bob is a Civil Engineer in
Columbus, Ohio.
Dixie Lee graduated from Chillicothe High School
in 1960, attended Miami University in Oxford, Ohio
for three years, then married. After four chil-
dren, whe has enrolled at Ohio State, Columbus,
Ohio to complete her degree in Dietitics and re-
lated fields.

VII-1. Anita Sue Lauer, b. 5 Sept. 1964, Columbus,
Ohio.

VII-2. Robert Frederick Lauer, b. 6 Jan. 1968,
Connelsville, Pa.

VII-3. Julia Marie Lauer, b. 3 June 1969, Lancaster,
Ohio.

VII-4. Daniel Emlyn Lauer, b. 21 Dec. 1971, Columbus.

RUTH GERALDINE GODWIN GADBURY

V-4. Ruth Geraldine Godwin, daughter of Enoch Godwin and
Nollie Hill, b. 17 June 1916, Long Cove Community
near Lometa, Tex., m. Farris Franklin Gadbury 9 Feb.
1937, Lampasas, Tex.
Farris b. 5 Sept. 1905, Ballinger, Tex., son of
Andrew Jackson and Leila Lewis Madison Rusler Gadbury.

Farris d. 17 March 1977 at home near Lometa, Lampasas
Co., Tex. of emphasema. Buried at Long Cove Cemetery.
Ruth went through tenth grade at Long Cove School,
finished her high school work and over a year of
college at John Tarleton College at Stephenville,
then came back to Long Cove as teacher for three
years, beginning in 1935-36.

Farris graduated from Lometa High School in 1925
and had attended John Tarleton College two years before coming back to Long Cove to farm the home place
in 1931.

Ruth and Farris lived most of their married live in
Long Cove except for the first summer in Bruni, Tex.
and the WW II years in San Antonio where they both
worked as machinests at Kelly Field.

Farris taught automobile mechanics in the G.I.
School at San Saba for 6½ years, then dairied for 15
years from 1949 to 1964. He then operated the Lampasas Tractor and Equipment business in Lampasas for
three years before retiring to the farm in 1967.

After their three girls were in their teens, Ruth
went back to college at Howard Payne College, Brownwood, earning a B.S. and M. Ed. degrees. She taught
at Killeen in 1956-57 and has taught fourth grade
at Lometa since.

Farris and Ruth and girls were active in the Long
Cove Baptist Church where Farris led the singing for
about 35 years and Nolliela and Farrisa played the
piano. Ruth taught Sunday School for some 38 years.

Ruth has compiled a local history book, One Hundred
Years in Long Cove and a genealogy book on Farris'
mother's family called A Branch of the Madison Tree.

VI-1. Nolliela Ann Gadbury
VI-2. Farrisa Joan Gadbury
VI-3. Bonita Sue Gadbury

VI-1. Nolliela Ann Gadbury, b. 23 July 1939, Long Cove,
       Mills Co., Tex., d. 17 Feb. 1957, Lampasas Co.,
       Tex., age 17, senior in Lometa High School, auto-
       mobile accident.

VI-2. Farrisa Joan Gadbury, b. 30 Oct. 1940, Long Cove,
       Mills Co., Tex., m. Lloyd D. Smith 26 Aug. 1960,
       Lometa Baptist Church. Lloyd b. 11 June 1938,
       Round Mountain, Blanco Co., Tex., son of Lincoln
       Smith and Geraldine Polvado.
          Farrisa and Lloyd have lived in La Feria, Nord-
       heim, Yorktown, La Pryor, Johnson City, and Kerens
       where they have been educators. At the last three
       assignments Lloyd has been superintendent and

Farrisa has taught in grade school. They are active Baptists.

VII-1. Laurie Ann Smith, b. 30 June 1961, Burnet, Tex., attending Baylor in Waco.

VII-2. Patti Sue Smith, b. 11 Dec. 1962, Cuero, De Witt Co., Tex.

VI-3. Bonita Sue Gadbury, b. 23 Mar. 1942, Long Cove, Lampasas Co., Tex., m. Darrel Roy Word 21 Aug. 1965, Long Cove Baptist Church, Lampasas Co., Tex. Darrel b. 15 Mar. 1938, son of Nolan Roy Word and Theda Irene White of Lampasas, Tex.

Bonita (Tudder) and Darrel lived in Austin for five years but are now at Cedar Park north of Austin. Darrel, with a Ph.D. in electrical engineering, is part owner of the firm of Geotronics of Austin. Bonita is a volunteer aid in grade school.

VII-1. Daris Sue Word, b. 12 Dec. 1970, Austin, Tex.

Ruth Godwin Gadbury Family

Front: Daris Word, Darrell Word, Patti Smith, Lloyd Smith
Back: Ruth Gadbury, Bonita Gadbury Word, Laurie Smith, Farrisa Gadbury Smith

Farris Gadbury
1905-1977

Nolliela Gadbury
1939-1957

LILLIAN MERLE GODWIN BROWN

V-5. Lillian Merle Godwin, dau. of Enoch Godwin and Nollie
Hill, b. 27 Aug. 1918, near Lometa, Mills Co., Tex.,
m. J. D. Brown 25 Dec. 1937, Gatesville, Coryell Co.,
Tex.
   J. D. b. 5 Sept. 1919, Lometa, Tex., son of John
James Brown and Annie Parolee Medart of the Atherton
Community east of Lometa.
   Lillian and J. D. met at Lometa High School their
senior year there. After graduation in May 1936 J. D.
attended Draughans Business College in Austin for a
year while Lillian attended John Tarleton College at
Stephenville that year and an additional summer.
   Lillian was teaching at Juno, Tex. when they married
during the Christmas holidays. After school was out,
they moved back to Lometa and operated a service sta-
tion until March 1943. Their first daughter, Anita
Lajuan, was born in the Rollins-Brook Hospital in
Lampasas while they lived at Lometa.
   In March of 1943 they moved to Dallas where J. D.
was employed at North American Assembly Plant for war
planes. In July of that year they moved to Grand
Prairie where they bought their first home at 314
Yeargan, living there for five years. While here
their second daughter, Judith Annette was born in
Methodist Hospital in Dallas.
   They invested in a half interest in a new and used
furniture business in 1945, called Grand Prairie Trad-
ing Post. They bought out the partner, Mr. Harold
Johnson, in 1948 and by 1963 decided to handle new
furniture altogether and changed the name to Brown
Furniture Company. They also operated a furniture
store in Brady from 1966 to 1971 and since March of
1965 have owned Brown Furniture Store in Ozona, Tex.
   They built and moved into their home on Church
Street in Grand Prairie in 1950 and have experienced
the growth of Grand Prairie from 7,500 to 55,000 pop-
ulation while they lived there.
   J. D. served on the Grand Prairie Commission for
three 2-year terms and was Mayor Pro Tem for the last
two terms.
   They were active in the Inglewood Baptist Church,
serving as Supt. and teacher of 3 yr-old for five
years. J. D. also served as building chairman for
the new church auditorium.
   Lillian has received further education from Arlington State, T.C.U., and El Centro. She does interior
design in connection with their furniture business.
She was a Girl Scout leader for 17 years, with her
daughters active scouts.

A nephew, Bennie Ray Ross, came to live with them in June 1959 and stayed to go through Jr. High and High School, with the exception of one year in Lometa High and a year at Allen Academy at Bryan.

Lillian and J. D. moved to Ozona, Tex. in July 1971, where they now reside.

VI-1.   Anita Lajuan Brown
VI-2.   Judith Annette Brown

VI-1.   Anita Lajuan Brown, b. 29 Nov. 1940, Lampasas, Tex., m. (1) Mehdi Raffi March 1969, Richmond, Va. Mehdi was born and raised in Tehran, Iran where his parents still live.

Anita m. (2) Henry Louis Salomonsky, Jr. 16 Aug. 1974, Richmond, Va. Louis b. Mar. 1939, Richmond, son of Henry Louis Salomonsky, Sr., and Elizabeth Ann Brockwell.

Anita graduated from Southwestern Medical School in Dallas in 1965, did her internship at St. Vincent's Hospital in New York City and is now Associate Professor of Anesthesiology at the University of Virginia Medical School in Richmond.

Children of Anita Brown and Louis Salomonsky:

VII-1.   Anita Louise Salomonsky, b. 4 June 1976, Richmond, Va., adopted.
VII-2.   Henry Louis Salomonsky III, b. 22 Nov. 1978, Richmond, adopted.

Children of Louis Salomonsky by previous marriage:
1.   Stephen David Salomonsky, b. 5 Aug. 1962.
2.   Mark Silvette Salomonsky, b. 4 Oct. 1963.
3.   Benjiman Louis Salomonsky, b. 1 Sept. 1965.
4.   Helen Elizabeth (Betsy) Salomonsky, b. 2 Nov. 1966.
5.   Daniel Henry Salomonsky, b. 12 Apr. 1968.

VI-2.   Judith Annette Brown, b. 13 July 1947, Dallas, Tex., m. Carroll Ray Boykin 13 Aug. 1966, Grand Prairie, Tex.

Ray b. 27 Aug. 1945, Uvalde, Tex., son of William Amos Boykin and Virginia Belle Hoag.

Judy has attended Texas Tech at Lubbock, Stephen F. Austin at Nacogdoches and Del Mar University in Corpus Christi, as well as San Angelo University.

Ray is a Methodist minister in Corpus Christi and was ordained in June 1979 at the South Texas Methodist Conference in San Antonio.

Children of Judy Brown and Ray Boykin:
VII-1. Michelle Leigh (Shelly) Boykin, b. 27 Jan 1968,
New Orleans, La.
VII-2. Kendanne Marie (Kendy) Boykin, b. 6 June 1972,
Greenville, Tex.

Lillian Godwin Brown Family

Seated:
Judy Brown Boykin, Kendy Boykin, Lillian Brown, Anita
Louise Salomonsky, Henry Louis Salomonsky III, Anita Brown
Salomonsky, Henry Louis Salomonsky, Jr.
Standing:
Shelly Boykin, Ray Boykin, J.D. Brown, Betsy Salomonsky.

BEULAH MERLINE GODWIN HOLLAND

V-6. Beulah Merline Godwin, dau. of Enoch Godwin and
Nollie Hill, b. 6 July 1921, Lometa, Mills Co., Tex.,
m. Rudolph Sherman Holland 14 Oct. 1944, Austin, Tex.
Rudolph b. 9 Sept. 1914, Marble Falls, Tex., son
of Clyde and Mabel Dunaway Holland. He passed away
30 Dec. 1977, San Antonio, Tex., buried Fairland
Cemetery out of Marble Falls, Tex.
Beulah attended the two-teacher Long Cove School
through the tenth grade, then rode the bus to Lometa

and graduated there in 1938 with 27 seniors that
year.

She was the sixth daughter of Enoch and Nollie
Godwin and, although the other girls had done some
college work, she was the first to earn her degree,
so was an inspiration to the others to continue
their schooling. Beulah attended John Tarleton
Agricultural College at Stephenville in '38, '39
and '40 then went on to TSCW in Denton where she
received her degree in Home Economics in September
1944.

She taught school at Morman Mills near Marble
Falls in 1941-42 and it was here that she met
Rudolph. She taught at Juno, Texas 1942-43, then
at Doole, Tex. 1943-44.

Beulah and Rudolph were married Oct. 14, 1944 in
Austin at the home of Mr. and Mrs. Steve Heffington,
then tax assessor of Travis County and an old friend
of the Holland family. Rudolph was home on furlough
from the Marines, having just completed 2 years in
the South Pacific during World War II. He was to be
stationed at Klamath Falls, Oregon and she was Home
Demonstration Agent at San Saba· Beulah stayed with
her job until the following May then joined Rudolph
in Oregon where she worked as 4-H Agent in Klamath
County until Dec. 1945.

Rudolph was discharged from the service in Oct.
1945 and worked in the potato harvest until they
came home to Texas for Christmas.

In January of 1946 Rudolph became foreman on the
Brownlee Ranch between Burnet and Marble Falls.
Gary, their first child, was born while they were
there. They left the ranch in July of 1949 and
lived for a time on the Bowman place in the Morman
Mills Community.

From April 1950 until Jan. 1953 they lived on
Valdina Farms where Rudolph was foreman of this
18,000 acre ranch in Uvalde and Medina Counties.
Jeanene, their daughter, was born in Hondo while
they lived there. Hondo was where they traded,
about 25 miles from Ranch Headquarters. Utopia,
where they attended church, was 18 miles away.

On May 1, 1953 they moved to the Snelling Ranch
near Spicewood out of Marble Falls, where Rudolph
was also ranch foreman. Here they were very active
in community and church work. Rudolph served as
Sunday School Supt. and was ordained a deacon in
Dec. 1964. Beulah taught a Sunday School class many
years.

Rudolph served on the Marble Falls school board for

Beulah Merline Godwin Holland Family

Standing:
Beulah Holland,
Jeanene Holland

Seated:
Gary, Craig, Trudy,
and Jodie Holland

Rudolph Holland
1914-1977

a number of years and Beulah substituted as a teacher often. She re-entered the teaching field full
time in 1968 when she began teaching eighth grade in
Johnson City, coming to Marble Falls as third grade
teacher in 1970, her present position.
 After Rudolph passed away with a brain tumor in
Dec. 1977, Beulah bought a home in Marble Falls, but
still operates a small ranch that she and Rudolph
had bought a few miles out of Marble Falls.
VI-1. Gary Rudel Holland
VI-2. Margerie Jeanene Holland

VI-1. Gary Rudel Holland, b. 24 Jan. 1948, Austin, Tex.,
    m. Trudy Elaine Hopper 28 Nov. 1970, First Baptist
    Church, Weslaco, Tex.
     Trudy, b. 4 June 1949, McAllen, Tex., is the
    daughter of Riley Edward Hopper and his wife,
    Bonnie Horton.
     Gary finished Marble Falls High School in 1966
    and attended Tarleton State College in 1966-67,

79

majoring in agricultural engineering. He earned
his degree from Texas A&M in Dec. 1972 in Mechan-
ized Agriculture.

Trudy graduated from Weslaco High in 1967 and
earned a degree in elementary education from Sam
Houston Univ. in Aug. 1970. She took additional
early childhood courses at Texas A&M to receive
kindergarten endorsement and is presently teaching 4-yr. olds and is curriculum director at
Timber Ridge Presbyterian Pre-school.

Gary and Trudy live at Spring, a suburb of
Houston, where Gary is employed as Field Mechanic
for Plains Machinery of Houston.

VII-1. Craig Douglas Holland, b. 13 July 1973,
        Houston.

VII-2. Jodie Kay Holland, b. 30 July 1976, Houston.

VI-2.   Margerie Jeanene Holland, b. 28 Oct. 1951, Hondo,
        Tex., m. Jerry J. Jackson 14 Oct. 1972, Spicewood
        Baptist Church, Spicewood, Tex. Divorced May
        1976.

After Jeanene graduated from Marble Falls High
School as salutatorian in 1970, she attended
Southwest Texas State College at San Marcos.
After marriage, she worked in clothing manufact-
ure and sales, then returned to college, earning
a degree in Interior Design at N.T.S. University
at Denton, Tex. in Dec. 1979.

RILEY ALVIN GODWIN

V-7.   Riley Alvin Godwin, first son but seventh child of
        Enoch Godwin and Nollie Hill, b. 18 Apr. 1923 near
        Lometa, Mills Co., Tex., m. Mary Yvonne Huepers
        Studer 2 July 1948, Austin, Travis Co., Tex.

Yvonne b. 28 May 1926, Galveston, Tex., dau. of
August Edward Huepers and Marjorie Rammer.

Riley attended the two-teacher Long Cove School
for the first nine grades with two girls in his
class beside himself, Alma Dean Parker and Annetta
Hereford. Some teachers he remembers well were
Miss Ruth Godwin, Miss Gladys Casbeer, Mr. Charles
Conradt, and Mr. Edward Smith. In the fall of 1939
he entered Lometa High School where he graduated in
the spring of 1941 in a class of 20 girls and 7
boys.

At John Tarleton Agricultural College where he
enrolled in Agricultural Education in the fall of
1941, he waited tables for his board. He lived off
campus in a rooming house with three other boys at

Mrs. Criswell's. The second year there he lived in the Agricultural Building with other students and did janitorial work for his room and board.

When WW II started he was 18. He volunteered for service but was allowed to remain in school until May 1943, then was inducted on June 4, 1943 at Camp Walters in Mineral Wells, Tex. His basic training was at Camp Maxey in Paris, Tex. then in Sept. he was enrolled in Northern State Teachers College to study engineering. This lasted two semesters until he was sent to Camp Rucker in Ala. to train for overseas duty in the 66th Black Panther Infantry Division as a machine gunner in a Rifle Company. It was to England in Nov. 1944 and on to France in December. After the cessation of the War, he was sent to Koblenz, Germany, Marsaille, France, and Vienna, Austria for tours of duty, then home to be discharged April 20, 1946.

He earned a B.S. degree at Texas A&M in July 1947 and began teaching Vocational Agriculture at Alvin, Tex. Aug. 1, 1947.

He taught in Alvin until 1952 when he and Mr. J. R. Beaver bought an International Harvester dealership, The Alvin Equipment Company. They operated a branch business in Angleton and lived there from 1952 to 1954, then moved back to Alvin where they are now living on West Cedar Lawn.

Riley and Yvonne met when he went for his interview for the teaching job at Alvin; she was secretary to the superintendent and by July of the next year they were married.

Yvonne graduated from Alvin High School in May 1943 and in June took the job as secretary, a job she held until March 1950. She had m. (1) Carl Studer.

VI-1. Lawrence Joseph (Studer) Godwin
VI-2. John Douglas Godwin
VI-3. Brian Gregory Godwin
VI-4. Judith Gail Godwin
VI-5. Enoch Edward Godwin

VI-1. Lawrence Joseph (Studer) Godwin, b. 17 Mar. 1946, Alvin, Tex., d. 8 Oct. 1964 in an automobile accident near Eagle Lake, Tex. Joe was Valdictorian of his high school class in Alvin and had enrolled in the University of Texas with 16 hours of advanced placement. Adopted by Riley.

VI-2. John Douglas Godwin, b. 31 Mar. 1950, Alvin, Tex., m. Flora Phyllis Harris 18 Dec. 1970, Alvin, Tex.

81

Riley Alvin Godwin Family

Left to right:
Judith Gail Moore
Enoch Edward Godwin
Mary Yvonne Godwin
John Douglas Godwin II
Riley Alvin Godwin
Shannon Marie Godwin
John Douglas Godwin

Lawrence Joseph
Godwin 1946-1964

Brian Gregory
Godwin 1952-1970

Phyllis b. 3 Jan. 1949, Marietta, Ga. dau. of
Clarence Harris and Juanita Smith Harris Wilson.
She was orphaned and was raised by Mr. and Mrs.
Newton E. Wilson.
John has done mechanical work and is now a mill
wright apprentice.
Children:

VII-1.   Shannon Marie Godwin, b. 28 June 1971, Texas
         City, Tex.
VII-2.   John Douglas Godwin II, b. 2 Dec. 1974, Web-
         ster, Tex. John and Phyllis were divorced
         19 Apr. 1979, both live in Alvin, Tex.

VI-3.   Brian Gregory Godwin, b. 3 April 1952, Galveston,
        Tex., d. 28 Feb. 1970 in John Sealy Hospital.

Galveston following an automobile accident.

VI-4. Judith Gail Godwin, b. 20 Aug. 1953, Angleton,
       Brazoria Co., Tex., m. Robert Alan Moore 24 Feb.
       1973, Alvin, Tex.
          Bob was b. 28 Aug. 1952, Gilmer, Upshur Co.,
       Tex. son of Richard Donald Moore and Erma Dean
       Hall.
          Judy earned her degree with a Physical Educa-
       tion major and is now teaching and coaching.

VI-5. Enoch Edward Godwin, b. 16 Sept. 1955, Angleton,
       Tex. Eddie was involved in a serious motorcycle-
       automobile collision 2 Oct. 1976 near Lake Travis
       out of Austin. He is now attending Southwest
       Texas State University in San Marcos, Tex.

MAY DELL GODWIN HUDGINS DUPUIS

V-8.   May Dell Godwin, seventh dau. of Enoch Godwin and
       Nollie Hill, b. 17 Dec. 1925, near Lometa, Mills Co.,
       Tex., m. (1) Harry Richard Hudgins 17 Dec. 1945,
       Grand Prairie, Tex.
          Harry b. 30 Sept. 1917, Pittsburgh, Pa., d. 3 Oct.
       1964, Beaumont, Tex., son of Stephen Francis Hudgins
       and Pearl Anna Szykawski. Harry is buried in Long
       Cove Cemetery, Lometa, Tex.
          May Dell was raised in Long Cove, attended the two-
       teacher school there and graduated from Lometa High
       School in 1942.
          She and Harry met in the fall of 1943 while she
       was attending John Tarleton Agricultural College at
       Stephenville, Tex. and he was in the Army stationed
       at Camp Bowie, Brownwood. When Harry went overseas
       in Oct. 1944, they were engaged and wrote every day.
       On his return in Nov. 1945 they were married in
       Grand Prairie at the home of Lillian and J. D. Brown
       on Yeargan.
          They lived in Grand Prairie where May Dell contin-
       ued to work for the office of Price Administration
       in Dallas checking sugar and gasoline ration stamps
       for stolen or counterfeit stamps.
          For the first year Harry owned a truck and moved
       furniture, then in Jan. 1947 he enrolled at North
       Texas Agricultural College in Arlington, Tex. By
       August 1948 they had moved to Bryan where Harry con-
       tinued his education at Texas A&M, receiving his
       degree in agronomy in May 1951. Furthering his edu-
       cation on the GI Bill, he earned his Masters Degree
       in Plant Pathology and Physiology in Jan. 1952.

Harry began employment with the Texas Experiment
Station in Yoakum in Feb. 1952 and then for Dow
Chemical in Lake Jackson in August of 1953.

In August of 1958 they moved to Beaumont, Tex.
where Harry joined the Texas Agricultural Experiment
and Research Station and was listed in American Men
of Science, 10th Edition, for outstanding work.

After three children, May Dell started back to
school at Lamar State College of Technology in Beaumont in the fall of 1962.

Harry became ill in the summer of 1963 and after
several doctors and hospital stays, his illness was
diagnosed as Acute Bacterial Endocarditis. He was
in John Sealy Hospital in Galveston from June 4 to
Sept. 4 of 1964, then home for a couple of weeks,
but passed away in Baptist Hospital in Beaumont Oct.
3, 1964.

May Dell remained in Beaumont with her three children ranging in ages from 9 to 13, and attended Lamar
Tech to earn her B.S. Degree in Speech Therapy in May
1967. She has taught speech therapy in Nederland
since Sept. 1967 and also advanced her education by
earning her M.S. in Special Education in 1973. She
moved to Port Neches in 1971.

She became a Baptist at an early age and Harry left
the Catholic church to join the Baptist Church in
1946. Their children joined the First Baptist Church
of Beaumont early in life.

VI-1.   Richard Lance Hudgins
VI-2.   Paul Andrew Hudgins
VI-3.   Glenna Francene Hudgins

VI-1.   Richard Lance Hudgins, b. 17 Jan. 1951, Bryan,
        Tex. (During Harry's semester finals in A&M.) m.
        Margaret Ann Dupree 8 July 1970, Beaumont, Tex.
        in Assumption Catholic Church. Margaret b. 26
        Aug. 1951, the daughter of Leon Dupree and Oma
        Cahanin of Beaumont.

        Richard served in the Air Force from Sept. 1969
        to Sept. 1973, received his honorable discharge
        Sept. 1975. He did his basic training in San
        Antonio, attended school in Illinois, then spent
        the remainder of his service time in the San
        Francisco area.

        Ricky and Margaret remained in the San Francis-
        co Bay area for several years after his release
        from service where Ricky was employed as a Certi-
        fied Bio-Medical Electronics Technician for Kaiser
        Foundation Hospitals.

        They now live in Lumberton near Beaumont where

Ricky is employed by Southwestern Bell Telephone
Company as a lineman. They moved into their own
home on 5 acres in 1979.

Margaret has an associate degree in Vocational
Nursing.

1. Anna Danielle Hudgins, b. 19 March 1974.
2. Erin Michelle Hudgins, b. 11 Nov. 1977. Both
   born Vallejo, California.

VI-2.   Paul Andrew Hudgins, b. 30 Nov. 1952, Yoakum,
Lavaca Co., Tex., m. Deborah Lynn Nelson 5 Jan.
1974, Bethlehem Lutheran Church, Beaumont, Jefferson County., Tex., daughter of Donald James Nelson
and Lucille Marian Simpson. Deborah b. 11 Feb.
1955, Beaumont.

Paul served in the Texas National Guard, receiving his honorable discharge March 1979. They
live at Nederland, Texas and just moved into their
new home in the fall of 1979.

Paul is a cable splicer for Southwestern Bell
Telephone Company and Debbie does clerical work.
One of Paul's interests is City League Baseball
at which he does well. They are Lutheran.

VI-3.   Glenna Francene Hudgins, b. 23 Aug. 1955, Lake
Jackson, Texas.

Francene graduated from Nederland High School
in 1974, then from Lamar University in Dec. 1978
with a major in Home Economics and a minor in
Social Work. She began employment in Feb. 1979
with Texas Department of Human Resources and has
been asked to be the Volunteer Coordinator. She
lives in Nederland, sharing a house with a girl
friend, Ginny Jordan.

Francene enjoys many interests such as animals,
sewing, cooking, reading, decorating, and travel-
ing.

May Dell m. (2) A.D. Nicks, 4 June 1971, divorced
10 May 1973.

She m. (3) Paul Francis Dupuis, Jr., 24 July 1976.
Paul was b. 19 Jan. 1932, Woodville, Tyler Co., Tex.,
son of Paul Francis Dupuis and Ninnie Best. He
earned a B.A. degree in Psychology in 1957 at East
Texas Baptist College, Marshall, Texas and is
presently (1980) attending McNeese University, Lake
Charles, La. working toward teacher certification
in education.

May Dell Godwin Hudgins Dupuis Family

Seated: Brian Haralson, Debbie Calvert, Alicia Haralson,
          Paul Dupuis, May Dell Dupuis, Danielle Hudgins,
          Erin Hudgins, children of Richard and Margaret,
          Francene Hudgins.
Standing: Billy Haralson, Diana Haralson, Donna Bridgers,
          Chris Bridgers, Margaret Hudgins, Richard Hudgins,
          Deborah Hudgins, Paul Hudgins.

IRA SMITH GODWIN

V-9.   Ira Smith Godwin, b. 2 Jan. 1929, Lometa, Tex.,
       ninth child and second son of Enoch and Nollie Hill
       Godwin, m. Kathleen Elizabeth (Kay) Kelley 4 Dec.
       1953, Tucumcari, N.M., First Baptist Church.
         Kay b. 16 Dec. 1929, Worcester, Mass., dau. of
       Frances E. Kelley and Elizabeth C. McGowan. She was
       educated in Catholic schools in Portland, Me. until
       high school. After graduating from Maine Eye and
       Ear Infirmary in 1951 as an R.N., she entered the
       Air Force, serving 18 months as an Obstetrical Super-
       visor.
         Smitty attended the Long Cove School, graduated
       from Lometa High School in 1946, attended John Tarle-
       ton College at Stephenville, then Texas A&M where he
       graduated in 1952 with a 2nd Lt. commission.
         He enlisted in the Air Force and was stationed at

Amarillo Air Force Base from April 1952 to April
1954. It was here that he and Kay met and later
married in nearby Tucumcari.
They were sent to Bartow Air Base, Fla. for pilot
training from April to Sept. 1954. Their first dau.
Deborah Kay was born while they were there. Their
next assignment was Goodfellow AFB in San Angelo,
Texas from Sept. of 1954 until Dec. 1957. Smitty
completed Pilot Training there and became an instructor in the Pilot Training Program. Gretchen joined
them there.
Then it was Mather AFB in California until July
1959 when they left for Taipai, Taiwan where they
lived until July 1961. They were then assigned to
Dubbins AFB, Ga. until Sept. of 1964. From then until Jan. 1966 they were at McDill AFB, Fla., then
Chanute AFB, Ill. until July 1966 when Smitty was
assigned to Vietnam and the family stayed in Vaca-
ville, Cal. until Oct. 1967.
They were at Kincheloe AFB, Sault St. Marie, Minnesota from 1968 to 1971, where Smitty was a KC 135
Stratotanker pilot and earned his Lt. Col. rating.
They were then sent to McConnel AFB at Wichita,
Kansas where a new air fueling wing was being estab-
lished. In 1974 they moved to Davis-Monthan AFB
near Tucson, Ariz. and there Smitty retired as a
Lt. Col. in 1975 after 23 years in the Air Force,
much of the time as a pilot.
After retirement Smitty and Kay went into the
photography business in Tucson where they had bought
a home. They are members of the Catholic Church.
VI-1.   Deborah Kay Godwin
VI-2.   Gretchen Joyce Godwin

VI-1.   Deborah Kay Godwin, b. 8 July 1954, MacDill AFB,
Florida, m. Scott R. Adams 25 Oct. 1979 at the
home of her parents in Tucson. Scott is the son
of Mr. and Mrs. Gordon P. Adams of Tucson.
Deborah graduated with a B.S. degree in Education from Southwestern College, Winfield, Kan. in
1976. She moved to Tucson and began working for
the Bob's Big Boy Restaurant chain.

VI-2.   Gretchen Joyce Godwin, b. 14 April 1956, Goodfellow AFB, San Angelo, Tex., m. David Clement
15 June 1974, Wichita, Kan. David is the son of
Mr. and Mrs. Don E. Clement.
Gretchen and David lived in Wichita until April
of 1977 when they moved to Colorado Springs, Colo.
where David was employed as a finisher in concrete

Ira Smith Godwin Family

David and Gretchen Godwin Clements
Deborah Godwin and Scott Adams
Kathleen and Ira Smith Godwin

construction. Gretchen had completed schooling in
Wichita as a medical technician and is employed in
Colorado Springs with an optometrist.

Gretchen m. (2) Joe Ciofalo 3 May 1980, Colorado
Springs, Colo. Joe is son of Mr. and Mrs. Joseph
J. Ciofalo.

V

Samuel Hill

Samuel Hill is the earliest proven ancestor in the Hill line from which we descend. He was in New Jersey, or "The Jerseys" as it was then called, in 1757 when his son Daniel was born. Possibly the line goes back to John Hill who came to Dorchester, Mass. in 1631 from England as is claimed by some Hill researchers.

There is a family story that the Hills were at one time prominent in the court of the King of England, but came into the King's disfavor and were exiled to Ireland, from whence they came to America.

In the 1760's Samuel Hill and family moved from the Jerseys to Loudoun Co., Va. near where Washington, D.C. is now located. Then about 1775-77 they came westward into Washington Co., N.C. which was established in 1777. This territory became Greene Co., Tenn. in 1783, then Jefferson Co., Tenn. in 1792.

In 1765 a Thomas Hill also came to Laudoun Co., Va. from New Jersey or Pennsylvania with children who had names similar to Samuel's family, possibly a brother, cousin, or uncle. This Thomas Hill family is included as a supplement in Our Hanks Family by Gladys Hanks Johnson.

In Northeastern Tennessee Samuel located in the area near the mouth of the Nolichucky River where it joins the noted French Broad on its way to the Tennessee. He located on the north side of these rivers, buying land near a James Hill who was one of the first settlers in Jefferson Co. James had located about three miles north of the mouth of the "Chucky" according to the History of Tennessee by Goodspeed. This James may have been Samuel's older son who came in advance of the rest of the family. They lived near each other with James selling land to both Samuel and his son Daniel.

Samuel Hill bought 220 acres of land in Greene Co., Tenn. in 1790, located on the Roaring Fork of Lick Creek and on Swan Pond Creek, a draft of Lick Creek.

In Dec. 1792, Samuel was granted 375 acres below the forks of Nolichucky and French Broad Rivers by the State of N.C., Grant #1044. This land ran down both rivers and was bought for 10 lbs. for each 100 acres. He also bought 60 acres north of the Chucky in 1795, then from James he bought 78 acres plus 30 acres of an island opposite that land located in the Nolichucky, both for $100. He sold this last 108 acres to Baldwin Harle in 1803 for $1500.00.

To his son Daniel he sold 191 acres, 100 of it for 5 shillings, gave another son Abraham 88 acres, then sold other parcels, until in his inventory after his death, he had only 200 of the 763 acres that he had bought (Jefferson Co., Tenn. Land Deeds).

In 1802 Samuel Hill was commissioned Justice of the Peace in Jefferson Co., Tenn. He and his sons are mentioned on jury duty and as workers and overseers on the county roads, beginning in 1790. In 1803 he was appointed Inspector of the Election held at Major McFarland's (Jefferson Co., Tenn. Court Minutes).

Life on the frontier in the late 1700's in Jefferson and Greene Counties, Tenn. is described by one historian as a daily routine of danger, toil, and unremitting privation. The people were isolated by forest and numerous ranges of mountains from outside sources. The last Indian raid was in 1793, but bears remained as co-tenants for many years. Only the hardy could withstand the rigors of frontier life, in fact may have found them appealing.

Children of Samuel Hill:
II-1. Susannah Hill
II-2. James Hill
II-3. Thomas Hill
II-4. Joseph Hill
II-5. Jonathan Hill
II-6. John Hill
II-7. Daniel Hill
II-8. Abraham Hill

II-1. Susannah Hill, only daughter of Samuel Hill, was provided maintenance during her natural lifetime by her father's will, so probably was unmarried.

II-2. James Hill, mentioned in Samuel's will, was likely one of the first settlers in Greene Co., Tenn., coming there in 1783. He received two grants from the State of N.C. in 1786, one for 400 acres in Greene Co., Tenn. on the north side of the Nolichucky, the other for 78 acres, an island in the Nolichucky (Greene Co., Deed B. 1, pp. 50-51).

James was listed on the first grand jury of Jefferson Co., Tenn. in 1792 after this county was formed from part of Greene Co. that year.

In 1794 James Hill obtained leave to keep a ferry on Nolichucky River, rates viz: Farmer and horse -4 pence, Waggon and team -3 p., Cart-2 p., Hogs and sheep, per. hd.-1 p., Cattle and horses - 2 p., Footman -2 p. (Jefferson Co. Court Min.)

James sold land to Daniel and Samuel Hill and also to Baldwin Harle in 1803.

II-3. Thomas Hill m. Molly Tillery 1 Oct. 1793.
II-4. Joseph Hill m. Susannah McMean 10 Mar. 1807.
II-5. Johathan Hill m. Jenny Hunter 9 Oct. 1792.
II-6. John Hill m. Eliz. Moore Jan. 1792, d. in War of 1812. He secured a land grant in Greene Co., Tenn. 20 Sept. 1787 for 368 acres in partnership with David Stewart.
II-7. Daniel Hill, b. 4 Sept. 1757, New Jersey, d. 1 Nov. 1846, McNairy Co., Tenn., m. Eleanor (Ellen) Nodding. Daniel Hill is the subject of the next chapter.
II-8. Abraham Hill, co-executor with Daniel of his father's will, sons: Samuel and John Hill. On 6 Nov. 1805, Samuel Sr. gave to Abraham Hill of Cocke Co., Tenn. 88 acres in Jefferson Co., Tenn. in the fork of the Nolichucky and French Broad joining Samuel, Sr. and Daniel Hill's places and including Abraham's buildings and improvements, being part of Samuel Hill, Sr.'s original land grant.

Abraham in turn gave 80 acres of the above land to his sons Samuel and John Hill of Cocke Co., Tenn. in April 1809. Cocke, Greene and Jefferson Counties corner in the area of the Hill places.

This Abraham and his brother Daniel had some court controversies after the death of their father. These are described in the Daniel Hill story.

Samuel Hill wrote his will 4 Dec. 1812 and died in 1814.

Samuel Hill Will
Jefferson Co., Tenn. Will Bk. #2, pp. 52-53

In the name of God, amen, I, Samuel Hill of Jefferson County and state of Tennessee, being aged and infirm but of perfect, sound and dis-posing memory, calling to mind the mortality of mankind, and knowing it is appointed of God for all men once to die, do make and ordain this my last will and testament-Imprimis.
First and principally, I recommend my soul unto the hands of the Almighty God who gave it and my body to the earth to be buryed in a decent Christ-ian-like manner. Nothing doubting but I shall receive the same again by the mighty power of God and as touching such worldly estate wherewith God has blessed me, I give and bequeath the same in the following manner.

Item-I give and bequeath unto my daughter Susannah one bay
mare and saddle and bridle, one bed and furniture and also
she is to receive her maintenance during her natural lifetime from the profits arriving of my plantation.
Item-I give and bequeath to each of my sons, James Hill,
Thomas Hill, Joseph Hill, and Jonathan Hill and to the
heirs and legal representatives of my son John Hill, deceased, the sum of three dollars, thirty-three and one
third cents each to them and their heirs forever.
Item-My will and desire is that all debts that I owe of
which there but few, be speedily and punctually paid before any other distribution of my estate takes place.
Lastly, I annominate constitute and appoint my two sons,
Daniel Hill and Abraham Hill and Francis I. Garston Carter,
Esqr. of Cock County, executors of this my last will and
testament and hereby revoking and making nul and void any
and all former will or wills, ratifying and confirming
this and no other to be my last will and testament. In
testimony whereof I have hereunto set my hand and affixed
my seal this fourth day of December 1812, one thousand and
eight hundred and twelve, sealed signed and published and
delivered the within will by the said Samuel Hill to be
his last will and testament in the presents of us this
day and year within written.

Samuel Hill   (Seal)

John Cooper
Thomas Griffin
John Hill, Jr.
James Hill, Jr.

An Inventory of the estate of Samuel Hill, Senr., dec'd,
taken the _____ day of 1814.

Jefferson Co., Tenn. Will Book 2, p. 77.

4 cows
3 three-yr. old heifers
1 two yr. old heifer
1 yearling heifer
1 black horse about 7 or 8
    years old
1 sorrel mare about 7 or 8
    years old
2 colts one a year old next
    spring, the other 2 years
    old next spring
1 bay mare about 14 or 15
    years old

19 head of sheep
19 head of hogs about 1
    year old
5 small pigs
1 copper still containing
    50 gals.
6 still tubs
8 or 9 syder and whisky
    barrels
about 50 gallons of whisky
    and brandy
1 old waggon and gear
1 large barshear plough

2 small barshear ploughs
1 broad axe
1 falling axe
1 old axe
2 mattocks
1 sprouting hoe
3 broad hoes
1 hand saw
2 chissells
3 augers
1 drawing knife
1 Frow
1 iron square
1 scythe
1 old crosscut saw
1 irontooth harrow
1 lock chain
2 pair fire dogs
1 pr. fire tongs
1 shovel
1 pr. smoothing iron
1 grid iron
1 pr. stilyards
1 copper teakittle
1 brass kettle
10 or 12 gals.(?)
1 frying pan
1 skillet
3 pots
2 dutch ovens
1 griddle for baking bread
Parcel of old iron-about 30
  weights
2 iron pot racks
1 nailing hammer
1 rifle gun
1 pr. pinchers
1 shoe hammer and some awls
6 feather beds
5 bedsteads and furniture
14 old chairs
1 cupboard and furniture
2 chests
1 small trunk
1 chest with drawers
3 flax wheels
2 large wheels
2 pr. old cotton cards
1 pr. wool cards

3 volumes of Erokines
  sermons
1 large bible
1 small bible
1 Watts Hymnes and psalms
1 Rippons selection
Few other books
2 womens saddles
1 old mans saddle
1 walnut table
2 washing tubs
2 tin buckets
3 water pales
1 churn
2 pewter dishes-large
2 pewter dishes small
2 large basons
3 small basons
7 pewter plates
3 poringers
2 quart measures
1 half-pint and 1 gill
  measure
6 pewter spoons
1 coffee pot
6 tincups
1 tin pan
1 tin half gallon measure
2 funnels
1 collander
1 loom and weaving gear
1 quill wheel
2 candlesticks
1 pr. snuffers
1 pr. shears
1 lantern
1 silver watch
1 old clock
1 looking glass
1 hone and
1 old razor
2 bottles
2 juggs
4 sack bags
6 or 7 bushels of flour
1 set of spools
4 crocks
1 pitcher
2 baskets

3 bushels or there abouts
  of salt
1 conk shell
6 sides sale leather
  and some small pieces
1 dressed deer skin
2 sides upper leather
1 large rawhide
3 small rawhides
2 flax hackles
3 turners chissels
2 meal sifters
32 lbs. machined cotton
1 pr. sheep shears
About 600 bushels of corn
About 12 bushels threshed oats
Supposed to be 80 bushels
  oats in the sheaf

Supposed to be 15 bushels
  rye in the sheaf
Supposed to be 8 or 900
  bushels of fodder
Supposed to be 4000 weights
  of hay
1 new spade
1 old spade
1 check reel
1 tin   plate stove
1 small piece blaster steel
1 half bushel
1 peck
1 half peck measures
1097 pounds pickled pork
126 pounds of dried beef
120 pounds of hogs lard
  and tallow

The following notes of hand were found amongst the papers of the afores'd decedent, towit:

John Neelly and James Neellys note for $95.00
  dated 13 Nov. 1807 and payable twelve months
  after date with the following credits $4.50, $6.00,
  $20.00,$16.66 2/3
William Griffin note for $25.00
  dated 20 Jan. 1809, payable one day after date
George Whittens note for   2 lbs. 10s
  dated 1 Feby 1797 and payable the 1 Dec.   5 barrels
  ensuing the date, credits 5 barrels corn   corn
  and interest up to 16 Jan 1798
James Hills note   16 lbs. 10s
  dated 18 June 1790
Abraham Hills note for $315.00
  dated 27 Sept. 1813, payable 1st Oct. next
  ensuing, credits $100.00 9 Dec. 1813
Daniel Hill and Abraham Hills note $80.00
  dated the 26 June 1812, payable three
  months after date
Cash on hand $115.06¼
  one very old Negro woman named Sylvey
  200 acres of land

Received in open court   Daniel Hill,
December 14, 1814   Administrator

Digressing for a personal story: In the summer of 1977 my sister Day Alva Trainer and I were in Greene and Jefferson Counties researching in the courthouses, old books in the attics, even old records stored in one jail. We had finished the research and desired to see the land where the Hills lived. We spent the night in the area and next morning drove toward the rivers. We stopped in the small village of White Pine to ask the way to where the Nolichucky River entered the French Broad. We were surprised to find the people we asked didn't know, but they pointed out a house back down the road and said if anyone would know the man there would.

We had said that morning almost prayerfully that there just must be somebody "out there" who could help us find the Hill land. We found him sitting on his front porch in his overalls, a short man of about 80 years. He didn't know much about Hill land, but when I told him they sold to Baldwin Harle, he warmed up immediately. He said that there never was a more honest man than Baldwin Harle, that Mr. Harle had been guardian of him and his sister and even after they thought they had all the money coming to them, he had paid them quite a bit more.

He could take us to the Harle Place and to the mouth of the Nolichucky, so he went with us for a nice drive down the Nolichucky, by the Baldwin Harle farm where we had a good view of the island in the river that our guide (We failed to make note of his name so excited were we.) said contained about 100 A in all. Then we drove right down to the mouth of the Nolichucky where James Hill and later Abraham had operated the ferry. The man pointed out the place where the house stood near the river. It was most like standing on hallowed ground.

When we took the kind man back home, he showed us his Indian artifacts, then picked up a worn, broken-handled eye hoe that had been found on the Hill land at the place where the rivers joined. (We had noticed cockleburrs there and an eye hoe is a tool used on them.) This hoe he offered to us and it is now one of my most treasured mementos of our trip, thanks to the kindness of the little man "out there."

95

VI

Daniel Hill

Daniel Hill, son of Samuel Hill, was b. 4 Sept. 1757, the Jerseys; d. 1 Nov. 1846, McNairy Co., Tenn. He m. Ellen (Ellender) Nodding who was b. ca. 1750; d. 1830 McNairy Co., Tenn., daughter of William and Mary Nodding who came to Washington Co., Tenn. from Montgomery Co., Maryland, just across the Potomac from Loudoun Co., Va.

Daniel had moved with his father's family to Loudoun Co., Va. when he was a few years old, then on to Washington Co., N.C. about 1775-77. This later became Jefferson Co., Tenn. His next move was when he migrated with several of his grown children and their families to McNairy Co., Tenn. in 1828. Daniel was a Revolutionary War veteran.

Children of Daniel and Ellen Hill:

III-1. Mary Hill, b. by 1780, m. Thomas Griffin, moved from Jefferson Co., Tenn. to McNairy Co. in 1828.

III-2. John Hill, b. by 1790, m. Anna Koffman, daughter of Daniel Koffman.

III-3. Samuel Hill, dec'd by Dec. 1814, m. Elizabeth (Conner?), daus. Harriet Elizabeth and Nancy.

III-4. James Hill, b. 17 Mar. 1789, Jefferson Co., Tenn., d. 31 Aug. 1881, m. Nancy Coleman, dau. of William Coleman and Nancy Bullard. Nancy b. 24 July 1791, d. 7 July 1883, Princeton, Mo.

III-5. Abraham Hill, b. 1790, d. 23 Feb. 1876, m. Martha (Patsy) Walker 22 Jan. 1818, moved from Jefferson Co., Tenn. to McNairy Co. in 1828. Martha b. 1799, d. 1873. Both are buried in Rose Hill Cemetery near Bethel Springs, Tenn. They were Baptist, raised nine children.

Abraham was a soldier in the War of 1812, enlisting at Dandridge, Jefferson Co., Tenn. He participated in the Battle of New Orleans under General Jackson, receiving a pension and 160 acres bounty land for his services. In his discharge papers he gives his home as 2 miles north of Purdy, Tenn. and is described as being five feet, eight inches high, has black eyes, brown hair, dark complexion and is by occupation a farmer.

Children listed for Abraham in the 1850 census of McNairy Co., Tenn. are Lucinda, Martha, Fisher, Almida, Mary, and Thomas.

III-6. Nodding Hill, b. 14 Jan. 1792, d. 16 Jan. 1831,
        Washington Co., Tenn., m. Ruth Brown, dau. of
        Jacob Brown, 27 Feb. 1823. Ruth b. 15 Oct. 1787,
        d. 27 May 1871. Children: Rufus, Massey, Jacob,
        Elizabeth, Eleanor, and James Monroe.

III-7. Sarah (Sally) Hill, b. 10 Feb. 1794, m. Joseph
        Graham 1 Aug. 1812. Joseph b. 29 Oct. 1792.
        Lived in Jefferson Co., Tenn. on the French Broad
        about 6 miles from Dandridge.

III-8. Elijah Hill, b. 1795 Jefferson Co., Tenn., d.
        1857, McNairy Co., Tenn., m. Rebecca Koffman
        (Coffman) 6 Jan. 1820. Greene Co., Tenn., moved
        1828 to McNairy Co., had 14 children, lost sever-
        al sons (some say seven) during a fever epidemic.
        Rebecca b. 3 July 1793, d. 27 Feb. 1897, dau. of
        Daniel Koffman and his wife, Elizabeth.
            Elijah and Rebecca Hill family comprise Chapter
        Seven.

III-9. Ellender Hill, b. 17 May 1799, d. 30 Sept. 1838,
        m. Isaiah Koffman 6 Nov. 1817, Jefferson Co.,
        Tenn., son of Daniel and Elizabeth Koffman. They
        both died in 1838 about 2 weeks apart, leaving
        six children. The children removed to Humboldt
        and Trenton Cos., Tenn. Ellender and Isaiah had
        moved from Jefferson to McNairy Co., Tenn. in
        1828 with the Hill migration.

III-10. Daniel Hill, Jr., b. 1800, m. Elizabeth (Betty)
        Koffman, bond 30 Oct. 1819, Greene Co., Tenn.
        Betty was dau. of Daniel and Elizabeth Koffman.
        They came to McNairy Co. in 1828, then on to
        Miss. Their daughter Maria m. Reuben Donnell,
        had 8 children and moved to Sherman, Grayson Co.,
        Tex.

III-11. Jeremiah Hill, b. 19 May 1801, m. Susannah
        Walker 10 Sept. 1826.

III-12. Massey Hill, b. 12 Mar. 1808, d. 10 Oct. 1873,
        m. (1) Elizabeth Mozel Jernigan Hogain 4 Sept.
        1834. Elizabeth b. 2 May 1815, d. Sept. 1837,
        one child.
            Massey m. (2) Lucinda Harle 23 July 1840 and
        had 11 children. Lucinda b. 5 June 1823, d. 27
        Nov. 1865, dau. of Col. Baldwin Harle and
        Isabella Miller. Isabella Miller was dau. of
        David Miller and Miss Washington, second cousin

to George Washington.
   Massey m. (3) Mrs. Madora Hill 28 Nov. 1867,
Madora was dau. of Prof. Carnes and widow of a
Mr. Hill, no kin to Massey.

III-13.   Jefferson Hill m. (1) Ellen Womack. He was
   Methodist, a school teacher who lost his wife
   while he was teaching in Polk Co., Ark. He had
   children Isabella, Annie, Bell, Massey, and R. C.
      Jefferson m. (2) a widow with 5 children, had
   one more child, Angie.

III-14.   Elizabeth Hill (Betsy) m. Jesse Driskill.

   Jesse and William Hill are given by other Hill
   researchers as sons of Daniel, but are not mentioned in Daniel's will.

   In records of Big Pigeon Primitive Baptist Church,
   East Tenn., Daniel Hill joined by letter 4 April
   1789 and was listed under Elders and Deacons in
   June, Bk. D, p. 4.

From Daniel Hill's pension application dated 24 June
1833, made in McNairy Co., Tenn. and obtained from the
National Archives we find much of his story. He states
that he was born in the Jerseys. (New Jersey was at that
time a colony with two capitals after having been divided
into East and West Jersey from 1674 to 1702.) Daniel was
a few years old when they moved to Loudoun Co., Va., then
"18 or 20" when they moved to Washington Co., N.C. known
later as East Tennessee, then in 1872 as Jefferson Co.,
Tenn. He was 71 when he and several other families made
the move to McNairy Co., Tenn. in 1828.
He states that while in Washington County he served
three three-month terms of enlistment in the Revolutionary
War. He volunteered for the first in 1780, then was drafted in 1781 and 1782. The first and third terms were
against the Cherokee Nation of Indians who were "commiting
a great many outrages against the whites."
The other term was against the British in the Swamps
of Santu in South Carolina. He served under Capt. James
Wilson and Col. John Sevier and they were with General
Marion, the "Swamp Fox" in South Carolina. In Daniel's
application he states that as a mounted horseman with
Gen. Marion, he was sent out "first one place and then
another to get provisions."
Col. Sevier was the renowned Indian fighter whose
Indian War Cry was "Here they are--come on, boys! Come
on!" Daniel stated that they marched through the (Indian)
Nation first one place and then another, killing a great

99

many Indians, destroying their crops, and taking Indian prisoners.

In the "Greenville (Tenn.) Sun Bicentennial Edition" the battles against the Indians that Daniel probably fought in are listed:
1780 John Sevier defeats Cherokee at Battle of Boyd's Creek.
1782 Sevier defeats Chickamonga Indians.

Testifying for Daniel's character and veracity as well as his military service were Parson Frances Beard, noted Primitive Baptist preacher of his community, and James Robertson of McNairy Co., who had served the last two terms of service with Daniel.

He was allowed a pension of $37.50 per annum to commence 4 March 1831.

Daniel Hill and four of his sons, Abraham, Daniel, Jr., Elijah, and Noddy are listed on the 1822 Tax List for Jefferson Co., Tennessee also two sons-in-law Thomas Griffin and Joseph Graham, all in Capt. Moore's Company and all listed as 1 white poll, no black polls, except that Daniel is exempted, probably due to age.

Land deeds for Daniel show that he was somewhat of a small landowner. From 1789 to 1827 he made six land purchases for a total of 273½ acres in Jefferson and Greene Counties, the first one being from James Hill for 34 acres, the lower part of an island in the Nolichucky River. All of the land was near the mouth and on the north side of the Nolichucky and French Broad at their confluence, very desirable river land, land that is now owned by the Tennessee Valley Authority.

After Daniel moved to McNairy County, he appointed his sons Jefferson and Massey Hill power-of-attorney to sell his last 200 acres in Jefferson and Cocke Counties (formed in 1797 out of Jefferson Co.) near the junction of the Nolichucky and French Broad, this document being made 26 Sept. 1831 in McNairy County, Tenn.

In 1828 when Daniel was 71 years of age several of
his sons and daughters and families, along with Daniel and
Ellen, made the pilgrimage from their homes in Jefferson
and Greene Counties, Tennessee to McNairy County located
in the southwestern part of the state.

Mr. Lucian R. Koffman writes of the trip: "It is
said by the old-timers that about 12 to 16 families made
the western migration together, with the women and children (plus drivers) making the trip overland by wagon, and
a convoy of rafts came down the river with all the household goods."

After this arduous trip, they settled three miles
north of Purdy on the headwaters of Cypress Creek. Purdy
was the county seat with only a few huts and a log courthouse. The county had been formed in 1823, the first
court was held in 1824, and early the town had a tavern
and a sheriff.

In Reminiscences of the Early Settlement and Early
Settlers of McNairy County, Tennessee by Gen. Marcus J.
Wright, LaFayette Hill says, "Then McNairy presented a
wild and desolate appearance. Wolves howled in the wilder-
ness; panthers screamed in the jungles; large herds of
deer grazed undisturbed on the sandy hills . . . There
was nothing of a civilized nature to be found."

LaFayette Hill further states that in the next two
years after their arrival, the first school was built with
Daniel Griffin as teacher. This teacher was likely a
grandson of Daniel Hill, son of his daughter Mary who
married Thomas Griffin.

The first church was organized under the management
of the Primitive Baptist with Parson Franklin Beard as
pastor. It is not known if the Hills were members of this
church, but Franklin Beard was given as a reference by
Daniel Hill when he applied for his Revolutionary War pension in 1833. (The church later excluded the Parson Beard
when he joined the Masons, but it was said that he continued to preach to large audiences anyway.)

This community of Hills north of Purdy was known as
the Hill Settlement and was among the largest in the county at that time. The Hills are described as generally
happy and contented, none having brought disgrace on the
name. They were of English and Irish descent, well-devel-
oped men and women and noted for their longevity. Their
chief occupation was farming and they preferred the warmth
of their own fireside with their loved ones to the pleas-
ures of the outside world.

Ellen, wife of Daniel, died at age 80 two years after
they moved to McNairy Co. Daniel was living with his son
John in 1830 census and with Elijah in 1840, passing away
Nov. 1, 1846 at age 89. Both are buried in Rose Hill
Cemetery, near Bethel Springs, Tennessee. Their stones read:

Daniel Hill
Born 1750
Died Nov. 1, 1846
Soldier 1775-81

Ellen Hill
Died 1830
Age about 80 yrs.

Rose Hill Cemetery
Bethel Springs,
McNairy County,
Tennessee

Note: Daniel had given his birthdate as 1757 in his pension application and stated that he copied the date from his father's Bible.

Before Daniel Hill left Jefferson County in east Tennessee for McNairy County he wrote a will which was evidently not recorded. He was 71 when he made this will, but lived 18 more years. The introduction to his will is

102

almost word for word like that of his father Samuel: (Taken from the Family Tree of Hill Family by May Hill Brewer.)

Will of Daniel Hill-1828

In the name of God, Amen, I Daniel Hill, of Jefferson Co., State of Tenn. being aged and infirm but of perfect sound mind and disposing memory, and calling to mind the mortality of mankind, and knowing it is appointed of God for all men once to die, do make and ordain my last Will and Testament.

Item: And principally, I recommend my Soul into the Hands of God that gave it; and my body to the Earth to be buried in a Christian like manner; nothing doubting but I shall receive the same again by the mighty power of God.

And as touching such worldly estate wherewith God has blessed me through His Grace, I give and bequeath the same in the following manner.

Item: I give and bequeath to my beloved wife Elender Hill all my movable property, which is to say, all my estate except my land, which shall go to her and at her disposal forever.

And with respect to my land estate, as I have given to some of my children their part of it, to their satisfaction, some in full, and some in part.

Whereas I traded with my son-in-law Thomas Griffin for a piece of land and gave it to my son-in-law Joseph Graham for his and his wife Sarah's claim of my estate which land to them so given is considered by me as their part in full.

Whereas my son Noding has received of me valuable consideration for his part in full.

My two sons Jeremiah and Elijah Hill have received each of them $500.00 out of my estate and given their receipt for the same, which is considered by me as their parts in full.

Whereas my son Abraham is gone from home and requested me to pay some debts for him, which I have done and he not being here to give his receipt for the same, I have counted it with a receipt he gave me before he left home of $55.00. I therefore give unto him out of my land estate the additional sum of $400.00

And as my son John has received out of my estate $138.00 and given his receipt for the same, I therefore give my son John unto him out of my land estate the additional sum of $362.00.

My son Daniel has received out of my estate the sums of $101.25 which he gave his receipt for, I therefore give unto him the additional sum of $398.75 out of my land estate.

I give and bequeath to my son James the sum of $500.00 out of my land estate.

I give and bequeath to my son Jefferson the sum of $500.00 out of my land estate.

I give and bequeath to my son Massey Hill the sum of my land estate (Possibly $500.00 was omitted in recopying.)

I give and bequeath to my son-in-law Thomas Griffin a piece of land I got of him and let Joseph Graham and his wife Sarah, my daughter, have for their part and claim of my land estate.

The said Thomas Griffin, therefore, is to have $500.00 out of my land estate.

I also give and bequeath to my daughter Mary Griffin $500.00 out of my land estate.

I also give and bequeath to my daughter, Elender, wife of Josiah (Isaiah) Koffman the sum of $500.00 out of my land estate.

Also to my daughter Elizabeth, wife of Jesse Driskill I bequeath and give to her the sum of $500.00.

Also I give and bequeath to the two daughters, Harriet and Nancy Hill (daughters of son Samuel, deceased) the sum of 3 dollars and 33 cents and no more, out of my land estate.

My intention in this is that each of my own children may have an equal part, and if my land does not sell for as much as I have laid off for each to have, they are each to have an equal loss, and if for more, they are each to have an additional made accordingly.

Item: My will and my dsire is that all my debts that I owe, which are but few, be hastily and punctually paid before any distribution of my estate takes place.

Lastly I nominate and appoint my two sons Jefferson and Massey, also my two sons-in-law Thomas Griffin and Jesse Driskill as Executors here making void and null all former wills ratifying and confirming this and no other, my last Will and Testament.

> Signed, Sealed and Acknowledged in the presents (sic) of us, this the 29th day of August 1828

> Daniel Hill   (Seal)

George Rodgers
Jesse Moore
William B. Helm   104

An inventory of III-3. Samuel Hill, Jr., son of
Daniel Hill, made in Jefferson Co., Tenn. to the June
Session of court 1815 by Daniel Hill and Elizabeth Hill:

One mare and one colt	One flax wheel
Two cows and calves	Two water pails
One 2-yr. old heifer	Four cups, eight spoons
Six head of hogs	Six knives and forks
One old side saddle	Two chears
One old man's saddle	One earthen crock
One oven and skillet	One old looking glass
Two beds and furniture	One Indian basket
One cotton wheel	One small tin trunk

One old Negro woman and three children
One hundred bushels of corn (supposed to be)

This property was sold at public auction 28 April
1815 with Elizabeth buying about half the items back.
Daniel and Abraham Hill also purchased items in the sale.
        Daniel Hill was appointed guardian of his grand-
daughters, daughters of Samuel, Harriet Eliza and Agnes
Hill. At the June 1817 court of Jefferson Co., Tenn.
Elizabeth Hill, widow of Samuel, sued Daniel for her one-
third share of her husband's remaining property which included four persons of color valued at $1230.00, plus
cash of $202.04. Elizabeth chose to take 2 of the Negroes,
Tye and March, valued at $200 each and the court ordered
them delivered to her along with $67.00 in cash. Daniel
was assessed the court costs. Tye and March were evidently the mother and youngest child; the others were
Isham valued at $530.00 and Stephen, $300.00.
        At the Sept. 1817 court session Daniel resigned his
guardianship of Harriet Eliza and Agnes Hill and the
court appointed Elizabeth, their mother, and James Conner
as guardians. They entered into bond with Baldwin Harle
for $6,000.00 for the faithful discharge of their duties.

Daniel Hill versus Abraham Hill

        Jefferson Co., Tenn Court Minutes show that there
was some disagreement between Daniel and his brother
Abraham over land that their father Samuel had not parti-
cularly deeded, but Daniel felt the land was meant to be
his. Samuel had died in 1814 naming Daniel and Abraham
and Francis I. Garston Carter executors. Daniel petitions
the court to appoint Jacob Harmon to execute the conveyance to him.
        In May 1817 Abraham Hill sent a letter by James Hill,

Godwin-Hill and Related Families

a witness, to Daniel:

May 28, 1817
    Daniel Hill, I wish you would come forward in
friendship and make a divide of the lands. I wish
no other but justice, you shall have a part in the
little island, if you will settle all in justice.
If you refuse to divide, I shall apply to our next
court for a divide, as this may be your notification
by

                          Abraham Hill

    Daniel filed this with the court in June 1817. In
the case Daniel Hill vs. Abraham Hill and others, the
jury deliberated for two days, but could not agree what
verdict to render, jury was discharged and a mistrial
entered and the cause was continued until next court.
    Later court, date not clear--Daniel Hill vs. Abraham
Hill and others Case No. 1396
    The jury heard the case, but could not agree what
verdict to render; they returned to the bar at divers
times during the day but were finally dismissed and a
mistrial declared. Cause continued until next court.

    March 12, 1818--Abraham Hill vs. Daniel Hill
    Appeal No. 1470

    This day came the parties and their attorneys and
thereupon came a jury (named) who being elected, tried
and sworn well and truly to try the matter and in contro-
versey, and because the jurors aforesaid are not agreed
what verdict to render, said are not agreed what verdict
to render. They are respited until tomorrow.

    March 13, 1818--Abraham Hill vs. Daniel Hill
    Appeal #1470

    This day came the Jury, who from rendering the ver-
dict in this cause on yesterday were respited, and
said they cannot agree; therefore by consent of both
parties and with the assent of the court a mistrial
is entered and this cause continued until next term.

    The case seems to be resolved, for in Jefferson Co.
Deed Book O, p. 401, dated 15 Sept. 1818 this conveyance
is recorded:

    Daniel Hill of Jefferson Co., Tenn. to Abraham Hill
of same Co. The conveyance is made in conformity with
an award to Abraham in which Daniel "relinquishes" part

of the estate "divised by my late father Samuel Hill,"
land to be divided between Daniel and Abraham. The land
relinquished to Abraham was near the mouth of the Nolichucky River and included a ferry landing on the west side of
Nolichucky and north side of French Broad at the mouth of
the Nolichucky.

Hills in Census of McNairy Co., Tenn. --1830

Page	Males		Females	
122	Jeremiah Hill	(m. Susannah Walker)		
	1	-5	1	20-30
	1	20-30		
122	Isaiah Koffman	(m. Ellender Hill)		
	1	5-10	3	- 5
	1	10-15	1	30-40
	1	30-40		
127	Abnery Hill			
	1	20-30	1	- 5
	1	40-50	1	30-40
137	Thomas Hill			
	1	- 5	2	- 5
	1	20-30	2	5-10
			1	20-30
150	Elijah Hill	(m. Rebecca Koffman)		
	3	- 5	1	- 5
	2	5-10	1	5-10
	1	30-40	1	30-40
150	John Hill	(m. Anna Koffman)		
	1	20-30	1	30-40
	1	40-50		
	1	70-80 (Daniel?)		
150	Thomas Griffin	(m. Mary Hill)		
	1	10-15	1	- 5
	3	20-30	2	5-10
	1	50-60	2	10-15
			1	40-50
151	Daniel Hill, Jr.	(m. Elizabeth Koffman)		
	1	5-10	1	5-10
	1	30-40	1	30-40
151	Abraham Hill	(m. Martha Walker)		
	2	- 5	1	- 5
	1	5-10	1	5-10
	1	10-15	1	30-40
	1	30-40		

In this Hill Settlement in McNairy Co., Tenn. in 1830
there were 15 men, 9 women, and 33 children with 16 of the
children under 5. Daniel, recently widowed, is in the home
of his son John.

Godwin-Hill and Related Families

Hill Family Bible owned by Mrs. Winnie Massengill, Rt. 1,
Bethel Springs, McNairy Co., Tenn. This Bible belonged
to Elijah Hill, son of Daniel Hill and his wife Elleanor
Nodding. Copied October 1965 by B. R. Randolph.

Daniel Hill son of Elijah and Rebecca his wife was born
24 May 1827
Samuel Hill was born 9 August 1830
Rhuphous Hill was born 7 June 1839
Sarah Jane Hill, John Hill's wife was born 8 July 1830
Catherine Hill was born 2 February 1844
Eleanor Hill was born 24 August 1829
Thomas Jefferson Hill was born 16 January 1847
Sarah King was born 8 August 1848
Mary Elizabeth Hill was born 29 July 1850
Drobert Pinkney Plunk was born 12 August 1868
Mary J. Hill was born 16 August 1848
Sallie Patsey Hill was born 10 September 1871

Marriage Register
Elizy Hill and Rheubeccak his wife was married 6 January
1820
John Case and Mary his wife was married 15 October 1845
Rufus Hill and Mary married 22 March 1871
Daniel Hill born 1834
John Hill son of Elizy and Rheubeccak Hill born 7 July
1822
William Hill born 1 February 1824
James Hill was born 26 August 1825
Jannie Brooks was born 1 June 1878

Death Register
Daniel Hill, Sr. died 1 November 184__?
William Hill died 15 September 184__?
Gideon Hill died 20 July 1855
Doctor Hill died 27 June 185__?
John Hill, Jr. died 4 October 1855
Mr. R. H. Hill son of Elijah and Rebecca Hill died 23
March 1919.
Mary Jane Hill died 14 January 1902
Ernest P. Brooks died 25 November 1914.
   * * * * * * * * * * * * * * * *
The edges of the old Bible were so worn that the last
digit on several dates was missing. BRR.

VII

Elijah Hill

Elijah Hill, son of Daniel Hill and Ellen Nodding, was b. 1795, Jefferson Co., Tenn., d. 1857, McNairy Co., Tenn. He m. Rebecca Koffman (Coffman) 6 Jan. 1820, Greene Co., Tenn. Rebecca b. 3 July 1793, d. 27 Feb. 1897, age 104 as per tombstone in Rose Hill Cemetery near Bethel Springs, Tenn. She was dau. of Daniel and Elizabeth Koffman.

Beckey
Hill
Bornd
July 3
1793
Died Feb. 27
1897

Eligah
Hill
Bor 1795
Died 1857

Rose Hill Cemetery,
McNairy Co., Tenn.

Godwin-Hill and Related Families

    Elijah Hill is listed in the 1822 Tax List of Jefferson Co., Tenn., then in 1830 in the census of McNairy Co., Tenn. with Elijah and Rebecca both in their 30's, 7 children under 10, 4 of them under 5. (See census p. 114)

    The trek with the rest of the Hill clan across Tennessee from Jefferson Co. in the northeastern part of the state to McNairy Co. in the southwest, some 375 miles, had been made in 1828. This pilgrimage included some 25 adults and 33 children.

    To this unsettled wild country they brought their livestock, limited tools, household goods, and such provisions as wagon and flat boat allowed. They shared the hardships and privations of pioneer travel and settlement of a new country, always hoping for a better life.

    Their new home was on Cypress Creek north of Purdy, the county seat, and out of present day Bethel Springs a few miles, in the area that came to be known as the Hill Settlement.

    Elijah Hill is spoken of in Reminescences of Early Settlers of McNairy County by Gen. Marcus J. Wright as one of the men who would come into Purdy when court was held, say on the first Monday in August, 1842, when the yoemanry of the county gathered from all quarters to Purdy, the common center. The majority came on horseback, some on foot, and some few in carriages. Court was a grave matter, for they had great reverence for law and order.

    In the idle crowds on the streets there would be "senseless bluster, rude jokes from the vulgar, dogmatic assertions from the ignorant, profanity from the drunken, and an incipient fight with the usual crowd of spectators."

    Purdy was the county seat until 1890 when a courthouse was donated at Selmer.

    By 1840 the Elijah Hills had 9 boys and 2 girls, all under 20 years old. In the 1850 census, another boy and girl have been added, but the 2 older boys and 2 older girls are no longer at home. There is a story which comes from several sources, one being my mother, that this family had 14 children but lost 7 sons and the father in a fever epidemic, probably typhoid.

    They lived in McNairy Co., Tenn. until after the 1850 census, but bought 160 acres of land in Tippah Co., Miss. on 13 Nov. 1849 for $1,250. Rebecca is listed in Tippah County in 1860, which is just over the state line from McNairy Co., Tenn.

    Between the 1850 and 1860 censuses, marriages and deaths had trimmed the family to three, with only Rebecca and the two younger children at home. Eleanor, a daughter who married a Hawkins, was now widowed and, with her two children, was living with her mother. James and

Samuel had married Tippah County girls and lived nearby.
(When Daniel Hill, Jr. died in 1855, his estate settlement mentioned 7 brothers and sisters.
By 1870 Rebecca 73, Rufus 31, and Catherine 24, are
back in McNairy County where Rebecca died in 1897.
Rebecca, or "Aunt Becky" as she was known to her
numerous nieces and nephews, was of German descent. Two
things that her grandchildren remembered about her were
that she took a toddy once a day and that she smoked a
little clay pipe. Often she would let P. G. Hill, her
grandson, light her pipe for her, but if he tried to
smoke it too long, she would say, "Give it to me or I'll
break the neck o' ya!"

Children of Elijah Hill and Rebecca Koffman:

IV-1.	John Hill	IV-8. Pleasant Hill
IV-2.	Mary (Polly) Hill	IV-9. Nichols Hill
IV-3.	William Hill	IV-10. Andrew Hill
IV-4.	James Hill	IV-11. Gideon Hill
IV-5.	Daniel Hill	IV-12. Rufus Hill
IV-6.	Eleanor Hill	IV-13. Doctor Hill
IV-7.	Samuel Hill	IV-14. Catherine Hill

IV-1. John Hill, b. 10 Nov. 1820, Jefferson Co., Tenn.,
d. 4 Oct. 1855, m. Sarah Jane _____, who was b.
8 July 1830.

IV-2. Mary (Polly) Hill, b. 7 July 1822, Jefferson Co.,
Tenn., d. 7 Dec. 1904, m. John A. Case 15 Oct.
1845, McNairy Co., Tenn. John b. 22 Oct. 1822,
d. 12 Jan. 1900, both buried in Rose Hill Cemetery,
McNairy Co., Tenn.
  V-1. William H. Case
  V-2. James D. Case
  V-3. Charles (Charlie) Case m. Nettie _____.
  VI-1. Mildred Case m. _____ McCaddon.
  VI-2. Clifton Case m. Velda _____.
  V-4. Jonas Case
  V-5. Andrew Case m. Martha Johnson Kirkpatrick.
  VI-1. Dora Case m. John Barton, six dau. Cora,
Ethel, Martha, Hattie, Alene, and Johnnie
Barton.
  V-6. Johnnie Case

IV-3. William Hill, b. 1 Feb. 1824, Jefferson Co., Tenn.,
d. 15 Sept. 184__ .

IV-4. James Hill, b. 26 Aug. 1825, Jefferson Co., Tenn.,
d. 16 Apr. 1918, age 92, Mills Co., Tex., m.

Lucinda Parolee Godwin, dau. of Allen Godwin and
his second wife, Martha, of Tippah Co., Miss.
Parolee b. 25 Dec. 1836, d. 10 Mar. 1909, both
buried at Comanche, Tex. They lived in Tippah Co.,
Miss. in 1860, Hardeman Co., Tenn. in 1870, and
Comanche Co., Tex. in 1880.

V-1.	Elijah Allen Hill	V-6.	Jennie P. Hill
V-2.	Mattie R. Hill	V-7.	Luther E. Hill
V-3.	P. G. Hill	V-8.	George W. Hill
V-4.	E. A. (Addie) Hill	V-9.	Jacob L. Hill
V-5.	James S. Hill		

James Hill and Parolee Godwin are the subjects of
Chapter 8.

IV-5. Daniel Hill, b. 24 May 1827, Jefferson Co., Tenn.,
d. 1855, unmarried.

IV-6. Eleanor Hill, b. 24 Aug. 1829, McNairy Co., Tenn.,
d. 1916 at 87, m. _____ Hawkins. Children: Thomas
and Mary H. Hawkins. Eleanor became a patient in
the State Hospital.

IV-7. Samuel Hill, b. 3 Aug. 1830, McNairy Co., Tenn., d.
16 Oct. 1915, m. Martha Jane Kinney Godwin, widow
of Elisha Godwin and dau. of James Kinney, Sr.
Martha b. 28 Dec. 1832, d. 14 Oct. 1911, lived
Tippah Co., Miss. Children: Mark, Tom, Will,
Carrie, Emma and Sallie.

IV-8. Pleasant Hill, b. ca. 1831, d. 1850's.

IV-9. Nichols Hill, b. ca. 1833, McNairy Co., Tenn.,
d. before 1850.

IV-10. Andrew Hill, b. ca. 1834, McNairy Co., Tenn., li.
McNairy Co., m. Elizabeth (Lizzie) ____. Children:
Rufus, Annis, Rachel, Mary, James, John, Susie,
and Betty Hill.

IV-11. Gideon Hill, b. ca. 1836, McNairy Co., Tenn., d.
20 July 1855.

IV-12. Rufus Hill, b. 7 June 1839, McNairy Co., Tenn.,
d. 23 Mar. 1919, m. (1) Mary Jane Harris 22 Mar.
1871. Mary b. 16 Aug. 1848, d. 14 Jan. 1902.
Rufus m. (2) Winnie Barnes, had no children of
his own, but raised 2 of Winnie's granddaughters,
Bertha and Martie Barnes. Martie m. Neel, li.
Memphis, Tex.

Rufus Hill visited his brother James Hill in Comanche, Tex. in 1913.

IV-13. Doctor Hill, b. ca. 1839, McNairy Co., Tenn., d. 27 June 1850's.

IV-14. Catherine Hill, b. 2 Feb. 1844, d. 1947, age 103, was blind. She m. Thornie Morris, li. near Bethel Springs, McNairy Co., Tenn. Children: Mary, Elec, Rufus, and Jennie Morris.

Information on above children from Elijah Hill Bible, owned by Mrs. Winnie Massengill, Bethel Springs, Tenn., copied by Bill Randolph, from census records, and family information from Mrs. Cora Barton Patterson of McNairy Co., Tenn.

Sons of Elijah Hill and Rebecca Koffman about 1885

James Hill
Samuel Hill

Know all men by these presents, that we, *Elijah Hill Rebecca Coffman* are held and firmly bound unto JOSEPH MC'MINN Esq. Governor of the State of Tennessee, and his successors in office, in the sum of Twelve Hundred and Fifty Dollars, to be void on condition there be no lawful cause to obstruct a marriage from being solemnized in the County of *Green* between *Elijah Hill* and *Rebeccah Coffman* Witness our hands and seals this **3** day of *January* ANNO DOMINI **1820**

Elijah + Hill

Sariah Koffman

Test

FAMILY CENSUS OF ELIJAH HILL (All b. Tenn.)

Married Rebecca Koffman (Coffman) Date 6 Jan. 1820 Place Greene Co., Tenn. Recorded Greene Co. Mar. Rec.

Census Year County, State	Sex	1830 McNairy Co., TN	1840 McNairy Co., TN	1850 McNairy Co., TN	1860 Tippah Co., MS	1870 McNairy Co., TN
Elijah b. 1795 TN	M	30-40	40-50	Elijah 55		
Rebecca b. 1793	F	30-40	30-40	Rebecca 50	Rebecca 55	Rebecca 73
1. John b. 1822	M	5-10	15-20			
2. Mary b. 1820-25	F	5-10	15-20			
3. William b. 1824	M	5-10	15-20			
4. James b. 1825	M	-5	10-15	James 25		
5. Daniel b. 1827	M	-5	10-15	Daniel 23		
6. Eleanor b. 1829	F	-5	10-15		Eleanor Hawkins 27	
7. Samuel b. 1830	M	-5	10-15	Samuel 21		
8. Pleasant b. 1831	M		5-10	Pleasant 18		
9. Nichols b. 1833	M		5-10			
10. Andrew b. 1834	M		5-10	Andrew 16		
11. Gideon b. 1836	M		- 5	Gideon 14		
12. Rufus b. 1838	M			Rufus 12	Rufus 21	Rufus 31
13. Doctor b. 1840	M			Doctor 10		
14. Catherine b. 1845	F			Catherine 5	Catherine 18	Catherine 24

114

VIII

James Hill

James Hill, son of Elijah Hill and
Rebecca Koffman (Coffman), was b. 26 Aug.
1825, Jefferson Co., Tenn., d. 16 Apr.
1918, Mills Co., Tex. at age 93. He m.
Lucinda Parolee Godwin, dau. of Allen
Godwin and his second wife, Martha.
Parolee b. 25 Dec. 1836, McNairy Co.,
Tenn., d. 10 Mar. 1909, age 73, Comanche, Tex. They were
married by 1852; both are buried at Comanche, Tex.
Children:

V-1. Elijah (Lige) Allen Hill
V-2. Martha (Matt) Rebecca Hill
V-3. Pleasant Gideon (P.G.) Hill
V-4. Elanor Adelaide (Addie) Hill
V-5. James S. (Jimmy) Hill
V-6. Jennie P. (Janie) Hill
V-7. Luther Ernest Hill
V-8. George W. Hill
V-9. Jacob Leslie (Jake) Hill

James Hill was about three years old when his family
migrated from Jefferson County in eastern Tennessee to
McNairy County in the southwestern part of the state, a
sparsely settled frontier, with the first church, school,
and mill being erected after his family clan arrived
there. The church was Primitive Baptist and the mill was
on Cypress Creek near his home on the place now known as
the McCallum Place.

The Hills were farmers, cotton being the chief money
crop. This they had to carry by wagon over 80 miles to
Memphis to be ginned and sold.

It was about 1852-53 when James married Lucinda
Parolee Godwin from Blue Mountain, Mississippi in Tippah
County just across the state line. Parolee's parents
gave them land in 1853 in Tippah Co. on Big Spring Run
joining her brother Jacob's land. Their post office was
Ripley, Miss.

They moved from Tippah Co., Miss. to neighboring
Hardeman Co., Tenn. just before the Civil War, an area
that was devastated by Federal troops. Some provision

was made for families of absent soldiers, but the country-
side became "overrun by armies of both sides but held
firmly by neither. Speedily life was reduced to its
simplest terms, a stark struggle for survival." This area
became known as "the belt of desolation." (History of
Tippah County, Mississippi by Andrew Brown)

The family story goes that James and Parolee buried
their cotton to keep it from being taken, later dug it up
and sold it for gold coins which Parolee put in a crock
container and covered with used cooking grease which
looked innocent enough near the stove. It was this money
they eventually used to come to Texas. (Told by Curtis
Hill to Ray York.)

James was conscripted and kept in a training camp for
some time, Aunt Minnie Scoggins Gunter relates. Parolee,
with Addie, her six-month old baby, went to visit him and
tried to get his release so he could care for his family
of four small children. Her plea was refused but as she
visited James many of the family men were so glad to see
a baby that they fondled little Addie until, as the story
goes, Parolee had to change the baby's dress six times
that day, so dirty did she get.

Parolee went home disappointed, but somehow the men
were released and James arrived home the same night that
Parolee and the baby did.

Grandpa P. G. Hill who was born in Aug. of 1859, remembered seeing soldiers come to their house and also
going by. His most humiliating privation as a little boy
was that he had to wear his older sister's dresses because
material could not be secured to make pants.

Minnie Gunter, daughter of Addie, also tells the
story of the family slaves. Parolee's parents gave her a
slave girl named Ann who later married another slave, Jeff,
owned by James. Though James often took Ann to work in
the fields, she was very devoted to both Parolee and James.
Ann had a baby about the same age as Addie and would nurse
both babies if Parolee had to be away. Their children
played together and once when Ann's little girl was holding a stick for P. G. to whittle, he cut off one of her
fingers.

At emancipation time James owned a number of slaves.
He had made it a practice to give them a jigger of whisky
each morning as they started to work. One enterprising
fellow would save his drink until he had a bottle full,
then sell it. When he was freed, he had enough money to
buy himself a plot of land.

When the slaves learned that they were free, they
went from farm to farm gathering their liberated friends.
When they came by the James Hill farm, Parolee was

churning on the rocks just outside the cellar where she kept
her milk. This cellar was in a
little house at the back of the
kitchen. Parolee always cared
for the milk and butter herself.

When the Negroes swarmed over
the place, they saw that churn
of buttermilk and began to dip
in and help themselves. Parolee was afraid to oppose them,
but when no one was looking
she quickly turned the churn
over. When the Negroes saw the
milk spilling over the rocks
"the cussing taken place."

Ann cried because Jeff made
her leave the Hills. She
begged Parolee to keep her
children, a boy and a girl, but
Jeff would not allow it and she
rode away with a wagon load of
other freed slaves, robbing as
she went.

Jeff didn't feel the same affection for his ex-owners.
He helped the other Negroes harness James' mules to the
wagon and load it with tools and provisions. He would say,
"Take this--it's mine. Take that!" Later James was noti-
fied that the mules and wagon could be picked up at a certain place, but fearing reprisals, he made no attempt to
recover them.

To Texas

James, Parolee, and children moved from Tennessee to
central Texas south of Comanche in 1878. It took them
about 10 weeks to come by wagon, leading their milk cow.
They are said to have traveled along with several other
families. Their oldest son Elijah was already in Grayson
County, but had moved near James by 1893.

They settled on the north side of a brushy hill in
southwestern Comanche County in the Brushy Gap area. First
they built a two-story log cabin with a lean-to of rough
lumber for a kitchen. The fireplace served for heating and
cooking and there was a pleasant porch on the east side.

The nearest post office was Mercers Gap about six
miles away until a post office was established in the Hill
home with a son, George Hill, as the postmaster. The post
office was called Democrat from which the community derived

James Hill Home, Democrat Community, Comanche Co., Tex.

Left to right: Parolee Godwin Hill, Nollie Hill, James
                Hill, Addie Hill Scoggins, holding Judge
     1904   Scoggins, Steve Scoggins, Iris Scoggins

the name it now goes by. When George married, Nollie, a
granddaughter, became postmistress. The only revenue was
from stamps cancelled there and stamps were 2¢ apiece.
Their home became the gathering place for people for miles
around and people who moved away often wrote back to Nollie
for the news.

When the family moved to Comanche in 1907, Mr. Ed
Dudley took the post office to his house, but it was soon
discontinued when rural free delivery came into being.

The farm where they settled is still known as "The
Hill Place." Two portions of tumbled rock fences, an open
well, some huge rotting logs, a few stones, and fireplace
brick are about all that remain. The dug water pond where
James Hill and his daughter Addie were baptized still has
water in it.

The Rocksprings Baptist Church records show that the
two were baptized by Bro. C. C. McCurdy July 25, 1896.
James was 71 and Addie was 35. It is thought that James
was Methodist before becoming Baptist. This Rocksprings
Baptist Church had been organized under an oak tree at
Mercers Gap in 1891. George and Lige Hill said they haul-
ed lumber and built the church house but were both later
"turned out" of it for infractions of Baptist practices.

Besides their nine children, James and Parolee raised
three grandchildren left them when the wife of P. G. Hill

died soon after the death of her third child.

Nollie, the granddaughter raised by this couple, described James Hill as a "good man." He was very serious and even-tempered, but could be angered on occasion. Parolee was very formal, always addressing her husband as "Mr. Hill," even though she was considered by some to be the manager of the household. She is said to have favored her sons in matters of discipline. She believed in working hard, considered it lazy to sit down to churn, Nollie remembered. Parolee had 11 children, raised 9 to adulthood.

The Hill Place in Democrat is now (1980) owned by Mr. and Mrs. Lynn Shelton.

Old Comanche Cemetery

James Hill	Lucinda Parolee Hill
Aug. 26, 1825	Dec. 25, 1836
Apr. 16, 1918	Mar. 10, 1909
Father	Mother

Children of James Hill and Parolee Godwin:

V-1. Elijah Allen Hill, b. 25 June 1853, d. 20 Aug. 1926, m. Sarah Louella Hudson.
- VI-1. Modina Hill
- VI-2. Lonnie W. Hill
- VI-3. Myrtie L. Hill
- VI-4. Arthur Hill
- VI-5. Philip Hill
- VI-6. William F. Hill
- VI-7. Everett A. Hill
- VI-8. Viola P. Hill

Elijah Hill Family treated in Chapter 9.

V-2. Martha (Matt) Rebecca Hill, b. ca. 1856, Tippah Co., Miss., m. J. Iris Groves by 1874, nine children, the first four born in Tenn. In Texas the family lived at Gorman.
- VI-1. Olga Susan Groves, b. ca. 1874, m. Tom Williams.
- VI-2. Herbert Groves, b. ca. 1876.
- VI-3. Mollie Groves, b. ca. 1877.
- VI-4. Sicily Groves, b. ca. 1879.
- VI-5. Jimmy Groves
- VI-6. Eddie Groves
- VI-7. Willie Groves, d. young.

119

James and Parolee Hill Family Group
About 1896

Front: Iona Scoggins, Jennie Scoggins, Mary Scoggins, Minnie Scoggins, Jim Scoggins, Achrol Hill, Alvin Hill, Arthur Hill, Willie Hill, Philip Hill.

Second: Lillie Scoggins held by Addie Scoggins, Luther Hill holding Olga Hill, Bessie Hill holding Whittie Hill, James and Parolee Hill, Nollie Hill, Myrtie Hill, Elijah A. Hill, Ella Hill.

Back: James Scoggins, George Hill, Jake Hill, Modina Hill, Lonnie Hill.

VI-8.   Luther Groves
VI-9.   Essie (Eppie) Groves m. _____ White.

Iris and Matt Groves

V-3.   Pleasant Gideon (P. G.) Hill, son of James Hill and
       Parolee Godwin, b.   28 Aug, 1859, d. 20 July 1948,
       m. (1) Kitty Bell Bishop.
   VI-1. Nollie Bell Hill   VI-3.   Achrol H. Hill
   VI-2. James Alvin Hill
       He m. (2) Vinnie Cavin
   VI-4. Lillian Hill   VI-8.   Parolee Hill
   VI-5. Cecil R. Hill   VI-9.   Mack Hill
   VI-6. J. D. Hill   VI-10. Ivanell Hill
   VI-7. Curtis B. Hill

       P. G. Hill Family comprises Chapter 10.

V-4.   Elanor Adelaide (Addie) Hill, dau. of James Hill and
       Parolee Godwin, b. 1 Dec. 1861, d. 4 July 1955, m.
       Jesse Burnett Scoggins.
   VI-1. James H. Scoggins   VI-6.   Minnie B. Scoggins
   VI-2. Iona Scoggins   VI-7.   Lillie E. Scoggins
   VI-3. Mary P. Scoggins   VI-8.   Mattie Iris Scoggins
   VI-4. Jennie V. Scoggins   VI-9.   J. Stephen Scoggins
   VI-5. Jimmie L. Scoggins   VI-10. Judge C. Scoggins

       Addie and Jesse Scoggins Family in Chapter 11.

121

V-5.   James S. (Jimmy) Hill, son of James Hill and Parolee
       Godwin, b. Feb. 1864, Tippah Co., Miss., d. 1895, m.
       Alice Wilson.
  VI-1.   Willie Hill, dau. m. Dr. _____ Land.
  VI-2.   Jimmie Hill, dau. b. Feb. 1896.
          Jimmy died of typhoid fever, leaving Alice with
          one small child and expecting another. She lived
          with James and Parolee Hill that winter and when
          the baby came in Feb. she named the little girl
          Jimmie also.
          Alice m. (2) _____ Boland and had several more
          children, three of whom died in a Christmas tree
          fire at Hobart, Oklahoma about 1916.

V-6.   Jennie P. (Janie) Hill, dau. of James Hill and Paro-
       lee Godwin, b. ca. 1868, d. at birth of her first
       child, m. Robert Meeks.
  VI-1.   Blanche Meeks, d. at age 3.

V-7.   Luther Earnest Hill, son of James Hill and Parolee
       Godwin, b. 19 Nov. 1873, Tenn., d. 25 Feb. 1948,
       Asborne, Kan., m. Mary Elizabeth (Bessie) Stovall
       20 Nov. 1892.
  VI-1.   Olga Hill, d. 29 Jan. 1970, Poway, Cal., m. (1)
          _____ Stevens, (2) _____ Macy.
    VII-1.   Curtis Stevens m. Pauline _____, Navy career
             man, li. Cal.
  VI-2.   Whittie Ann Hill m. Lee A. Pitcher, one son.
          Whittie and Lee were operating a tourist court
          in Berryville, Ark. when he stabbed her to death,
          then cut his own throat.
  VI-3.   George Leslie Hill
  VI-4.   Allen A. Hill m. Alma _____.
    VII-1.   Richard Allen Hill
      VIII-1.   John Hill (Adopted)
      VIII-2.   Allen LeRoy Hill
      VIII-3.   Robert Timothy Hill
      VIII-4.   Nancy Lee Hill
    VII-2.   Shirley Eileen Hill m. (1) ____ Thompson,
             (2) _____ Miller.
      VIII-1.   Eileen Ann Thompson
      VIII-2.   Clifford Allen Thompson
      VIII-3.   Sally Ann Miller
      VIII-4.   Janice Miller
      VIII-5.   Sherry Lynn Miller
      VIII-6.   Lori Lee Miller
    VII-3.   Edwin Claire Hill
      VIII-1.   Damon Otto Hill
    VII-4.   Leland LeRoy Hill
      VIII-1.   Michael Allen Hill

> VIII-2. Theodore Hill
> VIII-3. Nancy Lee Hill

V-8. George W. Hill, son of James Hill and Parolee Godwin,
      b. ca. 1874, Tenn., m. Bessie Davis, li. Zephyr, Tex.,
      later California.
  VI-1. Preston Hill, b. Zephyr, Tex.
  VI-2. Ervin Hill, b. Zephyr, Tex., lost at age 11 on
         a Sunday afternoon outing in Cal.
  VI-3. Gertie Hill, b. Zephyr. Tex.
  VI-4. Marie Hill, b. Cal.
  VI-5. Stanley Hill, b. Cal.

V-9. Jacob Leslie Hill (Jake), son of James Hill and
      Parolee Godwin, b. ca. 1877, Tenn., d. 12 Oct. 1954,
      m. Jessie Roberson. Jake went to Alaska during the
      Gold Rush there in 1898-99.

JAMES HILL

Married L. Parolee Godwin   Date ca. 1852   Place Tippah Co., Ms.(?)

Census Year County, State, Pg.	Sex	1860 Tippah Co., MS P. 130	Born	1870 Hardeman Co., TN		Born	1880 Comanche, Tex. F. 75-36	Born	1890 Comanche, Tex. P. 12, E36	Born
James b. Aug. 1826	M	35	Tenn	James	43	Tenn	50	Tenn	73	Tenn
Lucinda Parolee b. Dec. 1837	F	23	Tenn	M. P.	32	Tenn	43	Tenn	62	Mother of 11 7 ch living
Elijah A.	M	6	Miss.	L. A.	17	Miss.	25	Miss		
Martha R.	F	5	Miss.	M. R.	14	Miss.	23	Miss.		
Pleasant G.	M	9/12	Miss.	P. G.	11	Miss.	20	Miss.		
E. Adelaide (Addie)	F			E. M.	8	Tenn.	18	Miss.?		
James S.	M			J. F.	6	Tenn.	15	Miss.?		
Jennie P.	F			J. P.	2	Tenn.	11	Tenn.		
Luther E.	M						8	Tenn.		
George W.	M						6	Tenn.	25	Tenn.
Jacob Leslie	M						3	Tenn.		
Nollie B.	F								15	Tex. g. dau.
James A.	M								13	Tex. g. son
Achrol H.	M								11	Tex. g. son

124

IX

Elijah A. Hill

Elijah Allen (Lige) Hill, son of James Hill and Parolee Godwin, b. 25 June 1853, Tippah Co., Miss., d. 20 Aug. 1926, Mills Co., Tex., m. Sarah Louella (Ella) Hudson, dau. of G. W. Hudson and Susan Cox, 17 Oct. 1875 at Middleton, Hardeman Co., Tenn. Ella b. 12 Nov. 1860, Middleton, d. 10 April 1926, Mills Co., Tex. Both buried in Democrat Cemetery north of Mullin, Tex.

Elijah A. Hill Family
Front: Everett, Modina, Elijah, Viola, Ella, Myrtie, Willie
Back: Philip, Lonnie, Arthur

Lige and Ella Hill married at Middleton, Hardeman Co., Tenn. in 1875 where Ella had been raised and Lige's family had moved in the 1860's. He was 22 and she was nearly 15. They had moved to Grayson Co., Tex. by 1881 and were in neighboring Cooke County by 1886, then in the Democrat Community in Mills County by 1893 where they lived out their lives on a farm near the center of the community.

Coming from Tennessee with the Hills was a Stephen Hickman, 1825-1906, who had considerable money. He lived with the Hills, remained single, and died leaving his money to some nieces and nephews and the Elijah A. Hill family, except for $500 designated for his grave monument, 4 cypress cedars, and a fence around it all. The money left the Hill family caused considerable friction among the children and in-laws.

125

Grandparents

James Hill — Mrs. L. D. Hill

L. W. Hudson — Susan Hudson

Parents

E. A. Hill — Born June 25, 1853 at Ripley, Miss
Died Aug. 20, 1926

Ella Hill — Born Nov. 12, 1860 at Middleton, Tenn.
Died Apr. 10, 1926

They were married at Middleton, Tenn. on Oct. 17, 1875.

Children

Modena Hill — Born Sept. 13, 1877 at Middleton, Tenn.
Lonnie H. Hill — Born Jan. 23, 1881 at Whitesboro, Tex.
Myrtie Lee Hill — Born Dec. 31, 1883 at Whitesboro, Tex.
Arthur Hill — Born Nov. 7, 1886 at Roxton, Texas
Philip Hill — Born Mar. 16, 1890 at Roxton, Texas
died Mar. 9, 1950 at Dallas, Texas.
William F. Hill — Born Sept. 30, 1893 at Democrat, Tex.
Everett A. Hill — Born July 14, 1898 at Democrat, Tex.
Viola B. Hill — Born Mar. 16, 1901 at Democrat, Tex.
died March 1936

Elijah A. Hill family information in handwriting of Mary Hill, Philip's wife.

This money, with close management on Lige Hill's part, made it possible for him to loan his children and other kin money to finance homes and farming operations.

VI-1. Modina Hill, dau. of Elijah A. Hill and Ella Hudson, b. 13 Sept. 1877, Middleton, Tenn., m. John C. Beshears 29 July 1900, li. Eureka, Cal.

    VII-1. Robert Beshears, d. young.

    VII-2. Stephen Beshears m. Lola Singleton, li. Arcada, Cal., five children.

    VII-3. Earl Beshears, killed by a falling tree.

    VII-4. Lois Beshears, m. Joe Batich, li. Cal., no children.

    VII-5. Vogel Beshears, accidentally shot by his father at age 10.

VI-2. Lonnie Walker (L. W.) Hill, son of Elijah A. Hill and Ella Hudson, b. 23 Jan. 1881, Whitesboro, Grayson Co., Tex., d. 6 June 1964, San Antonio, Tex., m. Beulah C. Godwin 24 Nov. 1901, Goldthwaite, Mills Co., Tex.

Beulah b. 8 May 1883 Hopkins Co., Tex., dau. of J. A. Godwin and Liva Ann Smith, d. 29 Aug. 1963 at home, Lampasas Co., Tex. Both are buried in the Long Cove Cemetery north of Lometa, Tex.

Lonnie and Beulah lived near Mullin for a year or two, then moved to the Long Cove Community north of Lometa where they farmed for the rest of their lives.

Beulah Godwin Hill
Lonnie Walker Hill

Golden Wedding Anniversary
Nov. 24, 1951

127

He ran goats and cows and at one time operated an
extensive peach and pear orchard, selling fruit by
the truck load. He also had a syrup mill in the
late 20's when they were popular.

They were members of the Long Cove Baptist Church
from 1903 until their deaths. Beulah played the
pump organ and taught Sunday School, while Lonnie
was a deacon and often Sunday School Superintendent.

VII-1.   Allen Walker Hill
VII-2.   Zella T. Hill
VII-3.   Mattie Estell Hill (Adopted)

VII-1.   Allen Walker Hill, son of L. W. Hill and Beulah
         Godwin, b. 14 Aug. 1902 Mills Co., Tex., d. 16
         Nov. 1962 San Saba, Tex., buried San Angelo,
         Tex., m. Loma Mary Neeld 7 Aug. 1922, Lometa,
         Texas. Loma b. 26 May 1906 Lampasas Co., Tex.,
         dau. of Mr. and Mrs. W. Hugh Neeld.

Loma Neeld Hill

Allen Walker Hill

1960

Allen and Loma lived in San Angelo where
Allen worked for the Santa Fe for 20 years.
They then operated a dairy near Burnet for several years before opening a farm machinery
business in San Saba in the spring of 1953, a
business still known as Hill Implement.

Loma m. (2) Dr. R. C. Tennyson and lives in
Brownwood.

Children of Allen and Loma Hill:
VIII-1. Durwin Allen Hill, b. 27 June 1939 San
         Angelo, Tom Green Co., Tex., m. Paula Ann
         Bell 13 June 1959, Dublin, Texas. Paula
         b. 27 Aug. 1940, daughter of Herbert Bell
         and Pauline Hermann.
            Durwin finished high school in San Saba
         in 1956, attended Tarleton U. in

Stephenville and Texas Tech. in Lubbock
where he earned his degree, majoring in
agriculture. He taught 6 years at Graham
as V.A. teacher then went to A&M to earn
his Masters Degree, teaching V.A. in high
school while doing so. He is now vocational agriculture Area Supervisor, located at
Waco, Texas.

IX-1. Christi Lynn Hill, b. 16 July 1960,
Lubbock, Texas.

IX-2. Sherri Gale Hill, b. 2 Oct. 1962,
Graham, Texas.

VIII-2. Carrol Edward Hill, b. 5 July 1946, Lampasas, Tex., m. Chloe Jane Ratliff 10 June
1966, San Angelo, Tex. Chloe is daughter
of William P. (Bill) Ratliff and Eunice
Danford.

Carrol finished high school in San Saba
in 1964, attended Tarleton U. for two
years, then took a job in San Angelo with
the daily paper, later joining the First
National Bank as Loan Officer.

IX-1. Craig Allen Hill, b. 28 June 1967, San
Angelo, Texas.

IX-2. William Clint Hill, b. 16 July, 1970,
San Angelo.

VII-2. Zella T. Hill, dau. of L. W. Hill and Beulah
Godwin, b. 2 April 1909, Mills Co., near Lometa,
Texas, d. 15 Oct. 1971 San Antonio, Tex., m.
William Barton Hodges 23 Oct. 1933. Barton
b. 4 Oct. 1903, Mills Co., Tex., d. 16 Jan.
1977, San Antonio, Texas. Both buried in Long
Cove,Cemetery.

Zella T. and Barton farmed near Lometa until
1943 when they moved to San Antonio and worked
as Civil Service employees for some years,
later at the State Hospital.

VIII-1. Imogene Hodges (adopted), b. 23 April 1936,
m. (1) _____, (2) Terrell Fields, San
Antonio, Texas, live San Antonio.

IX-1. Terry Fields, b. May 1967.

VII-3. Mattie Estelle Hill, adopted dau. of L. W. Hill
and Beulah Godwin, b. 1 Nov. 1916, d. 7 Aug.
1962, San Saba Hospital, m. William Sykes (Bill)
Manning 28 Dec. 1935. Bill b. 3 Sept. 1902,
d. 30 May 1974. Both buried in Long Cove Cemetery.

Estelle and Bill farmed and raised their

family in the Long Cove Community near Lometa.

VIII-1. Ola LaVon Manning, b. 19 Feb. 1939, m. David Nunez Jenkins 8 Mar. 1958, Austin, Tex. David b. 16 Nov. 1935, Austin, son of William Les Jenkins and Reon Nunez.

LaVon and David have lived in Austin since marriage except for one year at De Ridder, La. They are active in Hillcrest Baptist Church work and motorcycling. David works for IBM, is in National Guard, and is active in sports, like playing roller hockey for 10 years. LaVon is church hostess, enjoys crafts, sewing, painting, and reading.

IX-1. Vicki René Jenkins, b. 19 Dec. 1960, Austin, Texas.

IX-2. Terri Lynn Jenkins, b. 7 Mar. 1963, Austin, Texas.

VIII-2. Frances Louise Manning, b. 14 Feb. 1940, m. Herbert Kenneth Grimsley, Jr. 4 June 1960, Austin, Tex. Herbert b. 11 Dec. 1933 Winter Haven, Fla., son of Herbert K. Grimsley, Sr. and Virginia Cook.

Louise and Herbert lived in Austin for a few years, then moved to Panama City, Fla. where Herbert continued in law enforcement, is now deputy sheriff of Bay County.

IX-1. William Kenneth Grimsley, b. 6 Apr. 1964 Panama City, Fla.

IX-2. Howard Jason Grimsley, b. 10 Feb. 1969, Panama City, Fla.

VIII-3. Mary Jo Manning, b. 25 Nov. 1941, m. Stephen Howard Study 24 Feb. 1962 Bergstrom AFB Chapel, Austin, Tex. Steve b. 3 Aug. 1941 Atoona, Penn., son of Fredrick LeRoy Study and Joyce Alberta Miller.

Mary Jo and Steve live in Austin, formerly in Pennsylvania, Steve employed by IBM in both locations as Customer Engineer. The entire family enjoys motorcycling, often going on trail rides. Mary Jo does oil painting and needlework, worked for First Federal Savings for some years, is now with Equitable Savings and Loan of Austin as Assistant Branch Manager.

IX-1. Stephen Douglas Study, b. 17 Jan. 1963,

Austin, Tex.
IX-2. David Howard Study, b. 17 Mar. 1969,
Camp Hill, Cumberland Co., Penn.

VIII-4. Janice Manning, b. 2 Aug. 1945, stillborn.
VIII-5. Linda Sue Manning, b. 14 Mar. 1947, li.
Austin, Tex.
VIII-6. William Dale Manning, b. 27 Nov. 1953.

VI-3. Myrtie Lee Hill, dau. of Elijah Hill and Ella
Hudson, b. 31 Dec. 1883 Whitesboro, Cooke Co., Tex.,
d. 7 Feb. 1973 Plainview, Hale Co., Tex., m. Will-
iam Pearl Deen 19 Aug. 1902, Mills Co., Tex. (Li-
cense Comanche Co.) Pearl b. 12 Jan. 1881 Blue
Mountain, Tippah Co., Miss., son of George Washing-
ton Deen and Lucinda Parolee Godwin, d. 26 Mar.
1967. Both buried Plainview, Tex.
   Both Myrtle and Pearl are great grandchildren of
Allen Godwin, Myrtie through his dau. Lucinda
Parolee and Pearl through his son Levi.
VII-1. Lee Ella Deen, b. 4 June 1903, Mills Co., Tex.,
d. 24 Nov. 1907.
VII-2. Stephen Hickman Deen, b. 4 April 1906, Democrat,
Mills Co., Tex., m. Nancy Emeline Emerson 6 Aug.
1927, Kress, Swisher Co., Tex. Nancy b. 30 Nov.
1906 Marion Co., Ala., dau. of Peter Scott
Emerson and Nancy Adline Avery.
   Hickman and Nancy live at Kress, Tex. He has
contributed valuable information and pictures
for this book.
VIII-1. Pearlene Deen
VIII-2. Ora Mae Deen

VIII-1. Pearlene Deen, b. 30 Dec. 1928, Tulia,
Swisher Co., Tex., m. Roger Melvin Francis,
Jr. 25 May 1947, Kress, Tex. Roger b. 2
Sept. 1919 Ochiltree Co., Tex., son of
Roger M. Francis, Sr., and Edith Mae
Stockton. Roger d. 23 May 1973 Waco, Tex.,
buried Plainview, Tex.
   IX-1. John Roger Francis, b. 24 Oct. 1948,
Tulia, Tex.
   IX-2. Phillip Melvin Francis, b. 11 Feb. 1950,
Tulia, Tex., m. Sharon Zimmerman 20
Nov. 1972.
   IX-3. Lynn Russell Francis, b. 15 June 1955,
Tulia, Tex.

VIII-2. Ora Mae Deen, b. 24 Nov. 1931, Tulia, Tex.,
131

m. Wayne Edward Stewartson 20 Dec. 1954,
Kress, Tex. Wayne b. 20 Nov. 1931 Santa
Anna, Coleman Co., Tex., son of John
Matthew Stewartson and Willie B. Scarbrough.

IX-1. Beverly Anne Stewartson, b. 9 Nov. 1957,
Plainview, Hale Co., Tex.

IX-2. Rebecca Sue Stewartson, b. 2 Sept. 1959,
Plainview, Tex.

VI-4. Arthur Hill, son of Elijah A. Hill and Ella Hudson,
b. 7 Nov. 1886, Rosston, Cooke Co., Tex., d. 28
Mar. 1911, m. (1) Ida A. Stevens 21 May 1908, one
child, stillborn, m. (2) Mabel Hodges. Mabel and
Arthur lived in Oildale, Cal.

VII-1. Theodore H. Hill (Ted), b. 12 June 1924, m. (1)
_____, m. (2) Betty _____.

VI-5. Philip Omer Hill, son of Elijah A. Hill and Ella
Hudson, b. 16 Mar. 1890, Rosston, Cooke Co., Tex.,
d. 9 Mar. 1950, Dallas, Tex., m. Mary Agnes Boland
17 May 1911, Brownwood, Tex.
    Mary b. 5 July 1888, Coleman, Tex., dau. of
Michael L. Boland and Angelina McCulloch, d. 12
Feb. 1955, Temple, Tex. Both are buried in Laurel
Land Cemetery, Dallas, Tex.
    Philip and Mary lived for a while at Mullin, Tex.
but spent most of their married life in Dallas
where Philip was a tire adjuster.

VII-1. Edith Louise Hill
VII-2. Madelyn Hill

VII-1. Edith Louise Hill, b. 28 Feb. 1914, Comanche,
Tex., m. Joseph Pickens Kirkland 14 Feb. 1936,
Little Rock, Ark. J. P. b. 28 Mar. 1907,
McClellan Co., Tex., son of Thomas Kirkland
and Mattie Vernon of the Kirkland Ranch near
Mount Calm, Tex.
    Edith and J. P. live in Ft. Worth where he
is employed with Real Estate Mortages. Both
are Baptist.

VIII-1. Patrick Boyd Kirkland, b. 17 Feb. 1943,
Ft. Worth, Tarrant Co., Tex., m. Judy Ann
Jolly 29 Dec. 1967, Ft. Worth. Judy b.
Japan, dau. of Earl and Dorothy Jolly.
They live in Richardson, Tex. while Pat
is employed in Real Estate Mortgages in
the Dallas office. Pat is a veteran of
the Marines.

IX-1. Kelly Boyd Kirkland, b. 27 May 1970,
Dallas, Tex.

132

IX-2. Kimberly Ann Kirkland, b. 23 Jan. 1972,
Dallas, Tex.
VIII-2. Thomas Philip Kirkland, b. 23 Dec. 1945,
Ft. Worth, Tex., m. (1) Anna Walker 31 Dec.
1969, m. (2) Barbara Ann Colley 29 Feb.
1972, Hawaii.
He served four years in the Navy, is now
in Real Estate Mortages in Ft. Worth.
IX-1. Sean Patrick Kirkland, b. 12 Aug. 1970,
Irving, Tex., son of Anna.
IX-2. Holly Blythe Kirkland, b. 17 Aug. 1973,
Ft. Worth, Tex., son of Barbara.

VII-2. Madelyn Hill, dau. of Philip Omer Hill and Mary
Agnes Boland, b. 4 May 1921, Dallas, Tex., m.
Clinton Lee Prestien 5 Dec. 1943, Dallas, Tex.
Clint b. 24 Sept. 1916 Denver, Bremen Co., Iowa,
son of Leo Charles Prestien and Dessie Violet
Coontz.
Madelyn and Clint have lived in Ft. Worth but
are now in Dallas where he is in real estate
development and sales. Clinton spent 5 years in
the Navy, 1941-1946, as a Pilot Radar Instructor,
was Prisoner of War in Japan from June to Aug.
1945, and a recipient of the Purple Heart.
Madelyn is an accomplished artist and does num-
erous kinds of crafts.
VIII-1. Richard Clinton Prestien, b. 5 Mar. 1945,
San Diego, Cal.
VIII-2. Dolores Jean Prestien, b. 8 July 1948,
Ft. Worth, Tarrant Co., Tex., m. Daniel
Richard Johnson 15 June 1974, Dallas, Tex.
Daniel b. 25 May 1949, Memphis, Tenn., son
of Charles Richard Johnson and Draper Oline
Parish. Jean and Dan have lived in Ventura,
Cal. and Dallas, but are now in Kansas City,
Mo. where he is attending Baptist Seminary
and she is teaching school.
IX-1. Daniel Richard Johnson II, b. 10 Apr.
1978, Dallas, Tex.
VIII-3. Larry Hill Prestien, b. 2 Mar. 1951, Dallas,
Tex.

VI-6. William Franklin (Willie) Hill, son of Elijah A.
Hill and Ella Hudson, b. 30 Sept. 1893, Democrat,
Mills Co., Tex., m. Minnie Blackburn 21 Feb. 1917,
Mullin, Tex., d. 8 June 1954. Minnie b. 14 Nov.
1895, Killeen, Bell Co., Tex., dau. of John Samuel
Blackburn and Mary E. Scoggin.

Willie enlisted in World War I soon after marriage. Later he and Minnie lived in Dallas where Minnie worked at Sears for many years, then at Democrat where they farmed and ran the Democrat Country Store. After Willie passed away, Minnie remained at Zephyr for several years but now lives at Goldthwaite and has recently recuperated from a broken hip. She has been very helpful in furnishing information for the Hill families.

VII-1.   W. F. Hill, Jr.
VII-2.   Jerry Boyd Hill

VII-1.   William Franklin (W.F.) Hill, Jr., b. 6 Oct. 1923, Dallas, Tex., d. 28 Jan. 1965, Irving, Tex., m. Gladys Caudill 9 Feb. 1946, Kentucky. Gladys b. 5 Feb. 1925, Ken.
         W. F. was in military service 1943-1946 in Germany, made Sgt., later was a pilot. W. F. and Gladys lived in Dallas, Pecos, and Irving where he was a salesman for Grace Chemical Co.

VIII-1. Sam Allen Hill, b. 10 Nov. 1945, m. Catherine Rushing 6 Dec. 1968, li. Arlington where he worked for a carpet company. m. (2) Janet Brewer, li. Orlando, Fla., works in electrical appliance store.

VII-2.   Jerry Boyd Hill, b. 4 Dec. 1928, Mills Co., Tex., m. Lucretia Taylor 31 July 1954, Pecos, Tex. Lucretia b. 3 Feb. 1925, Miss., dau. of M. O. and Pearl Taylor.
         Jerry and Lucretia lived at Kermit seven years and other towns as the job moved, but are now in Big Springs (1980) where Jerry works for Arco Oil Co. and Lucretia is doing volunteer hospital work. Jerry was in the service in Germany in the 1950's.

VIII-1. Minnie Catherine Hill, b. 21 June 1955, Miss., m. Mel Sutton 21 June 1975. Mel was in the Air Corps, now in the welding business in Houston.

IX-1.   Jennifer Lou Sutton, b. 11 Feb. 1976.

VIII-2. Patricia Hill, b. 5 Sept. 1956, Germany, Graduated from Hardin-Simmons University in 1979.

VI-7.   Everett A. Hill, son of Elijah A. Hill and Ella Hudson, b. 14 July 1898, Democrat, Mills Co., Tex., d. 24 July 1957, m. Minerva Josephine Vernon 19 Jan. 1918. Josephine b. 7 Nov. 1895, Sipe Springs, Tex., d. 21 Oct. 1967, Ft. Worth, Tex.

Everett and Josephine lived at Brownwood and Ft.
Worth.

VII-1. Marjorie Juanita Hill, b. 19 May 1919, Comanche
Co., Tex., m. L. D. Cole, lives Ft. Worth.
VIII-1. Karen Cole

VI-8. Viola Parolee Hill, dau. of Elijah A. Hill and Ella
Hudson, b. 16 Mar. 1901, Democrat, Mills Co., Tex.,
d. 19 Mar. 1936, m. Moss Boatwright 14 Aug. 1917.
Viola died of childbirth complications when her
eighth child was 10 days old and Moss died some
months later of a heart attack, leaving the eight
children ranging in age from infancy to 17 years of
age.
VII-1. Geneva Boatwright
VII-2. Jeanette Boatwright
VII-3. William Troy Boatwright
VII-4. Elna Boatwright
VII-5. Betty Lou Boatwright
VII-6. Billie Lloyd Boatwright
VII-7. Thomas Roy Boatwright
VII-8. Allene Joyce Boatwright

VII-1. Geneva Boatwright, b. 23 June 1918, Zephyr,
Mills Co., Tex., m. Jules Vernon Hillje 18 Apr.
1935, Cotulla, La Salle Co., Tex. Jules b. 22
Mar. 1905 Smithville, Bastrop Co., Tex., son of
Gerhardt Hillje and Mary Heger. Geneva and
Jules live at Cotulla.
VIII-1. Anna Mae Hillje, b. 19 Feb. 1937, Cotulla,
Tex., m. Gion Renee Laster 2 June 1957.
G. R. b. 30 May 1935, Roaring Springs,
Motley Co., Tex., son of Orie V. Laster
and Erzula Mae Smith.
IX-1. Karen J. Laster, b. 2 July 1960, Dilley,
Frio Co., Tex., m. Charles B. Starnes
Dec. 1978.
IX-2. Kathy J. Laster, b. 19 Feb. 1965, Alice,
Jim Wells Co., Texas.
VIII-2. Betty June Hillje, b. 23 May 1943, Cotulla,
La Salle Co., Tex., m. Walter Paul
Koricanek 10 July 1961, Cotulla, Tex.
Walter b. 22 May 1941, Flatonia, Fayette
Co., Tex., son of Charles William Koricanek
and Lena Syrinek.
IX-1. Walter Paul Koricanek, Jr., b. 19 Nov.
1962, Dilley, Frio Co., Texas.
IX-2. Bobby Lee Koricanek, b. 23 March 1967,
Alice, Jim Wells Co., Texas.
135

VIII-3.   John Vernon Hillje, b. 28 Feb. 1946,
          Cotulla, La Salle Co., Tex., m. Carolyn
          Ann Brumley 1 June 1968 Stanton, Martin
          Co., Tex.   Carolyn b. 17 Nov. 1948, dau.
          of Charles Brumley and Betty Cottongame.
   IX-1. Michael Scott Hillje, b. 28 Jan 1970,
          Alpine, Brewster Co., Tex.
   IX-2. Greg Allen Hillje, b. 19 May 1976,
          Alice, Jim Wells Co., Texas.
VIII-4.   Gary Lee Hillje, b. 6 Jan. 1948, Cotulla,
          La Salle Co., Tex., m. Saralyn Ann
          Matthews 21 Mar. 1970.   Saralyn b. 6 Nov.
          1946, Beeville, Bee Co., Tex., daughter
          of Norvil Cleo Matthews and Valesta Hilde-
          garde Gulley.
   IX-1. Stacie Lea Hillje, b. 5 Aug. 1975,
          Laredo, Webb Co., Texas.
   IX-2. Ricky James Hillje, b. 6 Oct. 1979,
          Laredo, Webb Co., Texas.

VII-2.   Jeanette Boatwright, dau. of Viola Hill and
          Moss Boatwright, b. 7 Dec. 1920, Johnson Co.,
          Texas, d. 25 Mar. 1973, San Antonio, Texas, m.
          Lee Brown 2 Nov. 1948, Austin, Texas.
             Jeanette came to live with Nollie and Enoch
          Godwin soon after her parents passed away.
          She finished high school at Lometa and her
          nurse's training at Breckenridge Hospital in
          Austin.   After marriage she nursed at Baptist
          Hospital in San Antonio, becoming Supervisor of
          Nurses.
   VIII-1. Riley Lee Brown, b. 21 March 1956, San
          Antonio, Tex.

VII-3.   William Troy Boatwright, b. 20 June 1922,
          Brown Co., Tex.   Troy was District Manager for
          Western Union in Manchester, Mo., now retired
          in Colo., three children.

VII-4.   Elna Mae Boatwright, dau. of Viola Hill and
          Moss Boatwright, b. 4 Mar. 1925, Brown Co.,
          Tex., m. Wilbert Matherne 17 Dec. 1947.   Wilbert
          b. 6 June 1905, son of Alexander Matherne and
          Lucy Porter of Fairfax, Okla.
             Elna and Wilbert live at Alice, Tex.
   VIII-1. Lucy Viola Matherne, b. and d. June 1952,
          Harlingen, Tex.
   VIII-2. James Troy Matherne, b. 4 Oct. 1954, San
          Benito, Cameron Co., Tex., m. Gladys Marie

Edwards 27 Dec. 1976, Alice, Tex. Gladys
b. 16 Mar. 1941, Stuart, Okla., dau. of
Joseph Freeland Edwards and Opal Veda
Conditt.

IX-1. Jamie Marie Matherne, b. 8 Nov. 1977,
Alice, Tex.

VIII-3. David Ray Matherne, b. 2 Aug. 1956, Harlin-
gen, d. same day.

VIII-4. Elna Inette Matherne, b. 9 Feb. 1958,
Tulare Co., Cal., m. Dennis Ray Bartholomew
28 Dec. 1974, Ducor, Cal. Dennis b. 8 July
1953, Ray, Minn., son of Carl Bartholomew
and wife, Helen.

IX-1. Vernon Allen Bartholomew, b. 26 Oct.
1976, Alice, Jim Wells Co., Tex.

VIII-5. Dale Allen Matherne, b. 15 Nov. 1962,
Porterville, Tulare Co., Cal.

VII-5. Betty Lou Boatwright, dau. of Viola Hill and
Moss Boatwright, b. 22 Jan. 1929, Mills Co.,
Tex., m. M. B. Cheshier, li. Dallas, Tex.

VII-6. Billie Lloyd Boatwright, son of Viola Hill and
Moss Boatwright, b. 26 Feb. 1931, La Salle Co.,
Tex., li. Spearman, Tex. where he does irrigat-
ed farming.

VII-7. Thomas Roy Boatwright, son of Viola Hill and
Moss Boatwright, b. 6 Oct. 1933, La Salle, Co.,
Tex., d. 1950's.

VII-8. Allene Joyce Boatwright, dau. of Viola Hill and
Moss Boatwright, b. 9 Mar. 1936, La Salle Co.,
Tex. She was raised in Buckner Orphans Home,
Dallas, Tex., now lives in Cleveland, Ohio, m.
_____ Stone, five children.

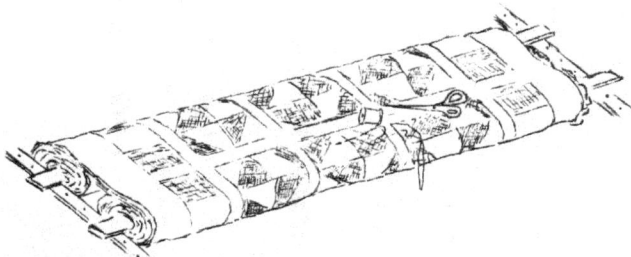

Printed and for sale by Jno. W. Hill, Proprietor of the Chief Job Office, Comanche, Texas.

(Class 8.)

CERTIFICATE OF REGISTRATION OF MARKS AND BRANDS.

NO.	OWNER AND PLACE OF RESIDENCE	KIND OF ANIMAL	MARK.	BRAND.	LOCATION OF BRAND.	DATE OF REGISTER N.
1844	E. A. & James Hill	Cattle	OO	E D	on left Sholder	March
		Horses		E D	on left Shulder	21 1879
		Hogs and other stock				

THE STATE OF TEXAS, } I, _____, Clerk of the
County of _____ } County Court in and for said county, do hereby
certify that the foregoing is a true copy of the record of the Mark and Brand of
E. A. & James Hill

Witness my hand and Seal of office, this 21 day of March, 1879

Clerk County Court _____ County.

138

X

Pleasant Gideon Hill

Pleasant Gideon (P. G.) Hill, son of James Hill and Lucinda Parolee Godwin, b. 28 Aug. 1859, Tippah Co., Miss., d. 20 July 1948, age 88, Brownwood, Tex., buried Comanche, Tex.

He m. (1) Kitty Bell Bishop 16 Aug. 1883, Comanche, Tex. Kitty, dau. of Alvin Bishop and Mary Jane Cox, b. 11 Mar. 1866, Middleton, Hardeman Co., Tenn., d. 21 June 1889, Ft. Davis, Tex., age 23.

Children of P. G. Hill and Kitty Bell Bishop:
VI-1. Nollie Bell Hill
VI-2. James Alvin Hill
VI-3. Achrol H. Hill

P. G. Hill m. (2) Vinnie Cavin 1 Oct. 1894. Vinnie b. 30 Aug. 1876, Burnet Co., Tex., dau. of Nathan Alexander Cavin and Sarah Augusta Powers. She d. 8 Aug. 1946, Taft, Cal.

Children of P. G. Hill and Vinnie Cavin:
VI-4. Lillian Hill
VI-5. Cecil R. Hill
VI-6. J. D. Hill
VI-7. Curtis Benton Hill
VI-8. Parolee Hill
VI-9. Mack Hill
VI-10. Ivanell Hill

The parents of both P. G. Hill and Kitty Bell Bishop came from Tennessee about the same time in 1878 and settled in adjoining communities in the southern part of Comanche County, Texas, the Bishops settling at Mercers Gap and the Hills at Brushy Gap, later called Democrat Community. Kitty was 12 and P. G. was about 19 when they came to Texas.

Kitty lost her mother when she was 13 and married P. G. when she was 17. Two letters from P. G. to Kitty written in Jan. and Feb. before they married in Aug. 1883 have been saved these almost 100 years.

Kitty Bell Bishop Hill

P. G. Hill

Children of Kitty and
P. G. Hill

James Alvin Hill
Nollie Bell Hill
Achrol H. Hill

Pleasant Gideon Hill

January the 12 1883

Miss Kittie Bishop
     the dearest one to me I got your wellcome
letter to day and was glad to her from you but
how glad I would be to see you and tell you how
much I thought of you and talk about the dance
and gay times you have had and hav some more as
gay   I have not got nary letter from Miss Jinnie
Stanley   She has gon back on me   I will come to
Comanch to see her but it wont be ___ as long as
you ar there   I hav saw Jim sence I got your
letter   Please tell me if you think I would
show your leters to eny body on erth   Miss Kittie
do you love me well enuff to for sake all for me
the more days that pass the more I think of you
If you aim to go back on me now is the time to tell
me but I hope you will not for I think a heep of
you more than tung could tell so I would close for
this time so pleas write soon as you get this to
your true lover   P. G. Hill
     Well I for got to tell you that Bud had got
back and I was glad to see him   he has gon to bed
and sleep the ciote howl and mak me lonly so good by
for this time   P. G. Hill

                    Ocland ranch
                    February the 20

Miss Kittie Bishop
     most dearist frind I seat my self to drop you
a few lines to let you know your kind letter came
saft to hand and the seal was brok and the contens
was red with egar eys and paced in the senter of
my hart but oh must I all way be put off yes your
leters ar dear to me but could be more so yes when
I see you it will be time a nuff to answer my question but it will be 3 month till I see you and oh
how long the time will be or seam to be and how
glad I be to hav a true lover ther   on (one) that
will never go back on me. if you aim to go back on
me let it be now the reson why I did not send you
that letter you did not send me yours and I thought
you did not want to see   I will show you my leter
and tell you all the nuse when I see you   I saw
Jim Collier (Kittie's bro-in-law) with letter
from you or Lida on (one) Miss Molie is a good
girl but the boys can hav them all if they will
giv me my chois do you think they will If you
know they will I am all right   That cuntry is
141

badly ingard (?) if the old lady Allen dont return
oh how sorry I most redy to cry but I guess I wont
Yes I would like to be at that dance if you would
injoy it eny beter if eny body in the world would
injoy your compy it would be me so I will close
write soon and ofton to your true lover so god by
for this time.

P. G. Hill

The location of Ocland Ranch is uncertain but it is known
that P. G. spent much time in west Texas on sheep ranch-
es, herding and shearing.

Kitty and P. G.'s first home was a log cabin just
north of Santa Anna Mountain. The cabin had a dirt floor
and they often had trouble with the skunks burrowing
under the walls. Their nearest neighbors were Kitty's
sisters Mollie Jackson and Mandy Simpson who lived 2 or 3
miles away.

Giddy was away from home much of the time and in
this lonely cabin Kitty stayed, bearing two children and
was expecting her third when they moved about 350 miles
to Marfa, Texas where P. G. got a contract to build some
"good sheep fence" in Presidio County on the Saucito
Ranch at $55 a mile. The contract was signed March 2,
1889 and the fence was to be completed by May 15, 1889.
It is presumed that he had Mexican labor.

Perhaps the fence was completed when Achrol was
about 6 months old and Kitty was ill with "after effects
of child birth." The family story goes that P. G. took
his family to Ft. Davis; Kitty died and was buried there.
The grave is unmarked. P. G. left the children, Nollie
barely 4, Alvin 2, and the baby Achrol, with someone
there, went back to complete his business, then came for
the children. Nollie said she remembered being sent to
get clothes out of a big trunk in the wagon while they
were there.

In searching for the grave of Kitty in 1973, we contacted the Supt. of the Ft. Davis Historic Site and he
very kindly checked the Post Surgeon's reports for the
years 1888 to 1891 and the Post Chaplain's "records of
births, marriages, baptisms, and deaths," for the same
period. No records for Kitty were found.

They may have stopped at the home of an individual
or at an inn and maybe Kitty is buried in the town of
Ft. Davis or in the old town cemetery on the Alpine-Ft.
Davis highway where markers have long since disappeared.

They came by train, probably boarding at Marfa, to
Democrat to P. G.'s parents, who raised the three little
ones as their own. Kitty had named the baby, but the
name had been forgotten, so his grandmother named him

Achrol for one of her brothers who had died.

P. G. met his second wife when he was in his early thirties. He had been working on a stock trade with Mr. Nathan Cavin and while visiting in their home near Marble Falls, Texas met the 17 yr-old Vinnie.

After marriage they lived near Del Rio, Ozona, and Sonora, then at Duran, N. Mex., moving back to Texas in 1918 when P. G. and his boys, Cecil and J. D., worked in the oil fields at Moran in Eastland County during the oil boom of 1918-1919. They operated trucks for hauling pipes used in the fields. After a year at Moran and another at Sipe Springs, the family moved to De Leon in the early 1920's.

P. G. was often away from home for long periods of time, usually leaving the family in some rural area with maybe a barrel of flour, some beans and molasses, but otherwise unfinanced.

He was an easy prey for someone needing a handout and seldom kept his money long. After listening to a hard luck story, he often brought men home to be fed, sometimes a table full. Once he brought a man home who had lice. Vinnie supervised while P. G. and the man washed and boiled the bedding after he had infested it.

In 1927 Vinnie took the children to the home of the oldest daughter in California where she lived until she passed away in 1946.

P. G. raised sheep and drilled wells, camping out most of the time until his health no longer permitted, then he came to live among his children, Parolee and Nollie rotating him until he was placed in a rest home in Brownwood where he passed away in 1948.

VI-1.   Nollie Bell Hill, dau. of P. G. Hill and Kitty Bell Bishop, b. 10 Feb. 1885, Santa Anna, Coleman Co., Tex., d. 13 Jan. 1974, buried Long Cove Cemetery, Lometa, Tex., m. Enoch Godwin 16 Aug. 1908, Brownwood, Tex.
  VII-1.   Glenna Mae Godwin
  VII-2.   Minnie Alba Tiana Godwin
  VII-3.   Julia Day Alva Godwin
  VII-4.   Ruth Geraldine Godwin
  VII-5.   Lillian Merle Godwin
  VII-6.   Beulah Merline Godwin
  VII-7.   Riley Alvin Godwin
  VII-8.   May Dell Godwin
  VII-9.   Ira Smith Godwin
  VII-10. Jeanette Boatwright (foster daughter)

    This family was treated in the Enoch Godwin Chapter.

VI-2.   James Alvin Hill, son of P. G. Hill and Kitty Bell
        Bishop, b. 5 May 1887, Santa Anna, Coleman Co.,
        Tex., d. 2 Feb. 1971, San Diego, Cal., m. Clarissa
        Adelaide Houschildt, 17 Mar. 1934. Clarissa b. 18
        Mar. 1901, Chicago, Ill.
    VII-1. Margaret Colleen Hill, b. 24 Dec. 1934, El
            Centro, Cal., m. Richard Douglas Mongan 17 Oct.
            1964, Los Alamitos, Cal. Richard b. 8 Mar.
            1935, Minneapolis, Minn., son of Donald Mongan
            and his wife Ruth Bolmgren. He was raised at
            McAllen, Tex., served in the U. S. Marine
            Corps, and is now an engineer, li. Santa Ana,
            Cal.
                Colleen was raised in California, living at
            San Diego, Hemet, and San Bernadino. She is
            a librarian. They are both Lutheran.
        VIII-1. Ryan Hill Mongan, b. 25 June 1966, Long
                Beach, Cal.
        VIII-2. Amy Lynn Mongan b. 7 July 1967, Long
                Beach, Cal.

        James Alvin Hill was called Alvin as he grew up,
but Jim in adult life. He began work with a telephone company early in life and followed this
trade until he retired, working for some time in
Texas, then for many years in California.
        In WW I he served in the army as a linesman in
the Signal Corps in France. Before he went abroad
he was stationed at Camp Merritt, New Jersey when
he wrote his sister Nollie this letter:

                    Camp Merritt New Jersey   12-27-17

Dear Sister received your letter yesterday. I am
getting along very well considering everything. We
have been under quaranteen 10 days and I guess will
be for about ten more on account of measles. Sure
is a fine Xmas we are having I don't think. It sure
makes me mad to think we are quaranteened here this
close to New York City on Xmas and can't go. I have
been in twice and seen a good part of the city but
we are not allowed to leave the Co. St. now. There
has been about 15 of our boys sent to the Hospital
with measles so far but I don't think I will get
them. We had a fire here two or three mornings back.
It broke out at Four Oclock A.M. We sure did have
to move out quick. It burned two of our Barracks but
we saved the most of our clothes. I have plenty of
good clothing and blanckets. I received a package
from Mr. Tadlock at Stamford the place where I roomed
four years. The package contained nearly everything

James Alvin Hill
Ryan Hill Mongan

Jim and Clarissa Hill
Amy Lynn Mongan

The Mongans
Amy, Colleen, Ryan, and Richard

1969

a person could use especially in a business like this. We are not allowed to carry but 75 lbs. across including our clothing and everything. But you can send some pecans if you can get any. They don't hardly know what they are up here. I have been fairing very well. The boys have been receiving cakes and nuts all during Xmas and I have had plenty all the time.

I guess we will be here about a month yet so you can send your mail here from now on. Maby I will get it. I have already had 3 boxes and 5 or 6 letters lost. They don't seem to handle the mail very well now especially around these army camps. There is about 40,000 troops here now and all of them gets lots of mail from home.

As ever
J. A. Hill

send some more letters from Lilly and others. They are news to me. Has any of the boys been drafted yet?

J. A. Hill Co. E 412 Tel. Bn. N. A.
Camp Merritt, New Jersey

He remained single until he was 46 living in California but coming back to Texas to visit his sister Nollie ever year or so. After marriage he and Clarissa continued to make trips to Texas. Alvin was a fun-loving fellow who enjoyed a good joke.

VI-3.   Achrol H. Hill, son of P. G. Hill and Kitty Bell Bishop, b. 10 Dec. 1888, Jeff Davis Co., Tex., d. 28 Aug. 1971, Denver, Colo.; m. Edna Mae Sims, dau. of Mr. and Mrs. Tom Sims of Lometa, Tex. Mae b. 7 Aug. 1893, d. 14 Nov. 1972, Denver, Colo.

Achrol's mother died when he was six months old and he, with his sister and brother, was raised by his grandmother and grandfather Hill in the Democrat Community north of Mullin, Tex. Like his brother Alvin, he began work early with a telephone company and followed this trade through his working years. Achrol and Mae lived at Cisco, Tex. some years then at Denver, Colo. for the rest of their lives.

VII-1.   James A. Hill, b. 30 May 1915, d. May 1936.
VII-2.   Mary Hazel Hill, b. 31 July 1916, m. (1) ____ Banta, (2) Dr. _____ Pharaoh, who d. 1967.
     VIII-1. Brook Banta m. M. R. (Rowe) Self.
         IX-1. James Self
         IX-2. David Self
         IX-3. Matthew Self

Hazel Hill Pharaoh is a chiropractor doctor, now
practicing in Seattle, Washington, living in nearby
Woodenville where she moved from Englewood, Colorado near
Denver, in 1973 after the death of her husband and
parents. Her daughter Brook, now divorced, lives near
with her three boys.

(My sister, Beulah Holland, and I contacted Hazel in
the summer of 1978 when we were in Seattle. She, Brook,
and the boys picked us up and took us out to a lovely
place for dinner for an enjoyable evening.)

VI-4.   Lillian Hill, dau. of P. G. Hill and Vinnie Cavin,
        b. 6 Aug. 1895 out of Del Rio, Val Verde Co., Tex.,
        m. (1) Claud Dunn, m. (2) Frank McMillan, and m.
        (3) A. Van Houtum.
            Lillian has lived in Taft, Cal., Ely, Nevada,
        Lake Buchanan, Burnet, Tex., and is now at Big
        Springs, Tex.
        Children of Lillian Hill and Claud Dunn:
    VII-1. Willard Dunn, b. 30 Mar. 1915, Rome, Tex.,
            was in the army in WW II. Estranged from
            family.
    VII-2. Murrel Dunn, b. 5 Jan. 1917, Ann Arbor, Mich.,
            d. 20 May 1945. He was first in the Navy,
            then called back into service in the army in
            WW II, was killed when a mine exploded under
            the truck he was driving on Luzon, buried
            Taft, Cal.

VI-5.   Cecil R. Hill, son of P. G. Hill and Vinnie Cavin,
        b. 24 Mar. 1898, Sonora, Tex., d. 1978, m. Helda

    VII-1. Lynn Hill, b. 12 June 1951, Alaska.
    VII-2. Cecilia Hill, b. 5 Feb. 1953, Nevada. Both
            live at Grass Valley, Cal.

VI-6.   J. D. Hill, son of P. G. Hill and Vinnie Cavin, b.
        14 Oct. 1903, Corona, Lincoln Co., N. Mex., m.
        Lillian Elderidge, li. Ely, Nev.
    VII-1. Lois Jean Hill m. M. F. Gilbert, 4 boys, 1
            girl.
    VII-2. Diane Hill m. Thomas C. Sheldon, 1 boy, 1 girl,
            li. Concord, Cal.
    VII-3. Alice Hill, m. Edward Torpey, 2 boys, 1 girl,
            li. Baldwin Pk., Cal.

VI-7.   Curtis Benton Hill, son of P. G. Hill and Vinnie
        Cavin, b. 18 Mar. 1906, Corona, Lincoln Co., N.
        Mex., d. 29 Sept. 1978, Big Springs, Tex., m.
        Gertrude Roman 26 Apr. 1935, Ely, White Pine Co.,

Children of P. G. Hill and Vinnie Cavin - 1946
Lillian Van Houtum, J. D. Hill, Curtis Hill,
Parolee Foster, Cecil Hill, Ivanell Cooke

Gertie and Curtis Hill, Vinnie Cavin Hill,
Helda and Cecil Hill, P. G. Hill
Front: Edith Foster, dau. of Parolee, and
         Lynn Hill, son of Cecil

Seated: Jim and Parolee
Foster holding grand-
children Denise Mosley and
Jill Prewitt
Back: Don and Edith
Prewitt, Joan and Paul
Mosley
Christmas, 1962

148

Nev. Gertrude b. 9 Mar. 1905, Jester, Navarro Co.,
Tex., dau. of Jacob Harmon Roman and Pauline
Williams.

VII-1. Douglas Roman Hill, b. 1 Oct. 1947, Taft,
Kern Co., Cal., m. Susan Gail Goering 13 Apr.
1974, Dallas, Tex. Susan b. 17 Sept. 1948,
Bay City, Matagorda Co., Tex.

VII-2. Donald Cavin Hill, b. 1 Oct. 1947, Taft, Cal.,
twin to Douglas, m. Keren Jenkins 9 Aug. 1971,
Houston, Harris Co., Tex., divorced 1972.

VI-8. Parolee Hill, dau. of P. G. Hill and Vinnie Cavin,
b. 7 Sept. 1908, Duran, Torrance Co., N. Mex., m.
Jim Foster 24 Aug. 1927, Santa Barbara, Cal. Jim
b. 15 Sept. 1904, Morgan, Tex.
Parolee and Jim have lived at De Leon, Stamford,
and Dublin, Tex., now live in active retirement
near Lake Buchanan, Burnet, Tex. where Jim enjoys
his productive garden and orchard. He had been
employed by a railroad company before his retirement. Parolee does some painting and other arts
and crafts.

VII-1. Joan Foster, b. 10 July 1929, m. Paul Mosley
27 Mar. 1947, Cisco, Tex. They now live on
Lake Buchanan and both teach at Burnet.

VIII-1. Michel Homer Mosley, b. 12 Dec. 1947, m.
Debbie Cox 3 Aug. 1974, Camp Pendleton,
Cal., li. Austin, Tex.

IX-1. Dawn Mosley, b. 25 Mar. 1976.

VIII-2. Viki Jean Mosley, b. 28 Oct. 1950, Cisco,
Tex., m. Howard Gregory 14 Aug. 1971,
Cisco, Tex., li. Austin, Tex.

IX-1. Staci Gregory, b. 17 Feb. 1977.

VIII-3. Karon Denise Mosley, b. 30 Apr. 1957,
m. Thomas Sloan Ellis of San Saba, Tex.
Thomas b. 1953, d. 24 Nov. 1975, auto
accident.

VII-2. Edith Mae Foster, b. 30 Mar. 1934, m. Don
Prewitt 23 Feb. 1952, Stamford, Tex., li.
Midland, Tex. Edith Mae and Don have lived in
Stamford, Odessa, Midland, Houston, and were
on assignment in Teheran beginning in 1970.
Now in Midland, Edith Mae teaches school and
Don works for an oil company.

VIII-1. Jo Don Prewitt, b. 11 May 1953, d. 27
Jan. 1971, Teheran, Iran. He was active
in school and served as teacher aide in
1st and 2nd grades, was a member of
Alamo Heights Baptist Church at Midland
at the time of his death. He and two

other American boys were struck down on a
Teheran street by a drunk taxi driver.
Buried at Pearland, Tex.

VIII-2. James Cal Prewitt, b. 5 Mar. 1956.
VIII-3. Vonda Jilene Prewitt, b. 8 Oct. 1959.

VI-9. Mack Hill, son of P. G. Hill and Vinnie Cavin, b.
1910, Duran, N. Mex., d. at 6 mo. of whooping
cough and measles.

VI-10. Ivanell Hill, dau. of P. G. Hill and Vinnie Cavin,
b. 30 Mar. 1912, Duran, Torrance Co., N. Mex.,
d. 25 Dec. 1957, Great Lakes Naval Base, Ill.,
buried Libertyville, Ill., m. (1) _____ Singuette.

VII-1. Beverly Singuette Cooke (adopted name) m.
Paul Babyer, li. Houston, Tex.

VIII-1. Debbie Babyer, b. ca. 1955.
VIII-2. Catherine Babyer, b. ca. 1958.
VIII-3. Steven Babyer, b. ca. 1965.

Ivanell m. (2) Robert H. Cooke (Cooky) who was in
the Navy. They traveled with assignments, were
in Pearl Harbor when it was attacked.

Parolee Hill Foster has very kindly furnished the
material on the family of P. G. Hill and Vinnie
Cavin.

XI

Elanor Adelaide (Addie) Hill

Elanor Adelaide (Addie) Hill was the fourth child of
James Hill and Lucinda Parolee Godwin, b. 1 Dec. 1861,
Middleton, Hardeman Co., Tenn., d. 4 July 1955, age 93,
m. Jesse Burnett Scoggins 9 May 1880, Comanche Co., Tex.
at the home of her parents.

Jesse Scoggins b. 4 Sept. 1853, Washington Co., Tex.,
son of Isaac H. and Mary Ann Stafford Scoggins. Jesse
was raised in Bell Co., Tex. where his father was a
Methodist preacher. He d. 1 Aug. 1915. Both are buried
in the Democrat Cemetery, Mills Co., Tex.

Children of Addie Hill and Jesse Scoggins:

VI-1.   James Hamilton (Janus) Scoggins
VI-2.   Iona Scoggins
VI-3.   Mary Parolee Scoggins
VI-4.   Jennie Victoria Scoggins
VI-5.   Jimmie (Jim) Lee Scoggins
VI-6.   Minnie Bell Scoggins
VI-7.   Lillie Elanor Scoggins
VI-8.   Mattie Iris Scoggins
VI-9.   Jesse Stephen (Steve) Scoggins
VI-10. Judge Carroll Scoggins

Addie and Jesse farmed and Jesse taught school while
raising their family of 10 robust children. Jesse had
lost his left arm above the elbow in a shooting accident
when a young man, but managed to do most jobs well. The
children worked with their farm crops and chores and often
also picked cotton and hoed crops for their neighbors.

Addie was quiet and even-tempered, a very pleasant
person to be around. My mother felt closest to Addie and
her daughters of all her kin. The girls were like sisters
to her and it was in their homes that we visited every
summer as we grew up, which provided us with some of the
most memorable times of our childhood.

The active life in this family of ten children is
described by a daughter, Minnie Scoggins Gunter at age 85
as she relates on tape:

> I don't know--What little I used to know, I've
> forgot, but maybe I can think of one or two little
> things. I'm a doing as well as you could expect.
> Don't get around too good yet. But I can't expect

151

that at my age and falling like I did. (She broke her hip 4 Jan. 1975 at age 83.)

As to Mother and Daddy and their times--Mother was born and raised in Tennessee, married in Comanche and I have their marriage license.

There were ups and downs in their married life. Daddy taught school. Fer as money, they just didn't have it. I never went to school the first day (of a term) in my life. And Daddy would keep us out to work their own crop and everybody's crop around fer us to have a little bit of money to buy things. We never did go hungry, but there were lots of times we'd a liked to changed diets, I'm sure. And they sold eggs. Mother'd raise a big bunch of chickens.

Mother made all of our clothes. Nine times out of ten you could go to town and for 10¢ a yard you could get the nicest--what was called print that day and time--or calico. And she made all our clothes and everything 'til it helped I know real well.

You could get 20 pounds sugar for a dollar, get 20 pounds of coffee for a dollar, and 20 pounds of rice to the dollar, which went a long ways in that day and time--but money didn't go--in fact we didn't hardly have any money to go anywhere. Daddy would buy a barrel of sugar, 360 pounds for $22.00. It would cost a fortune now.

Nine times out of ten we milked 8 or 10 cows and the only school I ever went to in my life I walked 4 and a half miles, night and morning. We didn't start until we were eight, but Mother let Jim go a year before and paid on him because Daddy'd have him out a plowing and everything and he wouldn't get to go to school much, so consequently he was a year ahead of me. (They were twins.) Only he'd come home at night and show me the reading he'd done, but I didn't like arithmetic and wouldn't have nothing to do with that.

And I can remember when my mother was baptized as well as if it was yesterday. Her and Grandpa Hill was baptized at the same time. I was only 5 years old and that was in 1896. I guess the reason it made such an impression on me, I'd never seen anyone baptized or nothing, and taking her out in that water and all. I remember how scared I was that they was going to drown her. So little things like that is in a child's mind a whole lot more than a feller realizes that it is.

And Grandma and Grandpa--I can remember (being told about) when they first came to Texas and he was plowing a little field across the hill there and run onto

a polecat and he'd never seen one or heard of one,
so he taken his lines and whipped the thing to death.
It just made him sick and his team sick and he went
to the house and wanted Grandma to tie a rag of tur-
pentine around his head so he couldn't smell that
smell. Just things that way, why, stays with a kid
when other things don't.

That Jeff and Ann, why I've heard Grandma talk of
them so much. They were slaves, you know, and Grandma and Grandpa had 'em and Jeff was taken off to
the army. And he stayed so long and he come back and
taken the team from the plow and hitched 'em to the
wagon. Th' was a whole bunch with him. He told them
to load up everything because they were his, and they
weren't no more his than nothing on earth. He'd say,
"Get that, it's mine! Get this, it's mine!" And
this whole bunch--Grandma was a churning out on the
back--it was kinda a rock outfit where she was churning and kept her milk and butter--they had cups tied
to their belts where they could get water to drink
and each one taken his cup and they uncovered that
there churn that Grandma was churning and was just
drinking that milk, cream and all. And when Grandma
seen their backs turned one time, she just slipped
over and taken her foot and turned that there churn
over and spilled all that--poured all that milk on the
rocks and everything. And when they come back
around and seen it, oh, they was mad and the cussin'
taken place.

But, well I don't know, Grandpa heard several months
after that if he'd come to a certain place, he could
have that wagon and team, but Grandpa was afraid to
go and they never did go.

Grandma thought lots of Ann--and Jeff too, until
he went off to the army. She thought Ann was a good
person.

When we worked in the field for the other fellow,
we would take our dinner, we didn't get to come home,
just rest in the shade of a tree and go right back to
hoeing or whatever we uz a doing.

Daddy would go to the gin with a load of cotton.
There'd be so many there and with just one gin, that
maybe he'd be gone all day and all night before he
could get his cotton ginned.

Daddy accidentally shot his arm off one time when
he went to shoot an antelope. They were 100 miles
from a doctor. They traveled day and night 'til they
got to where this doctor was and it was just hanging
by a little flesh. He finished cutting it off and
they buried it in a cigar box. He was about 17 years
153

old when that was done.
  Lots of things he couldn't do. He couldn't tie his
shoes and lots of other things. But there were lots
of things he could do. He could cut wood and he could
hoe and he could plow. He drawed water out of the
well with a bucket and rope. He had a hard time doing
that. He would pull it (the rope) down fer as he
could and then he'd reach back and catch it before it
flew back and he'd finally get the water up to the top.
There were so many things.
  He used to make syrup--all that we could use and
sold lots of it too. All of us kids just hated syrup
making because we didn't like to work at the syrup mill.
  It was at the syrup mill we'd like to eat the foam
off the syrup before it got too cool. We'd get us a
piece of cane and eat that. One time me and Jim run
on to get some of the fresh foam that had just been
run off that morning. Jennie was a tagging away long
behind. When Jim touched that bung to that there little barrel, it flew out and just covered him with the
warm syrup.
  Well Jennie could see that something was on him and
she thought a cane knife had fell out of the tree.
She screamed back to the house that a cane knife had
fell out of the tree and cut Jim's head off. Well it
just scared Mother nearly to death, but it was just the
syrup on him. That's all there was to it.

VI-1.   James Hamilton (Janus) Scoggins, son of Addie Hill
        and Jesse Scoggins, b. 15 Feb. 1881, d. 28 April
        1950, m. Pearl Ethridge, who was b. 1877, d. 1958.
          James was an oil field worker, living for some
        time at Houston, Tex., but retiring to Zephyr,
        Tex. They are buried in Democrat Cemetery, Mills
        Co., Tex.
   VII-1.   Ethel Scoggins m. ____ Jarman, li, Ft. Worth,
            Tex.
   VII-2.   Hettie Lee Scoggins m. Bill Walker.
   VII-3.   Irene Scoggins m. K. Kuykendall.
   VII-4.   May Scoggins m. C. A. Wood.
   VII-5.   J. H. Scoggins, d. unmarried, 1918, flu.
   VII-6.   Burnett Scoggins, d. unmarried, 1918, flu.
   VII-7.   Billie (dau.) Scoggins m. (1) Forrest Dailey;
            m. (2) Clarence Wilson.

        The girls were all alive in 1975, all widows.

VI-2.   Iona Scoggins, oldest daughter of Addie Hill and
        Jesse Scoggins, b. 20 April 1883, Mills Co., Tex.,

Elanor Adelaide (Addie) Hill

The Addie and Jesse Scoggins Family
Seated: Judge, Addie, Stephen; Inset: Jesse Scoggins
Standing: Minnie, Iris, Jim, Janus, Iona, Jennie, Mary and Lillie
(Taken 1 Aug. 1915 at Jesse's death.)

155

d. March 1948 in the hospital at Brownwood, but
was living at Carbon near Rising Star, Tex.
   Iona (Oney) m. John Bell, son of John Bell, Sr.
and Ruth Bell. John b. 29 July 1875, Ellis Co.,
Tex., d. 24 Jan. 1955, Rising Star, Tex. Both
are buried at Democrat Cemetery, Mills Co., Tex.
   Hard work was a challenge to Oney. She was
active on the farm as a young girl and after
marriage she canned, crocheted items for her home
and for sale, and also helped with the farm work.
She liked to do productive work so well that it
thrilled her to get to pick in good cotton. She
enjoyed helping others; both she and John were
very free-hearted.
VII-1. Addie Ruth Bell
VII-2. Robert Jesse Bell
VII-3. Minnie Katherine Bell

VII-1. Addie Ruth Bell, b. 14 May 1906, m. Andrew
        Calvin (Cal) Duncan. Cal was b. 7 Sept. 1892,
        Cooper, Delta Co., Tex., d. 21 Apr. 1968,
        Banning Cal. Addie Ruth still lives in
        California.
    VIII-1. Ruth Duncan
    VIII-2. Frances Duncan

VII-2. Robert Jesse Bell, b. 10 May 1908, d. 3 Jan.
        1975, San Angelo, Tex., m. (1) Hazel Baker,
        m. (2) Cleo ____ of Cal.
          Robert worked several years in the shipyards
        at Beaumont, but spent most of his life farm-
        ing, which he loved. He also lived at Rising
        Star and San Angelo, Tex.
          Children of Robert Bell and Hazel Baker:
    VIII-1. James Dale Bell
    VIII-2. Bobby Gene Bell

VII-3. Minnie Katherine Bell, b. 16 May 1911, Mills
        Co., Tex., m. Ruby Ernest Cornelius 10 Dec.
        1932, Comanche, Tex.
          Ruby was b. 4 Sept. 1909, Zephyr, Brown Co.,
        Tex., son of Walter Cornelius and Jesse Locke,
        d. 10 Jan. 1967, buried at Zephyr.
          Minnie recalls from her childhood days a
        trip that she made with her parents from their
        home near Weatherford to visit the kin north
        of Mullin. The trip was made in a covered
        wagon, lasting several days, during which they
        camped along the way and spent the nights in
        the wagon.

Minnie and Ruby farmed most of their married life in the vicinity of Zephyr and Minnie has worked in the Zephyr School lunchroom for many years since.

VIII-1. Wayne Cornelius, b. 12 Dec. 1933, Zephyr, Brown Co., Tex., m. Virginia Lewis 12 Jan. 1960. Virginia b. 30 Dec. 1932, dau. of Leon Lewis and Mildred Kelly. Wayne is a welder.

    IX-1. Roger Cornelius, b. 24 Oct. 1962, Brownwood, Tex.

    IX-2. Donna Cornelius, b. 2 June 1964, Brownwood, Tex.

    IX-3. Terri Cornelius, b. 11 Jan. 1969, Brownwood, Tex.

VIII-2. Joyce Cornelius, b. 3 Oct. 1937, Zephyr, Brown Co., T-x., m. Billy Singleton 9 Mar. 1956, Zephyr Methodist Church. Billy b. 1 Mar. 1934, Regency, Tex., son of Otto Singleton and Gladys Lee.

Joyce and Billy lived at Rankin, Tex. for seven years where Billy worked in the oil fields. They now live in Early, Tex. Billy is employed at the water plant and Joyce is a beauty operator.

    IX-1. Carla Singleton, b. 29 Nov. 1956, Brownwood, m. Timothy Hickey 22 Aug. 1975, Early, Tex.

        X-1. Joey Allen Hickey, b. 9 Aug. 1976, Brownwood, Tex.

    IX-2. Brenda Singleton, b. 4 July 1960, Rankin, Upton Co., Tex.

    IX-3. Timmy Singleton, b. 19 Mar. 1963, Sonora, Sutton Co., Tex.

VIII-3. Jo Etta Cornelius, b. 24 Feb. 1943, Brownwood, Tex., m. Billy Cook 31 Nov. 1968, Zephyr, Tex. Billy b. 8 Aug. 1943, son of George and Mary Cook.

    IX-1. Tonya Cook, b. 20 Mar. 1973, Brownwood, Tex.

Information on Iona Scoggins Bell family furnished by Minnie Bell Cornelius of Zephyr, Tex.

VI-3. Mary Parolee Scoggins, dau. of Addie Hill and Jesse Scoggins, b. 29 Sept. 1885, Mills Co., Tex., d. 28 June 1938, Mills Co., Tex. She m. George Young Tomlinson 2 Dec. 1906.

George b. 14 April 1879, d. 30 Jan. 1958, son of John W. Tomlinson and Mary Jane Stephavens. Mary and George lived in the Democrat Community north of Mullin where they are both buried. George was a successful farmer and Mary was known as a wonderful cook.

VII-1. Clara May Tomlinson
VII-2. Lillie Alice Tomlinson

VII-1. Clara May Tomlinson, b. 9 May 1907, Mullin, Tex., m. Johnnie T. Johnson 10 May 1923, Johnnie b. 4 July 1904, Comanche, Tex., d. 24 Jan. 1956.
    VIII-1. Dorothy Marie Johnson, b. 13 Feb. 1924, Mullin, Tex., m. Lewis Ray Cunningham 25 May 1941. Lewis b. 24 Dec. 1920, Okla.

VII-2. Lillie Alice Tomlinson, b. 15 April 1911, Mills Co., Tex., m. Robert (Dick) Glenn Jones 21 July 1930, Waurika, Okla. Robert b. 12 April 1909, Haskell Co., Tex.
    VIII-1. Peggy Jean Jones, b. 27 July 1936, Brownwood, Tex., m. Charles Lynn Ross 12 July 1964. Charles b. 7 Feb. 1930 Gorman, Tex.
        IX-1. Shawna Alice Ross, b. 9 Oct. 1960, Brownwood, Tex.
        IX-2. Mamie La Sha Ross, b. 2 Sept. 1965, Brownwood, Tex.
        IX-3. Clifton Glenn Ross, b. 10 Jan. 1969, Brownwood, Tex.
    VIII-2. Mary Alice Jones, b. 21 July 1940, Brownwood, Tex., m. Thomas Marion Stalcup who was b. 29 July 1938.
        IX-1. Shelley Dawn Stalcup, b. 9 May 1962, Lubbock, Tex.
        IX-2. Thomas Chad Stalcup, b. 26 June 1965, Enid, Okla.

Information on Mary Parolee Scoggins Tomlinson family supplied by Lillie Tomlinson Jones of Mullin, Tex.

VI-4. Jennie Victoria Scoggins, dau. of Addie Hill and Jesse Scoggins, b. 19 Feb. 1888, d. 26 Mar. 1966, Ft. Worth, Texas, buried in Mt. Olivet Cemetery, Ft. Worth, Tex., m. (1) Dave Crockett Spivey, who was b. 14 Dec. 1892, son of Henry Clay Spivey and Kathleen Fletcher, d. 18 Feb. 1920, buried in Democrat Cemetery, Mills Co., m. (2) Albert Bishop, m. (3) Bennie F. Brown.
Children of Jennie Scoggins and Dave Spivey:

VII-1. Ola Ellnor Spivey
VII-2. Virgil Spivey

VII-1. Ola Ellnor Spivey, b. 14 Sept. 1906, Zephyr,
Brown Co., Tex., d. 7 Feb. 1965. Ola m. John
Roma Fitzpatrick 26 May 1925. John b. 30 Nov.
1894, Horatio, Ark., d. 28 Mar. 1974, Tyler,
Tex. Both are buried in Pleasant Grove Ceme-
tery No. 1, Decatur, Tex. John was the son of
Henry Young Fitzpatrick and Sarah Elizabeth
Bishop and a veteran of World War I.
   John m. (2) Mrs. Dora Fulner.
   Ola and John moved about as John worked in
the oil fields, but settled near Decatur where
he worked for General Dynamics in Ft. Worth.
The children all graduated from Decatur High
School and the three girls graduated from
Decatur Baptist College.

VIII-1. Parolee Juanita Fitzpatrick, b. 1 Oct.
1926, Idabel, McCurtan Co., Okla., m. (1)
James Douglas Wilson 21 July 1950, Chicago,
Ill.
   James Douglas b. 15 April 1922, Selmer,
Tenn., son of Taylor Douglas Wilson and
Martha Elizabeth McCullar.
   Juanita is a graduate of Decatur Baptist
College and North Texas State University,
taught school 4 years, has been a book-
keeper for the last 18 years at Arlington,
Tex.
   Juanita m. (2) Ray Scott Homan.
   James m. (2) Mrs. Shirley Baum.
IX-1. Donna Re Wilson, b. 18 June 1951,
Chicago, Cooke Co., Ill., counselor in
the Houston school system.

VIII-2. Clarence Virgil Fitzpatrick, b. 29 Oct.
1928, Zephyr, Tex., m. Jeanette Bratcher
24 May 1959, Arlington, Tex. Jeanette b.
10 Nov. 1932, Ft. Worth, Tex., dau. of
Ira Bratcher and Augusta Pauline Parson.
Clarence is a veteran of the Korean War,
now involved in building grain elevators
and concrete work for water systems.

VIII-3. Nelda Lou Fitzpatrick, b. 28 Jan. 1932,
Brownwood, Tex., m. Bobby Eugene Rust 26
June 1960, Ft. Worth, Tex.
   Bobby b. 7 Jan. 1935, Cleburne, Tex.,
son of Willie B. Rust, Sr., and Elon

Teresa Bell.
Nelda is a graduate of Decatur Baptist
College, now working on art degree from
University of Houston.

IX-1. James Robert Fitzpatrick Rust, b. 12
Sept. 1961, Houston, Tex.

IX-2. Crystal Adele Rust, b. 19 Sept. 1963,
Houston, Tex.

VIII-4. Bettye Sue Fitzpatrick, b. 13 Mar. 1934
Saton City, Rusk Co., Tex. After graduat-
ing from Decatur Baptist College and North
Texas State University, Bettye joined the
staff of the Alley Theater in Houston,
where she is Production/Company Manager
and also does some acting.

VII-2. Virgil Spivey, b. 7 Aug. 1908, d. 6 Nov. 1923,
buried Democrat Cemetery, Mills Co., Tex.

Information on Jennie Scoggins Spivey family
furnished by Juanita Fitzpatrick Homan.

VI-5. Jimmie Lee (Jim) Scoggins, son of Addie Hill and
Jesse Scoggins, b. 3 July 1891, (twin to Minnie)
d. 14 Sept. 1965, buried Democrat Cemetery, Mills
Co., Tex., m. Mayme Morris, lived Victorville,
Cal.

VII-1. Jessie Lee Scoggins m. Mona _____.
VIII-1. Jimmie Scoggins
VIII-2. Mona Lee Scoggins
VIII-3. Eddie Scoggins
VIII-4. Sharon Scoggins
VIII-5. Shannon Scoggins, twin to Sharon.

VII-2. James Morris (Marcie) Scoggins m. Charlotte
Morris.
VIII-1. A. J. Scoggins
VIII-2. Steve Scoggins
VIII-3. Angela Scoggins
VIII-4. Barbara Scoggins
VIII-5. Marsha Scoggins

VII-3. Evelyn Sue Scoggins m. (2) Jim Elrod.
VIII-1. Barbara   VIII-2. Mark

VII-4. Patricia Scoggins m. Medie _____.
VIII-1. Debbie   VIII-3. Medie
VIII-2. Donna   VIII-4. Gabor

VI-6. Minnie Bell Scoggins, dau. of Addie Hill and Jesse
Scoggins, twin to Jim, b. 3 July 1891, m. Claburn
Cooper Gunter 21 July 1912.

160

Cooper b. 28 June 1892, son of John L. and Mary
Northcut Gunter, d. 19 Oct. 1954. Minnie and
Cooper farmed near Mullin, then Zephyr, Tex. They
operated a laundry in Zephyr for many years.

After Cooper's death Minnie continued to live in
Zephyr for several years before moving to Hico,
Tex. She broke her hip 4 Jan. 1975 at age 83, but
made recovery enough to be able to live alone again.
She entered Arlington Villa, a retirment complex in
1978.

VII-1. Mattie Burdell Gunter
VII-2. Claburn Scoggins Gunter

VII-1. Mattie Burdell Gunter, b. 21 Mar. 1914, d. 19
Sept. 1954, m. Elton Levi Horner 29 Jan. 1934,
Zephyr, Tex.
VIII-1. Linda Lee Horner, b. 8 Mar. 1941, m. Roy
Lee 7 July 1961. Roy b. 9 June 1936,
employed as aircraft mechanic at L.T.V.
in Grand Prairie, Tex.
IX-1. Terry Allen Lee, b. 6 Aug. 1963.
IX-2. Elton David Lee, b. 29 Aug. 1965.
IX-3. Sharon Renee' Lee, b. 9 July 1970.
VIII-2. Kayrene (Kay) Horner, b. 13 July 1945,
Zephyr, Tex., m. Florian Milton Schramm
26 Dec. 1965. Florian Milton b. 1 July
1938, Waco, Tex., is employed at Bell
Helicopter, Ft. Worth as an electrical
engineer. He is the son of Florian
Adolph Schramm and Selma M. Behoke.
Children:
IX-1. Kevin Milton Schramm, b. 13 Dec. 1969,
Dallas.
IX-2. Keith Elton Schramm, b. 13 Feb. 1971,
Dallas.

VII-2. Claburn Scoggins Gunter, b. 22 April 1927, m.
Anna Jo Green 16 Aug. 1947. Anna Jo b. 16
April 1930. Claburn is semi-retired with a
heart condition and Anna Jo is employed by
Shop Rite Foods, a division of Piggly-Wiggly.
They live in Arlington, Tex.
VIII-1. Claburn Lynn Gunter, b. 5 Nov. 1951, m.
Mary Welch 10 Oct. 1970. Mary b. 8 Sept.
1953. Lynn is also employed at Shop Rite
Foods.
VIII-2. Lexie Flynn Gunter, b. 16 Nov. 1953, m.
Peggy ____, 10 July 1973. Peggy b. 2
March 1951. Lexie is employed by Time
Corporation, Waco, Texas.

Children:
IX-1. Lela Michelle Camp (Missy) Gunter (dau.
       of Peggy) b. 7 June 1972.
IX-2. Jo Anna Marie Gunter, b. 29 April 1974.
VIII-3. Lisa Gwen Gunter, b. 19 July 1956, attend-
         ed college at T.C.J.C. in Ft. Worth, m.
         Wayne Everett Morris 24 June 1979, Botanic
         Garden, Ft. Worth, Texas.

Material on this family furnished by Minnie
Scoggins Gunter and Kayrene Horner Schramm.

VI-7. Lillie Elanor Scoggins, dau. of Addie Hill and
       Jesse Scoggins, b. 27 Sept. 1894, d. 12 Jan. 1973,
       m. Thomas Elbert (T.E.) Stevens. They spent most
       of their married life in Brownwood, Tex. while
       carrying on ranching activities nearby. T. E. d.
       1961.
   VII-1. Dorris D. Stevens
   VII-2. Miriam Judabeth (Judy) Stevens

   VII-1. Dorris D. Stevens, b. 21 Sept. 1920, Desdemonia,
           Tex., m. Coy L. Evans 2 Dec. 1939. They lived
           much of their married life in Ft. Worth, Tex.
           Coy d. 20 April 1975.
      VIII-1. Gerald T. Evans, b. 7 July 1941, Brown-
               wood, Tex., m. (1) Rebecca Butcher Adams,
               m. (2) Sharon K. Morzan, dau. of Bert B.
               Morzan. Sharon b. 25 Sept. 1943,
               Portales, N. Mex. They have lived in
               Tex. and Fla. where he has been a sheet
               metal mechanic for nearly 20 years.
                  Sharon m. (1) Tex Belcher.
                  Children of Gerald and Sharon Evans:
         IX-1. Gerald Thomas Evans, Jr. b. 20 Sept.
                1959.
         IX-2. Shari Alexandria Evans, b. 7 Aug. 1963.
                Both b. Ft. Worth, Tarrant Co., Tex.
      VIII-2. Donald L. Evans, b. 16 Sept. 1944, Brown-
               wood, Tex., m. Alice F. Colburn Anglin
               24 Nov. 1968, Brownwood. Alice b. 27
               April 1942, Birmingham, Ala., dau. of
               J. A. Colburn, Sr. and wife, Eula. They
               live in Ft. Worth where Donald is in
               insurance.
         IX-1. Donna Evans, b. 27 Mar. 1970, Jackson-
                ville, Onslow Co., N.C.
         IX-2. Janelle Evans, b. 18 Nov. 1973, Jack-
                sonville, N.C.

Alice Colburn m. (1) Kenneth Anglin.
Children:
1. Angela Anglin, b. 31 July 1962,
   Birmingham, Ala.
2. Carol Anglin, b. 10 Apr. 1964,
   Birmingham, Ala.

VII-2. Miriam Judabeth Stevens, dau. of Lillie Scoggins
and T. E. Stevens, b. 1 Mar. 1931, Brownwood,
Tex., m. Herman L. Moore 9 July 1949.
  Judy and Herman live in Brownwood where Judy
operates a school of dance and Herman taught
school before going into ranching.
  Three daughters.

VI-8. Mattie Iris Scoggins, dau. of Addie Hill and Jesse
Scoggins, b. 12 Feb. 1897, m. William Arthur Jenkins
5 Oct. 1913. Will, son of William E. Jenkins and
Lathio Smith, b. 12 Nov. 1889, Mullin, Mills Co.,
Tex., d. 3 Jan 1979, Hico, Tex., buried Stephenville,
Tex.
  Iris and Will farmed in the Democrat Community
north of Mullin, then moved to Stephenville to send
their children to Tarleton College. They later mov-
ed to Hico where they operated a laundry several
years before retiring there. They belonged to the
First Baptist Church in Hico, Tex.

The Iris and Will Jenkins Family

Front:
Leonard Jenkins,
W. A. Jenkins, Jr.,
Wanda Jenkins Mayfield
Back:
Herman Jenkins,
Iris Scoggins Jenkins,
Will A. Jenkins,
Day Alva Jenkins Ross

VII-1. Day Alva Irene Jenkins
VII-2. Herman Edward Jenkins
VII-3. Leonard Burnett Jenkins
VII-4. William Arthur Jenkins, Jr.
VII-5. Wanda Sue Jenkins

VII-1. Day Alva Irene Jenkins, b. 16 Feb. 1916, Mullin, Mills Co., Tex., m. Rowe Lamar Ross 29 April 1939. Rowe, son of Edward D. Ross and Marie Wood, was b. 19 May 1913 at Stephenville, Tex., d. 29 Oct. 1961.
Both Day Alva and Rowe attended Tarleton College, later living at Iraan and Ft. Worth, Tex. Rowe was a tooling engineer and since his death, Day Alva has been associated with T.C.U. in Ft. Worth. Both belonged to the Disciples of Christ Church.

VIII-1. Nancy Sue Ross, b. 30 Dec. 1939 at Iraan, Pecos Co., Tex., m. Robert K. Schomp 3 Sept. 1960 at Stockton, Cal. Robert b. 6 Aug. 1936, Stockton, Cal., son of Kenneth K. Schomp and Lorena Fox, is a graduate of Chapman College and Texas Christian University. Nancy Sue is also a graduate of T.C.U. and teaches school. Robert is a minister in the Disciples of Christ Church.
Children:

IX-1. Timothy Robert Schomp, b. 11 Nov. 1963, Ft. Stockton, Tex.
IX-2. Sara Elizabeth Schomp, b. 29 May 1963, Richardson, Tex.
IX-3. David Rowe Schomp, b. 9 Mar. 1972, Houston, Tex.
IX-4. Erin Mikal Schomp, b. April 1975.

VIII-2. Rowe Ann Ross, b. 5 Mar. 1945, Ft. Worth, Tex., m. Darrell D. Biggs 29 Jan. 1965, Darrel was b. 4 Sept. 1940, Kansas, son of Virgil Biggs and Gertrude Peters. Rowe Ann attended Tarleton College and is now a bank teller; Darrell is a graduate of Mexico State and T.C.U., is a minister in the Disciples of Christ Church, were in Minnesota, now Oklahoma.

VII-2. Herman Edward Jenkins, son of Iris Scoggins and Will Jenkins, b. 15 July 1920, Mullin, Tex., m. Mildred Mills 31 Aug. 1940. Mildred b. 11 Nov.

1921, Crosscut, Brown Co., Tex., dau. of Robert
L. Mills and Lillie Chambers.
  Herman was a Second Lt. in WW II, for several
years a real estate appraiser, is now retired
on the Jenkins homestead near Mullin, Tex.
Mildred teaches school. They are both Methodist.
VIII-1. Robert William Jenkins, b. 15 Dec. 1947,
         Coleman, Tex., graduate of Texas University,
         now a civil engineer, m. Candice (Candy)
         Jane Spinosa 15 Aug. 1970, Ft. Worth, Tex.
   IX-1. Shannon Paige Jenkins, b. 20 Dec. 1971.
   IX-2. Alden Rebecca Jenkins, b. 13 Jan. 1976.
VIII-2. Charles Edward Jenkins, b. 16 Aug. 1950,
         Coleman, Tex., graduate of Texas U. in
         electrical engineering, m. Pamela Kay
         De Pauer 22 Aug. 1969, Ft. Worth, Tex.
   IX-1. Jacob Robert Jenkins, b. 9 Mar. 1977.
   IX-2. Logan Jenkins, b. Aug. 1979.

VII-3. Leonard Burnett Jenkins, son of Iris and Will
        Jenkins, b. 1 Aug. 1922, Mills Co., Tex., m.
        Hattie Lou Davis 23 July 1941. Hattie Lou b.
        15 Feb. 1924, Mills Co., Tex., dau. of George
        Davis and Maggie Ann Gray. They live in
        Saginaw, Tex. where Leonard does body and
        fender work. They both belong to the Christ-
        ian Church.
VIII-1. William Burnett Jenkins, b. 8 Jan. 1943,
         Ft. Worth, Tex., m. Donna Lynn Schumach
         20 Nov. 1962. Donna b. 21 Mar. 1944,
         Ft. Worth.
   IX-1. William Lynn Jenkins, b. 21 Oct. 1963,
          Ft. Worth, Tex.
   IX-2. Cynthia Ann Jenkins, b. 19 Feb. 1969,
          Ft. Worth, Tex.
VIII-2. Sandra Lenora Jenkins, b. 3 July 1944,
         Brownwood, Tex., m. (1) William Larry
         Owens 17 Apr. 1961. Larry b. 28 Oct.
         1942, Ft. Worth, Tex.
   IX-1. Kari Owens, b. 3 July 1963, Ft. Worth,
          Tex.
   IX-2. Karin Owens, b. 15 Oct. 1964.
          Sandra m. (2) Johnnie Reagan 21 May 1974.
          Johnnie b. 17 Aug. 1947, Ft. Worth, Tex.
VIII-3. Kenneth Wayne Jenkins, b. 22 Nov. 1953,
         Ft. Worth, Tex., m. Leahsa McLaury 23
         July 1973. Leahsa b. 3 July 1953, Ft.
         Worth, Tex.
   IX-1. Tyler Leigh Jenkins, b. 29 July 1977.

VII-4. William Arthur Jenkins, Jr., son of Iris
        Scoggins and Will Jenkins, b. 23 Oct. 1925,
        Mills, Co., Tex., m. Billie Jean Evans 28 Nov.
        1947. Billie Jean, dau. of Everett Evans
        and Louise Sutton, b. 13 July 1926, Ft. Worth,
        Tex.
            Junior is a veteran of WW II.
        VIII-1. Patricia Ann Jenkins, b. 24 Aug. 1949,
                 Ft. Worth, Tex.

VII-5. Wanda Sue Jenkins, dau. of Iris Scoggins and
        Will Jenkins, b. 29 Sept. 1927, Mills Co.,
        Tex., m. Ethridge Vernon Mayfield, son of John
        Earl Mayfield and Jessie Richey, b. 28 Apr.
        1920, Erath Co., Tex.
            Wanda Sue is employed by Del Rio Book and
        Trust Co. and Ethridge, who was a S/Sgt. in
        U.S.A.F. in WW II, is a mechanic in Del Rio.
        They are both Presbyterian.
        VIII-1. Kathy Sue Mayfield, b. 6 Jan. 1961, Ft.
                 Worth, Tex.
        VIII-2. Dowd Lamar Mayfield, b. 22 May 1963,
                 Ft. Worth, Tex.

            Information on Mattie Iris Scoggins Jenkins
            furnished by Iris Jenkins, Day Alva Jenkins
            Ross and other members of the family.

VI-9. Jesse Stephen (Steve) Scoggins, son of Addie Hill
       and Jesse Scoggins, b. 14 Feb. 1900, d. 3 July
       1967, m. Ruth _____. Steve was an army career
       man, serving most of the time in San Antonio, Tex.
       VII-1. Lucille Scoggins
       VII-2. Shirley Scoggins

VI-10. Judge Carroll Scoggins, son of Addie Hill and
        Jesse Scoggins, b. 20 Feb. 1904, d. 25 Oct. 1960,
        m. (1) Addie May McCurdy. Lived in O'Donnel,
        Tex. in 1948.
        VII-1. Billy Joe Scoggins (girl)
        VII-2. Macky Jean Scoggins
                Judge m. (2) Lila Hicks
        VII-3. Bobby Ray Scoggins

XII

Smith Family

I. PETER SMITH

From the time of the first three boatloads of English immigrants in May of 1607 on the shores of James River in present Virginia to the time our Peter Smith made his will in 1738, settlers had scattered over the coastal plains, the Piedmont Plateau, and had crossed over the Blue Ridge highlands, settling the Valley of Virginia hundreds of miles from the coast. But Peter Smith is in Westmoreland County of the tidal area, bordered by the Potomac and Rappahannock Rivers, the county where George Washington was born in 1732.

Peter willed over a thousand acres of land to his children in Prince William County and an unstated amount to two other children in Westmoreland County, showing he was of the landed gentry. But the heavy immigration into Virginia caused a demand for land and the grandsons of Peter looked to the south and west as their frontiers, many going to South Carolina, at least one to Kentucky.

Peter Smith made his will in Westmoreland Co., Va. 10 Jan. 1738, it being proved 28 April 1741. The complete will follows, but this is a list of his children mentioned and the major bequests to them.

II-1. Dau. Mary Fleming, 48 acres land where she lives.
II-2. Son Peter Smith, remainder of land in Westmoreland Co., Va.
II-3. Son James Smith, 325 acres in Prince William County on Bull Run where he lives.
II-4. Son Thomas Smith, 325 acres in Prince William Co., where he lives.
II-5. Son William Smith 325 acres in Prince Wm. Co., to his liking out of remaining land.
II-6. Dau. Abigail Flemine and G. dau. Anne Bailey, remainder land in Prince Wm. Co., Abigail to pick first.
II-7. Heirs of John Smith, one shilling sterling.
II-8. Dau. Anne Thomas, one shilling sterling.
II-9. Dau. Hannah Ware, one shilling sterling.
II-10. Dau. Martha McClanahan, feather bed.

Peter was to get the remainder of the movable estate and be the sole executor.

Godwin-Hill and Related Families

Peter Smith Will
Bk 9, p. 140, Westmoreland Co., Va.

In the name of God amen, the tenth day of January 1738.
I, Peter Smith, of the County of Westmoreland in Virginia being in health and of perfect mind and memory
thanks be given unto God therefore calling to mind the
mortality of my Body and knowing that is appointed for all
men once to die do make and ordain this my last will and
Testament that is to say Principally and first of all I
give and Recommend my soul unto the hands of God that gave
it and my body I recommend to the Earth to be Buryed in
decent Christian Buryal at the discretion of my Executors
nothing doubting but at the general Resurrection I shall
receive the same again by the mighty Power of God and as
touching such worldly Estate wherewith it has Pleased God
to bless me in this life I give demise and dispose of the
same in the following manner and form.
Imprimis I give and bequeath to my Daughter Mary Fleming forty Eight acres of land where she now lives according to the courses that a survey that Barber made Beginning at a corner tree of Whetstones land to her and her
heirs for Ever.
Item I give to my son Peter Smith the Remaining Part of
all Land that I possess in Westmoreland County to him and
his heirs for Ever.
Item I give to my son James Smith three hundred and twenty
five acres of Land in Prince William County lying and being
upon Bull Run where he now lives to him and his heirs for
Ever.
Item I give and bequeath to my son Thomas Smith three hundred and twenty-five acres of land in the aforesaid County
where he now lives to him and his heirs for Ever.
Item I give to my son William Smith three hundred and
twenty five acres of land in the aforesaid County to his
Liking out of the Remaining Part of the same tract of Land
to him and his heirs forever.
Item I give to my daughter Abigail Flemine and my Grand
Daughter Anne Bailey the Remaining part of that tract of
land in Prince William County aforesaid my Daughter Abigail
having the first choice, to them and their heirs for Ever.
And as for what movable estate it hath pleased god to
bestow upon me I give and bequeath as followeth.
Item I give and bequeath to the heirs of my son John Smith
one Shilling Sterling money.
Item I give to my son James Smith one Shilling Sterling
money.
Item I give to my son Thomas Smith one Shilling Sterling
money.

168

Item I give to my son William Smith one Shilling Sterling
money.
Item I give to the heirs of my daughter Anne Thomas one
Shilling Sterling money.
Item I give to my Daughter Mary Fleming one Shilling
Sterling money.
Item I give to my daughter Hannah Ware one Shilling
Sterling money.
Item I give to my Daughter Martha McClanaham a feather
bed at the discretion of my Executor hereafter named.
Item I give to my Daughter Abigail Fleming one Shilling
Sterling money.
Item and the rest of my movable estate not already
Bequeathed I give and bequeath to my son Peter Smith whom
I likewise Institute make and ordain my whole and sole
Executor of this my last will and Testament and I do here-
by utterly Disallow Revoke and disannul all and every
other former Testaments Wills Legacies and Bequests and
Executors by me in any way before named willed and be-
queathed Ratifying and confirming this and no other to be
my Last will and Testament In witness whereof I have here-
unto set my hand and seal the day and year above written.
Witnesses:
James Walker   Peter Smith
Stephen Bailey Jun
Hugh Thomas   Proved 28 April 1741

II-4. THOMAS SMITH

Thomas Smith, son of Peter Smith of Westmoreland Co.,
Va., d. 1778, m. Elizabeth Fleming about 1740 and lived in
Prince William Co., Va. near where Washington, D.C. is now
located. He was supposed to have been of Welch descent
and Elizabeth was French, according to Dr. J. B. O. Lan-
drum in History of Spartanburg County, S.C.
Thomas Smith was a planter in Virginia, his main crops
being corn and tobacco. Besides the 325 acres that his
father willed to him in 1738, land where Thomas lived at
the time, he also leased 133 acres of land from Francis
Watts on Bull Run in Prince Wm. Co. in May 1749. The provisions of the lease were for 99 years in consideration of
500 lbs. of tobacco due each Dec. 25th, beginning in 1751.
Thomas agreed to build a "sufficient dwelling house and
tobacco house and corn house and to plant an apple orchard
of 150 trees fenced in and not to make sale or willful
waste of timber."
When Thomas died in 1778, the remainder of the lease
was sold by his son Charles Smith, executor, for 120 pounds
sterling to Alexander Henderson, who at the same time
bought a tract of land from Charles for 100 pounds.

Four of Thomas' sons, Daniel, Thomas, Peter, and James, were in S.C. when their father died. Now Charles and John followed them there, also John Gibbs who had married their sister. Also in 96 Dist. S.C. were cousins Handcock and William Smith, sons of Wm. Smith, brother to Thomas.

Sept. 12th 1778--An Inventory of the Estate of Thomas Smith

	£	S	D
Lease of Francis Watts for 99 years, seventy years of which is to come	100	0	0
1 cow	8	0	0
2 beds	14	0	0
a cupboard	0	12	0
A Dutch oven and skillet	2	5	0
A frying pan	0	12	0
pewter	2	0	0
Two spinning wheels	1	0	0
One old wooling wheel	0	10	0
Six old hand tubs	1	0	0
A hand mill	1	0	0
Cooppers (sic) tools	1	0	0
A grindstone and iron pessle	0	9	0
Three old barrels and a tan tub	0	18	0
Two tables and a Sadle tree	0	12	0
A loom and flour tub and candle cop	1	2	3
	£ 135	0	3

The Estate of Thomas Smith, dec'd with Charles Smith as Administrator.

Sept. 1778 by amount of the inventory	£ 135	0	3
To Elizabeth Smith widow her third part	45	0	1
Fleming Smith, one ninth	10	0	0
John Smith, one ninth	10	0	0
John Gibbs, do	10	0	0
Elizabeth Smith, do	10	0	0
Charles Smith (to my own share)	10	0	0
Remainder in hand for			
Daniel Smith			
Thomas Smith			
Peter Smith			
James Smith			
Sons of the deceased now in the state of South Carolina for each £10	40	0	0
	£ 135	0	3

Receipts are shown for each of these except the four boys in South Carolina, with John Gibbs signing for his brother-in-law, John Smith.

Children of Thomas Smith and Elizabeth Fleming:
(Not especially in order.)

III-1. Fleming Smith, b. 1745, m. Prudence Bland, dau. of
        John Bland, bought the Hanniah Lincoln farm in
        Cumberland Co., Ky. in 1814, it later becoming
        part of Monroe County where he drew a Rev. Soldier's
        pension of $25, beginning 21 Oct. 1833 at 88 years
        of age. He had a dau. Dorcas who m. John Page and
        probably a son Samuel.
III-2. John Smith, lived Spartanburg, S.C. when his father
        d. in 1778, had son, Thomas, dau. Susanna who m.
        Thomas Finch and one other dau., crippled.
III-3. Dau. Smith who m. John Gibbs, lived in Union Co.,
        S.C., were active in the Padgett Creek Baptist
        Church from 1784 for several years.
III-4. James Smith, 1751-1840, m. (1) Elizabeth_____, (2)
        Martha Peek Howard, li. Spartanburg and Union Cos.,
        S.C.
III-5. Elizabeth Smith
III-6. Charles Smith m. Catherine Rhodes ca. 1760, li.
        Spartanburg Co., S.C., made deacon in Philadelphia
        Church (Baptist) 1805, d. 1824, Rev. Sol.
        Ch.: Elijah, Sanford, William, Daniel, Moses,
        Aaron, Martha, Abigail, Elizabeth, Rachel Ann,
        Mary.
III-7. Daniel Smith
III-8. Thomas Smith, unmarried.
III-9. Peter Smith

III-4. JAMES SMITH

        James Smith, son of Thomas Smith and Elizabeth
        Fleming of Prince William Co., Va., b. 9 June 1751,
        d. 11 Sept. 1840, age 90, in Union Co., S.C.
        m. (1) Elizabeth _____, who d. 11 Dec. 1810.
        m. (2) Martha Peek Howard who d. 9 Nov. 1840.
        Children of James Smith and first wife Elizabeth:
   IV-1. John Fleming Smith, b. 14 Mar. 1793, m. Nancy
          Tollison 26 Mar. 1835, lived Union Co., S.C.
          Children:
      V-1. Franklin Smith, d. during War unmarried.
      V-2. Thomas W. Smith, Baptist minister of note,
            d. 1883.
   IV-2. Elizabeth Smith, b. 29 Mar. 1797, d. 2 Oct.
          1841, unmarried.
   IV-3. Sarah Smith m. John Eubanks, lived Union Co.,
          S.C.
   IV-4. Anna Newton Smith m. (1) Thomas Eubanks, (2)
          John Tollison.

IV-5. Enoch Smith, b. 19 May 1806, d. 10 June 1885, m.
Jane Moore 22 Dec. 1835.
IV-6. Priscilla Smith, d. unmarried 25 Sept. 1843.

Above from William Smith Bible and James Smith
Will.

James was in Spartanburg Dist., S.C. when he
entered the Service in 1778 at age 27. He was
probably about 40 when he married first and 60 the
second time. The name Newton for a daughter may
indicate that his first wife was Elizabeth Newton.
James and Martha had no children
James Smith applied for and received a pension
for service in the Revolutionary War in July, 1833
at age of 81, living in Union County, South Carolina at the time. He was allowed 30 dollars per
annum to commence 4 March 1831, was paid arrears
of $60. He was three times a draftee in the War,
for three months each time.

James Smith Pension Application

STATE OF SOUTH CAROLINA
UNION DISTRICT   TO WIT:

On this 5th day of October 1832, personally appeared
in open Court, before the Judge of Common Pleas and Sessions, now sitting for the District aforesaid, JAMES SMITH,
a resident of Union District, aged Eighty one years, who
being sworn according to Law, doth, on his oath, make the
following Declaration, in order to obtain the benefits of
the Act of Congress, passed June 7th 1832, that he entered
the Service of the United States under the following named
officers and services herein stated--"I entered the Service
about the 15th September 1778, in Spartanburg District,
S. C. in Captain John Thomas's Regiment as one of the
drafted Militia, to serve against the Indians, and marched
to a place between Philips's Blockhouse and the Oconee
River, where we arrived while our time had expired and were
then marched back and discharged. In the year 1781 I joined a company commanded by Major White (acting as Captain)
and marched to the Siege of Ninety Six, where the Fort
being then occupied by Colonel Cruger with the British and
Tory. We remained besieging the Fort under Command of Gen.
Greene until the enemy were reinforced by Colonel or Lord
Lawdon from Charleston, when the siege was lifted by Greene
and were marched home and discharged. I afterwards joined
the company commanded by Major John Ford, acting as Captain,

under Command of Gen. Pickens, and marched to Bacon's
Bridge on Ashly River and joined the Army of Gen. Greene,
where we were stationed as a check upon the British Army
to prevent them from aiding the City of Charleston. I
continued at this place until my time had expired and was
finally discharged. I have no documentary evidence of my
services and I know of no person who served with me except
Captain Hanna and Major William Smith, who served with me
and who now live in Spartanburg Dist. S.C. I do herewith
relinquish any claim to a pension or annuity except the
present, and declare that my name is not on the pension
Roll of the Agency of any State.--In answer to the Inter-
rogation put by the Court, I answer 1 and 2 I was born in
Prince William County, Virginia on the 9th June 1751, as I
have been informed, having no record of my age.
3--I lived in Spartanburg when I was in the Service, and
have lived in Union and Spartanburg ever since the War and
now live in Union District.
4--I always served as a draftee.
5--In written.
7--I refer to the Hon. Willie Walker and to John Rogers to
prove my character for truth and moral deportment.

Sworn to & Subscribed   Signed
the day & year afrsd.

        Jno M. O'Neall   *James Smith*
        Pres. Judge.

        A combination will and deed made in Union District,
S.C. 26 Jan. 1836, Deed Bk. Y, p. 55, is a conveyance from
James Smith to his single daughters, Priscilla and Elizabeth, of 114 acres of land "whereon I now live," also 2
horses, all cattle, cows, hogs, tools, provisions, outstanding debts, whatsoever he was entitled to at his
death, exept "my man, Dave." To his wife he gave the
Negro man Dave.
        In June of the same year Priscilla and Elizabeth gave
the land and property back to James. Deed Bk. S 12, pp.
58-60, Union Co., S. .
        Then in Jan. of 1839, James made his will, which was
recorded 25 Sept. 1840.
        At the same time his wife Martha made her will which
was recorded 15 June 1851. Both wills follow:

        WILL OF JAMES SMITH, UNION COUNTY, SOUTH CAROLINA

State of South Carolina)
Union District   )
In the name of God, Amen--
I James Smith of the said State and District being weak in

body but of sound and disposing mind and memory and calling to mind the uncertainty of Human Life and being desirous to dispose of my Earthly possessions with which it has
pleased God to bless me with, do make this my last Will
and Testament in manner and form following.

1st--I bequeath my soul to God, and my body to the dust
from whence it came.

2nd--It is my desire that as soon as possible after my
death that the Expenses of my buriel and all of my just
debts be speedily paid.

3rd--I give and bequeath to my beloved son, John F. Smith
the sum of five dollars in cash in addition to what I have
heretofore given him.

4th--I give and bequeath to my beloved son, Enoch Smith,
the sum of five dollars in cash in addition to what I have
heretofore given him.

5th--I give and bequeath to my beloved daughter Elizabeth
the sum of five dollars in cash in addition to what I have
heretofore given her.

6th--I give and bequeath unto my beloved daughter Sarah,
the wife of John Eubanks the sum of five dollars in cash
in addition to what I have heretofore given her.

7th--I give and bequeath to my beloved daughter Anna Newton, wife of James Tollesin the sum of five dollars in
cash in addition to what I have heretofore given her.

8th--I give and bequeath to my beloved daughter, Priscilla
Smith, who now lives with me and renders me all the service in her power in my old age, all the remaining part of
my Estate, consisting of the tract of land whereon I now
live containing One Hundred and Fourteen Acres, bounded by
lands of S. S. Meng, Absolom Barnett, James McBride and
others. to her and her heirs and assigns forever--I further give as aforesaid to my daughter, Priscilla Smith,
my stock of cattle, hogs, sheep, one gray mare and colt,
my household furniture and kitchen furniture, plantation
tools and generally of everything of which I am possessed
in any manner or means.

And I do hereby constitute and appoint my said beloved
daughter Priscilla my sole Executrix of this last Will and
Testament.

James Smith   (Seal)

Signed, Sealed and Acknowledged
published and declared as my last
Will and Testament
Hereby revoking, making null and
Void all others this the 16th day
of January, One thousand eight
hundred and thirty nine
In the presence of D. Wallace
J. E. Peek (wife's son)
Absolom Barnett

Recorded in Will Book
B page 271 File Box 26
Pkg. 8
Recorded 25th of Sep-
tember 1840
J. J. Pratt, Ordinary

174

WILL OF MARTHA SMITH Union, South Carolina

In the name of God, Amen--I, Martha Smith, wife of James
Smith of Union District, South Carolina, being old and
weak in body, but of sound and disposing mind and memory,
and being desirous of disposing of such Earthly goods as
it hath pleased God to bless me with, do make this my last
Will and Testament in manner and form following:
1st--I give and bequeath unto my beloved grandson, Isaac
E. Peak my tract of land lying in the said District of
Union, on Morriss's Branch bounded by lands of Repp Edwards
and Jesse Clark and others, it being the same land whereon
my daughter, Mary Howard now lives and containing seventy-
five acres, more or less. The same to him and his heirs
in fee simple forever.
I also give and bequeath unto my said grandson, Isaac E.
Peak, my cupboard, one chest, one table and all my beds
and furniture, except one bed and furniture. Also I give
him one cow and calf.
2nd--I give and bequeath unto my beloved daughter, Mary
Howard, my negro man, named Dave to the sole use, benefit
and behalf of said slave, Dave, during her live. It is
my expressed desire that the husband of the said Mary
Howard shall not have any control of the said slave either
by himself or any creditors or by any manner of means whatsoever derive any benefit from the labor or service of said
slave. I also give and bequeath unto the said Mary Howard,
one bed and furniture to her and to the heirs of her body,
free as above stated with the case of the slave, Dave,
from all control or power of her husband or his creditors.
And I do hereby nominate, constitute and appoint my said
Grandson, Isaac E. Peak, my sole executor to carry this my
last will and Testament into effect. To whom I also give
whatever property I may be possessed of at my death not
above named in this will

                          her
              Martha X Smith   (Seal)
                          mark
Signed, Sealed, published
and X underlined before signing.
D. Wallace
Acknowledged and declared as my last Will and Testament,
this the Sixteenth day of January, One Thousand Eight
Hundred and Thirty-nine.
In the presence of
D. Wallace   Recorded in Will Book B page 274
Absolom Barnett   Recorded June 15, 1851
James Smith (her husband)   File Box 26 pkg. 18

IV-5. ENOCH SMITH

Enoch Smith, son of James and Elizabeth Smith was b.
19 May 1806, d. 10 June 1885. He m. Jane Moore
(More) 22 Dec. 1835. Jane b. 23 Dec. 1814, d. 29
Oct. 1885. Enoch and Jane died a little over 4
months apart, are buried in the Old Caney Cemetery
out of Pickton, Tex. near Sulphur Springs.
They had four boys and five girls. All of the
boys fought in the Confederate Army, one of them
losing his life in the service.

V-1.	Elias M. Smith	V-5.	Newton E. Smith
V-2.	Miles G. Smith	V-6.	Julia Ann Smith
V-3.	Sarah E. Smith	V-7.	Olivia (Liva) Ann Smith
V-4.	John Fleming Smith	V-8.	Rhoda A. Smith
	V-9.	Mary C. Smith	

Enoch and Jane Smith lived near Spartanburg in South
Carolina before coming to Alabama about 1840, first
to Randolph County before settling in Calhoun County
in the beautiful Chocoloca Valley about 3 miles west
of Jacksonville, Ala., an area surrounded by wooded
hills. Two children were born in Spartanburg Co.,
S.C., one in Randolph Co. and the other six in
Calhoun County. They made the long move to northeast Texas in the fall of 1870 when Enoch was 64
and their youngest daughter 15.
Land records in Calhoun Co., Ala. show that Enoch
and Jane sold 1/4 section of land in the Coosa Land
District in Sept. of 1869 for $600.00. Jane made
her mark.
Their son Elias also sold 160 acres in 1869 but
for $1500.00. Elias had several land deeds; John
Fleming Smith also owned land in Calhoun County.
Jane was the daughter of Aaron and Bettie Moore
who were listed in the 1800 Census in Pendleton
District of South Carolina in the Little River area,
which is now in Abbeville County.
From John Fleming's ledger we have this information:

Children of Aaron and Bettie Moore:

Ruth Shurbert	Julia Pinson
Mary Vice (John, 7 ch.)	Elizabeth Guinn
Nancy Wood	Sarah Teague (Elijah T.)
Rhoda Galahar	Jane Smith (Enoch)

All of these sisters came to Alabama from South
Carolina except Elizabeth. All lived to a ripe old
age and all raised families except Rhoda.

When we visited in Anniston, Alabama in 1969 we contacted Mary Vice, granddaughter of Mary Vice above, also Clifford Vice, her nephew, who was a multiple-sclerosis victim in a wheel chair making a living by doing furniture repairs in a shop beside his house. We also talked with George R. Teague, descendent of the Teagues who came from Spartanburg.

Enoch Smith and Jane Moore Smith

Enoch Smith	Jane Smith
Born	Born
May 19, 1806	Dec. 23, 1814
Died	Died
June 10, 1885	Oct. 29, 1885

Caney Cemetery near Pickton, Texas

177

V-1. Elias M. Smith, oldest son of Enoch Smith and Jane
      Moore, b. 17 Oct. 1837, Spartanburg, S.C., d. 26
      Mar. 1925, Stratford, Oklahoma, m. Harriett Sarah
      Nesmith 10 Jan. 1861.

Elias Smith and wife Harriet (Hoss)

In the Semi-Weekly Farm News of
Dec. 1, 1922 in a column headed
"Pioneers and Veterans" Elias M.
Smith tells his story:

Celebrates 85th Birthday
E. M. Smith, Stratford, OK.

I wish, through The Farm News, to greet on this,
the eighty-fifth anniversary of my birth, all of my
good old friends who may be readers of the paper. I
wish for all of them prosperity and happiness through
life and in the end an eternal home in Heaven.
      I was born in Spartanburg, S.C., Oct. 17, 1837. In
1840 my father, Enoch Smith, moved to Calhoun County,
Ala., and located near Jacksonville, where I was
reared in poverty and almost in obscurity, not having
the advantage of an education. Here I grew to man-
hood. I was married to Miss H. S. Nesmith Jan. 10,
1861. In 1862 I was called upon to volunteer and
take up arms in defense of my country, which call I
obeyed at once. I enlisted in Captain S. D.
McClellan's company, Ninth Alabama Volunteers, on Feb.
11, 1862. I served until July 1, 1863. I was captured then and held as prisoner of war at Ft. Delaware.
I was released June 15, 1865, returning home June 23
with naught but willing heart and hands to work.
      To our union three sons and two daughters were born.
The sons were all too old for the late war, their
ages ranging from 44 to 54 years. The two younger
sons died since the war closed.
      I moved to Texas in 1869 and settled in Hopkins
County, fifty-two years ago. I am a Jeffersonian
Democrat and have followed by always voting a straight
ticket. Am a reconstructed rebel, farmer and have

followed the plow on injunction of the master for
seventy-five years. My offspring number sixty-eight.
I am sending a picture of four generations, myself,
85; my daughter, Mrs. R. L. Beckham, 50; my grandson,
Roy Beckham, 28; and my great-grandson, Lee Roy
Beckham, 4.
(Uncle Elias Smith had reached his 85th birthday in
October, 1922. He lived to be 87 years, 5 months old.)

Elias' claims to no educational advantages did not
keep him from learning to write a pretty hand, whether
letter, poem, or prose. In a letter to Aletha Cane (Cain)
dated May the 31st 1892, Sul Springs, Texas, he writes:

Mrs. Aletha Cane   Big Valley, Texas
Respected Madam--Mother and Sister in Christ, It
affords me untold pleasure to read But a few lines from
an old friend from whome I have long since learned to
love, and as an appreciation of your kind letter I Seat
myself to try to respond to Same, you Said you gladly
received my Kind words and that you had not forgotten
us and that you was Glad that Tea was getting better
her health is still improving and I think She will
finely recover. But it will take time. you said you
was very feeble and had heart disease. (Aletha, his
sister's mother-in-law, was 77 at the time.) One of
the inspired appostles Said that these light Afflictions which are But for a moment Shall work out for us
a fare more and Exceeding and Eternal weight of Glory
Beyond this vale of tears. Earth has no Sorrows that
Heven cannt heal. The Christians hope is a Blessed
hope. I often wonder why there is so much affliction
in the world. But God works in misterious ways his
wonders to perform So we conclude it will take all the
afflictions and troubles of this life to ripen us for
the life that is to come, In one of the Ancient Battles
we read that a cannon Ball Struck a fort and defaced the
Buty of it and tore up the Earth and from that ugly casm
Sprand up a fountain of never failing water. the more
you Bruse the Rose the Sweeter the perfume--to the
Christian Death it is Said is only a Dream and if so
how peaceful the Slumbers how pleasant the wakening But
to the ungodly Death will be a dreadful reality This is
a sad thought and one upon which we do not like to
think about or talk about. . .
When I take in all my surroundings I can But Exclame
as did David that Surely goodness and mercy has followed me all the days of my life and then Exclame What
Shall I render unto the Lord for all his Benefits unto
me. We close Praying that God may add his Blessings to
179

us all and that the remnant of our days may be spent
to his Prase.
                    Yours in love E. M. Smith

    To J. A. Godwin at the same time he writes of his
farm,

    "We are having rain in abundance.. . . It has been
too wet and cold for cotton--corn and oats are very
promising. I commenced cutting wheat yesterday. . .
My Reaper works fine. . . I can plow 12 or 14 acres
a day and soon run over my crops I expect to cut wheat
and oats for the Public. We have a good garden plenty
of chickens milk and butter in abundance.
                    Yours Truly
                    E. M. Smith

    Children of Elias M. Smith and Sarah Nesmith:
VI-1. Millie Jane Smith, b. 15 Oct. 1861, m. R. E.
       White 17 Jan 1877.
VI-2. James Elbert Smith, b. 2 May 1866, m. Belle O.
       Short 27 Aug. 1896.
VI-3. William Enoch Smith, b. 12 Sept. 1867, m. Tex
       Anderson 17 June 1890.
VI-4. Dau. _____ b. 1872, m. Robert L. Beckham Oct. 1893.
VI-5. Sidney Alonzo Smith, b. 26 May 1875, m. Ona Page.
VI-6. Rosa E. Smith, b. 3 Aug. 1877, d. 8 Sept. 1879.

V-2. Miles G. Smith, son of Enoch Smith and Jane Moore,
      b. 15 Nov. 1838, Spartanburg, S.C., d. 23 Apr. 1862,
      age 23, at Okolona, Miss. in the Confederate Army.

V-3. Sarah E. Smith (Sally), dau. of Enoch Smith and Jane
      Moore, b. 23 May 1841, Calhoun Co., Ala., d. 23 July
      1926, m. J. B. Posey 22 Sept. 1861. Sally and J. B.
      Posey were living in Montague Co., Tex. in 1914.
VI-1. Nora Posey   VI-3. Miles Posey
VI-2. Robert Posey   VI-4. Penn Posey

V-4. John Fleming Smith, son of Enoch Smith and Jane
      Moore, b. 20 Jan. 1843, Randolph Co., Ala., d. 11
      Aug. 1932, Como, Tex., age 89, m. (1) Rosa Catherine
      (Kate) Wingo 27 Sept. 1866. Kate b. 27 Oct. 1845,
      dau. of Willis Seay Wingo, d. 28 Mar. 1925. Both
      are buried in Old Caney Cemetery out of Pickton,
      Hopkins Co., Tex.
         Fleming enlisted in the Confederate Army 1861,
      Jacksonville, Ala., served in Tenn., Miss., and
      Ala. He came to Lamar Co., Tex. in 1866, on to
      Hopkins Co. in 1870 where he engaged in general
                          180

merchandising with partners in Como Mercantile Co.
He also took part in developing Como Lignite Co.
    Fleming m. (2) Adeline L. Meek Dec. 1925 at age
82.
    Children of John Fleming Smith and Kate Wingo:
VI-1. Ida Smith, b. 8 Mar. 1868, d. 20 Jan. 1930, Paint
Rock, Tex., m. Joe L. Williams.
  VII-1. Silas Williams m. Jessie Hampton.
  VII-2. Wallace Williams m. Van Haglestein, li. Paint
Rock, Tex.
  VII-3. Kate Williams m. M. N. Taylor, li. Como, Tex.
  VII-4. Ben Williams
  VII-5. Ted Williams
  VII-6. Helen Williams, unmarried, teaches Ballinger,
Tex.
  VII-7. Hester Williams, m. Jeff Beard, li. Paint
Rock, Tex.
  VII-8. Josephene Williams m. Byron Estes, teaches
Abilene, Tex.
VI-2. Talulah Ann Smith, b. 7 Dec. 1869, d. 25 Dec.
1952, m. W. C. Johnston.
  VII-1. Mildred Johnston m. _____ Taylor.
  VII-2. Roy Johnston
VI-3. Charles Edward Smith, b. 1 Apr. 1873, d. 27 Mar.
1963, m. Lutie Gresham.
  VII-1. Mabel Smith m. D. S. Isom.
  VII-2. Edwin J. Smith m. Jewell Garrett.
  VII-3. Madeline Smith m. Robert Triplett Smith.
(Treated in more detail following this list of
children.)
VI-4. Benjamin Newton Smith, b. 14 Feb. 1876, d. 31
Jan. 1956, m. Frances Gass.
  VII-1. Catherine Smith, m. _____Schultz, li.
Alexandria, La.
  VII-2. Eloise Smith, m. _____Le Grendre, li.
Thibadeaux, La.
  VII-3. Ruth Smith
  VII-4. Irene Smith m. _____Cook, li. Shreveport, La.
VI-5. Laura Josephene Smith, b. 12 Apr. 1878, d. 31 Jan.
1965, Greenville, Tex., m. (1) Augusta Wood 1896.
Augusta d. 1905. m. (2) _____ Milton.
  VII-1. Gladys Wood m. _____ Saunders, li. Greenville,
Tex.
  VII-2. Robert Wood, li. Ft. Worth, Tex.
  VII-3. Julian Wood, li. Dallas, Tex.
  VII-4. A. D. Wood, li. Cuero, Tex.
VI-6. Bessie May Smith, b. 19 Feb. 1880, d. Nov. 1939,
Pollack, Tex., m. Luther Hampton.
  VII-1. Fred Hampton
  VII-2. Tom Hampton, retired Co. Clerk, Angelina Co.,
Tex.

VII-3. Herman Hampton, li. Carthage, Tex.
VII-4. Hallie Hampton, li. Houston, Tex.
VII-5. Robert Hampton, twin to Hallie, li. Lufkin, Tex.
VII-6 & 7. Maurine and Laurine Hampton, twins, dec'd.
VII-8. Hazel Hampton, li. Houston, Tex.
VII-9. Lucille Hampton, li. Richmond, Tex.
VII-10. Nell Hampton, li. Pasadena.
VII-11. Luther Hampton, Jr., U.S. Army.
VI-7. Walter Lewis Smith, b. 24 Jan. 1883, d. 1967, m. Maude Graham.
VII-1. J. T. Smith, li. Dallas, Tex.
VII-2. Rosa May Smith, dec'd.
VII-3. Ollie Edna Smith.
VII-4. Mack Smith, li. Sulphur Springs, Tex.
VII-5. Donald Smith, dec'd.
VII-6. Clarice Smith.
VI-8. Willis Enoch (Will) Smith, b. 15 July 1885, d. 1 Sept. 1951, m. Mattie Morgan.
VII-1. Bill Smith, Methodist minister.
VII-2. Martha Lee Smith m. _____ Thurman, li. Mesquite, Tex.
VI-9. Oscar Fleming Smith, b. 27 Oct. 1889, d. 14 Nov. 1958, m. Edna Jernigan.

VI-3. Charles Edward Smith, son of John Fleming Smith and Rosa Catherine Wingo, b. 1 April 1873, Hopkins Co., Tex., d. 27 Mar. 1963, Henderson, Tex., m. (1) Mary Lucinda Jane (Lutie) Gresham 24 Dec. 1895.
Lutie b. 2 Dec. 1878, Lauderdale Co., Ala., dau. of Harris James Gresham and Masury Ann Young, d. 10 May 1939, Como, Tex. Both buried in Como Cemetery.
He m. (2) Mrs. Grace Carroll of Como, Tex., she d. 23 Oct. 1958, buried Como Cemetery.
Charles Edward Smith was a merchant in Como, continuing a business his father had started in 1892.
Children of Charles Edward Smith and Lutie Gresham:
VII-1. Mabel Clare Smith, b. 28 Oct. 1897, Como, Tex., m. Dewey Spurgeon Isom 14 Mar. 1922. Dewey, son of John Isom and Lelia Tyre, li. Como, Tex.
VIII-1. John Charles Isom, b. 2 Nov. 1924, Como, Tex., m. Hazel Euphenia Crawford 16 Aug. 1952. Served in Naval Air Corps in South Pacific in WW II, now works for Chance-Voight.
IX-1. Eva Muriel (Midge) Isom, b. 1 Nov. 1956.

Hazel d. 1956, car crash, John Charles
m. (2) Frances Dean 10 Sept. 1966.
VIII-2. Dewena Jane Isom, b. 4 July 1928,
Como, Tex., m. Odis Durward Crowell
30 July 1948. Odis, son of Odis M.
Crowell and Eva Ruth ____, served in
7th Armored Division in WW II.
IX-1. Odis Conrad Crowell, b. 20 Jan.
1950.
IX-2. Patric Isom Crowell, b. 28 Sept.
1962.
VIII-3. James Smith Isom, b. 26 Sept. 1930,
Como, Tex., m. Marjorie Sue Hicks 9
Jan. 1953. Marjorie dau. of Eunice
Everett Hicks and Clara M. Barrett,
li. Bridgeport, Tex. Served in Navy
1948-1952.
IX-1. Larry Dale Isom, b. 14 Nov. 1953.
IX-2. Dewey Everett Isom, b. 22 Sept.
1956.
IX-3. Kenneth Charles Isom, b. 9 Dec.
1958.
IX-4. Donna Jean Isom, b. 12 Apr. 1960,
lived 2 days.
VIII-4. Kenneth Phil Isom, b. 15 Oct. 1932,
Como, Tex., m. 10 Aug. 1956, Eleanor
Patricia McManus Argibright, dau.
of John and Mary Ann McManus, Provi-
dence, R.I. Phil served in the Navy
1952-1956, li. in Bridgeport, Tex.
IX-1. Mary Alice (Argibright) Isom, b.
24 July 1951.
IX-2. Vonda Gay Isom, b. 18 Nov. 1963.

VII-2. Edwin Jack Smith, son of Charles Edward
Smith and Lutie Gresham, b. 20 July 1900,
Como, Tex., d. 20 June 1967, m. Stacy
Jewell Garrett 7 May 1926. Stacy dau. of
Wilburn Thomas Garrett of Ala. Edwin and
Stacy li. Dallas.
VIII-1. Edwin Jack Smith, Jr., b. 13 Oct.
1928, Dallas, Tex., m. Joanne Wasoff
17 Oct. 1959. Joanne dau. of Harry
K. and Amelia Shipley of Dallas.
Edwin Jack, Jr. was with the U.S.
Embassy in Ecuador, Germany and
Argentina, was an oil company execu-
tive in London, England.
IX-1. Mark Garrett Smith, b. 11 June
1961, Buenos Aires, S.A.
183

IX-2. Susan Amelia Smith, b. 16 Feb. 1963,
       Buenos Aires, S.A.

VII-3. Madeline Smith, dau. of Charles Edward Smith
        and Lutie Gresham, b. 4 Feb. 1903, Como, Tex.,
        m. Robert Triplett Smith 7 Nov. 1929. R. T.
        is son of Samuel Leonard Smith and Katie
        Augusta Triplett. He is a cattle raiser
        and owner of R. T. Smith Welding and Press
        Co. of Henderson, Tex.
           Madeline attended Wesley College, Green-
        ville and East Texas Teachers College,
        Commerce, Tex. and taught school before
        marriage.
    VIII-1. Richard Robert Smith, b. 18 Nov. 1934,
             Louisville, Miss., m. Zelda Irene
             Morriess 1 Aug. 1964. Zelda is dau.
             of Luther Morriess and Retha Latting.
                Zelda teaches music in elem. school
             and Richard is Sec'y-Treasurer of the
             R. T. Smith Welding and Press Co. of
             Henderson.

        Madeline Smith has furnished the material on
     the John Fleming Smith line. She has been most
     helpful and encouraging over the years as we
     gathered data on the Smith lineage.

V-5. Newton E. Smith, son of Enoch Smith and Jane Moore,
      b. 10 Apr. 1845, d. 27 Feb. 1923, Lockney, Floyd
      Co., Tex., m. Amanda Caroline Godwin 16 Jan. 1873.
      Amanda b. 15 Oct. 1857, dau. of Martial Godwin and
      Sarah J. Odom. She d. 29 Mar. 1933, buried Peters-
      burg, Tex.
         "Uncle Newt" was a farmer, moved to Lockney,
      Texas when he could no longer farm. Both he and
      Amanda were devout Baptist; he led the singing in
      church and his daughter Lois played the organ.
      A granddaughter, Irene Foster, remembers the Smith
      family get-togethers when they would sing. One of
      her fondest memories was of her grandfather sitting
      on the front porch, rocking and singing "Amazing
      Grace."
         Newton had come with his family from Calhoun Co.,
      Ala. to Hopkins Co., Tex. in 1870, but he soon came
      to Mills Co. where he met and married Amanda Godwin.
      They moved to Bonita in Montague Co. in 1897 then
      on to Hale Co. in the Panhandle in 1919, shipping
      their belongings by frieght. Eva's husband had
      died during the flu epidemic of 1878, so she and

her two children moved with them. Roy's family,
Cager's, and Maude went too, occupying one whole
car of a slow-moving passenger train. They settled
in Hale and Floyd Counties.

Children of Newton Smith and Amanda Godwin:

VI-1. Marshall H. Smith, b. 18 Dec. 1874, d. 3 Feb. 1884.

VI-2. Rhoda A. Smith, b. 5 Nov. 1876, d. 28 Aug. 1880.

VI-3. Bertha Jane Smith, b. 12 Sept. 1878, d. 27 Oct. 1889.

VI-4. Eva Nevada Smith, b. 23 Nov. 1880, d. 5 Feb. 1952, m. Lee Snodgrass 25 Feb. 1900. Ch.: George and Mildred Naomi Snodgrass.

VI-5. Enoch Vigor Smith, b. 20 Apr. 1883, d. 7 March 1966, buried Abilene, m. Beulah Carter 10 Nov. 1902. Ch.: Hoyt, Chronco, Flossie, Joyce, Doris, Alma, E. V., Jr., Jay C., and Freda Smith.

VI-6. Lela Belle Smith, b. 5 Nov. 1885, m. Quinton Sylvester Howard 17 Dec. 1913. In 1979 Lela is in nursing home in Lubbock at age 94.

   VII-1. Louise W. Howard, b. 14 April 1917, m. (1) John R. Wells. Ch.: Diana G. Wells. m. (2) Donald D. Chapman Sr. Ch.: Don. J. and Quinton D. Chapman.

   VII-2. Audrey Marjetta Howard, b. 26 Feb. 1921, d. 6 Nov. 1930, Lubbock, Tex.

   VII-3. James Dayle Howard, b. 26 June 1927, d. 18 May 1949, Columbia, Miss., buried Lubbock, Tex.

VI-7. Jesse M. Smith, b. 18 April 1888, d. 20 Mar. 1958, buried Plainview, Tex., m. Grace Pearce 25 Nov. 1910. Ch.: Ferrel, Vivian, Lafern.

VI-8. Roy Montrue Smith, b. 12 Dec. 1890, d. in the 1970's, buried Plainview, Tex. m. Willie Snapp, Ch.: Joy, Christina, Floreno, Avadell, Mozello, and Roy, Jr. Smith.

VI-9. Cager Monroe Smith, b. 28 Feb. 1893, d. 5 Aug. 1950, buried Plainview, Tex. m. Carrie Admiro 4 Aug. 1912. Ch.: Irene, Norman, Leola, J. C., Junelle, Bill and Lowell Smith.

VI-10. Maude Anna Smith, b. 26 Jan. 1895, d. 19 Feb. 1968, m. J. H. Corbin, no children.

VI-11. Lois Naomi Smith, b. 5 Feb. 1897, m. Rufus Martin 26 Oct. 1919. Ch.: Buster Howard, J. W., Caroline, Helen, Wayne, R. B., Lindell. Albert, and Norma Louise.

VI-12. Sadie Ray Smith, b. 6 Mar. 1900, m. Bob Veltzon 24 Dec. 1916. Ch.: Garland, Glenn, Pauline, and Olene.

Godwin-Hill and Related Families

Newton E. Smith family material furnished by Louise Howard Chapman and Irene Smith Foster.

V-6. Julia Ann Smith, daughter of Enoch Smith and Jane Moore, b. 25 Dec. 1847, Calhoun Co., Ala., d. 28 Oct. 1932, buried Old Caney Cemetery out of Pickton, Tex., m. Woods Miller 26 Sept. 1893 at age 46, lived in Big Valley Community, Mills Co., Tex.
Woods Miller, b. 13 Oct. 1843, son of Wm. Goodloe Miller, was raised near Bastrop, Tex. He m. (1) Margaret Hemphill in 1870 and came to Mills County. Margaret d. in 1891, both buried in Big Valley Cemetery.
Children of Woods Miller and Margaret Hemphill:
C. H. Miller   Wm. Goodloe Miller
Cornelia E. Miller   Woodie Miller, d. young.
Margaret L. Miller   Eva Adrene Miller
          Charles (Charlie) Miller
Woods and Julia Miller adopted Viola Cherry who m. Omar Warren 5 Feb. 1921, Mills Co., Tex. Julia died at Como, Texas.

LAST WILL AND TESTAMENT OF JULIA A. MILLER, COMO, TEXAS
To Whom it May Concer:
Know ye that I, Julia A. Miller, do hereby make, ordain and declare this to be my last will and testament, hereby revoking all other wills heretofore made by me.
1st--I will that all my just debts be paid.
2nd--That $100.00 be used to place a tombstone at my grave.
3rd--That the residue of my estate be divided as follows, towit:
To my adopted daughter, Viola Warren, I give one eighth of my estate and to Manda Smith one eighth of my estate and one eighth to be divided equally between Tiny Webb (niece) and Julia Ferguson and the remainder of my estate I desire will be divided one eighth to each of my brothers and sisters or their heirs for their sole use and benefit forever and I hereby appoint my brother J. T. Smith and my nephew C. E. Smith as my executors without bond and without any legal process whatsoever except to file and have this will recorded on the probate docket. My said executors shall have full power to sell, mortgage or lease in any way or manner to dispose of the whole or any part of said estate and to collect all debts that may be due me.
This 7th day of March 1923
                    Signed Julia A. Miller
                    186

Julia had lived with her sister Mary after her parents
died until she married, and Mary had helped take care of
her after her husband died, so the administrator, B. N.
Smith, son of J. T. Smith, wrote to her sisters and
brothers asking permission to assign their rights to the
inheritance, total assets $1,141.85, to "Aunt Mary" Gaines,
dated 8 April 1935. Much of the assets were unsecured
notes, so hard to collect in the depression.

V-7.   Liva Ann Smith, dau. of Enoch Smith and Jane Moore,
        b. 11 Oct. 1850, Calhoun Co., Ala., d. 28 Apr. 1935.
        m. John Allen Godwin 15 Oct. 1874, Hopkins Co., Tex.

        This family is the subject of Chapter 3.

V-8.   Rhoda E. Smith, dau. of Enoch Smith and Jane Moore,
        b. 8 Nov. 1852 Calhoun Co., Ala., d. 9 Sept. 1882,
        age 29. She m. Richard Teer 4 Nov. 1875, li.,
        Hopkins Co., Tex. 1880. Richard b. ca. 1852, son
        of William Teer and his wife Margaret.

V-8.   Mary C. Smith, youngest dau. of Enoch Smith and
        Jane Moore, b. 19 July 1855, Calhoun Co., Ala., d.
        22 Nov. 1950, at 95, m. (1) Benjamin Williams 4 Nov.
        1875, m. (2) Dr. S. G. Gaines of Tenn., 26 Mar. 1893,
        Mills Co., Tex., li. Greenville, Tex.
    VI-1.   Claudia Jane Williams, b. 8 Nov. 1879, d. 22 Jun.
            1899, 20 years.
    VI-2.   Kate Lucy Gaines, b. 31 Jan. 1894, m. William W.
            Bowles 1 Nov. 1931, Durant, Okla. Kate taught
            school for many years.
        VII-1. Rosa Lee Bowles, foster child, b. 22 Sept.
                1929, m. J. I. Morgan 1963.
            VIII-1. Katiebeth Morgan, b. 10 Feb. 1966,
                     Lubbock, Tex.

Mary Smith Gaines, on
 her 87th birthday
Dr. S. G. Gaines

Standing:
Daughter Kate Lucy
 Gaines Bowles
    1942

SMITH CHART

I. PETER SMITH, Westmoreland Co., Va., Will proved 1741

II. Mary m. Fleming | Peter | James | Thomas -1778 m.Elizabeth Fleming | William | Abigail m.Fleming | John | Anne m.Thomas | Hannah m. Ware | Martha m.McClanahan

III. Fleming 1745- m. Prudence Bland | John | Daughter m.John Gibbs | Elizabeth | Charles -1824 m.Catherine Rhodes | Daniel | Thomas unmarried | Peter | James 1751-1840 m.(1)Elizabeth (2)Martha Peek Howard | Priscilla -1843 unmarried

IV. John Fleming 1793-1861 m.Nancy Tollison | Elizabeth 1797-1841 unmarried | Sarah m. John Eubanks | Anna Newton m.(1)Thomas Eubanks (2)John Tollison | Enoch Jane m. Moore

V. Elias M. 1837-1925 m. H.S. Nesmith | Miles G. 1838-1862 unmarried | Sarah E. 1841-1926 m. J.B. Posey | John Fleming 1843-1932 m.(1)R.C. Wingo (2)Adeline Meek | Newton E. 1845-1923 m. Amanda C. Godwin | Julia Ann 1847-1932 m. Woods Miller | Liva Ann 1850-1935 m. John Allen Godwin | Rhoda A. 1852-1882 m.John Teer | Mary C. 1855-1950 m.Richard (1)B. Williams (2) S.C. Gaines

GODWIN

Orilla C. 1875-1876 | Rena E. 1877-1878 | Essie D. 1879-1880 | Riley M. 1880-1907 | Beulah C. 1883-1963 m.L.W. Hill | Enoch 1886-1971 m.Nollie Hill | Effie May 1888-1973 m. E.H. Roberts | Della Maud 1891-1966 m. Barney Alexander

188

XIII

Spencer Family

Aletha Spencer who married John Allen Godwin, Sr. about 1836, probably in Madison Co., Tenn., was a descendant of William Spencer who has been researched and documented by Henry W. Rigby in Descendants of William Spencer of Montgomery Co., N.C.

WILLIAM SPENCER

William Spencer was in N.C. as early as 1757 when he and a John Spencer bought land in Craven Co., N.C. William soon sold this land and is found to have bought land in Anson Co., N.C. in 1763 consisting of 100 acres bought from Thomas Suggs, Jr. bordering Thomas Suggs, Sr., who may have been, or become, his father-in-law. Later William bought more land out of this Thomas Suggs grant from Thomas, Sr. and his wife Mary "on a branch of the Pee Dee called Little River." When Montgomery County was formed from Anson County in 1779, most of William's land was in Montgomery County, 1,310 acres of his total 1,460 acres.

William Spencer m. Hannah (Suggs?) about 1765 and appeared on the 1790 census of Montgomery Co., N.C. as head of household with:

```
          2  m.  + 16              5  f.
          2  m.  - 16
```

He served in the Revolutionary War. His will was probated 6 July 1805, Montgomery Co., N.C. with sons Johnson and Seymore executors. His wife Hannah then appeared on these census of Montgomery Co., N.C.

```
          1810        1  f.  + 45,  2 slaves
          1830        1  f.  70-80
          1840        1  f.  90-100
```

Known children of William and Hannah Spencer:

II-1. Johnson Spencer   II-4. Elias Spencer
II-2. Terah Spencer   II-5. Seymore Spencer
II-3. Elijah Spencer   II-6. Sarah (?) Spencer
           II-7. Daughter, m. _____ McLeod
Two more daus. as per 1790 census.

189

Godwin-Hill and Related Families

II-1. Johnson Spencer, b. ca. 1765, m. Annie Tucker by
1790 when he is shown as head of household on census of Montgomery Co., N.C.
Children: William, Elijah, James, Clark, George,
Nathan, Ama, Elizabeth.

II-2. Terah Spencer, dau. of William and Hannah Spencer,
b. 1766, m. Thomas Sugg, son of George Sugg, had
7 children, all b. N. C., first one b. 1784. Thomas, a Rev. Sol., d. Franklin Co., Ala. 5 Sept.
1829.

II-3. Elijah Spencer, son of William and Hannah Spencer,
b. 1774-1780, probably Montgomery Co., N.C., m.
Sarah _____, d. Aug. 1843.
Children: Hannah, Elijah, Jr., Robison, Serena,
Branson, Clark, Nancy, Sarah, Harbert, William,
Elizabeth, Mary.
Charges of arson were brought against Elijah and
his son Harbert in 1843 when the Montgomery County
Courthouse burned. There articles appeared in
issues of the Charlotte Journal dated 13 April and
20 April 1843, respectively, and were reprints of
items that had been reported earlier in the
Fayetteville Observer:

DISASTROUS FIRE. We stop the press to announce that
on Friday night last, the Court House of Montgomery
County, with every book and paper belonging to the
offices of the two Clerks and Register, was totally
destroyed by fire. It was discovered between 10 and
11 at night, and had made such progress in the interior of the old combustible building, that it was
impossible to save anything. There had been no fire
or candle in the building for a week, so that it was
evidently set on fire.
On Saturday morning a negro accidentally discovered
in the woods, a place where horses had been tied, and
the tracks of a man leading to the Court House, about
a mile off. A party pursued, first the man's tracks,
and then those of the horses, following them all that
day, and Sunday morning, through an unfrequented road
until they led to the house of Elijah Spencer, about
18 miles off. The man's tracks agreed in size with
Spencer's, and the horses' with those of two found in
his stable. A fresh rain had made all these tracks
distinct. Spencer and his son Harbord were immediately arrested, and carried to Lawrenceville jail. They
were to have had an examination before a Magistrate on
Monday, the result of which we have not heard.--
FAYETTEVILLE OBSERVER.

MONTGOMERY COURT HOUSE.--We learn that the examination of Elijah and Harboard Spencer, resulted in their full commitment for trial for burning the Court House. The 7th section of the 34th chapter of the Revised Statutes, makes the burning of a Court House or other public building, felony, punishable with death, without benefit of clergy.

The motive for the perpetration of this crime was at first supposed to be, to destroy the evidence of a forgery, for which Elijah Spencer, the father, was under indictment in Montgomery Court, in altering a deed; but it is now stated, that in addition to this motive, there was an execution against him for some $200, and a heavy bond filed in the Court House, for the forthcoming of a number of negroes, who had been seized to prevent their being run off to the South. These were all destroyed. The only thing belonging to the offices which was saved, was one of the Register's books, which happened to be at the house of a gentleman of the bar. The loss of all the wills, deeds, dockets, bonds, settlements of estates, &c.&c., must be a source of incalculable and irreparable evil.-- FAYETTEVILLE OBSERVER.

On July 6, 1843 Elijah and Harbert Spencer jointly gave power-of-attorney to Jesse Smitherman, Harbert's brother-in-law, to conduct business affairs for them in North Carolina, Montgomery Co., Deed B.15, p. 140. Harbert was in Texas by 1845 when a daughter was born there.

Elijah died the next month after giving the power-of attorney, but it is not known if the trial took place.

Elijah had extensive land holdings as well as slaves in Montgomery Co., N.C.

His wife married George Allen 28 Aug. 1844, marriage bond Montgomery Co., N.C.

Other descendants of Elijah also came to Texas and it may have been that these series of events led to our own ancestor moving to Texas also. Aletha Spencer Godwin Cain brought her family from Arkansas to Upshur Co., Tex. where Elijah's son and daughter, William M. Spencer and Serena Spencer Callicutt were both living.

My father was uncertain as to whether Aletha's maiden name was Spencer or Callicutt. The close association with Serena Speneer Callicutt's family may have led him to think it was Callicutt. Many unproductive hours were spent hunting a family for Aletha Callicutt, but answering a few genealogical queries on Spencer brought happy results.

The burning of the Montgomery Co., N.C. Courthouse was a great loss to our family research. Our patriarch,

Godwin-Hill and Related Families

Allen Godwin, lived there in the 1830's and may have married the second time there. His daughter Pennie probably married her husband, James Callicutt, there and of course many Spencer records were lost.

II-4.   Elias Spencer, son of William and Hannah Spencer, b. 11 Apr. 1778, probably Montgomery Co., N.C., d. 6 Sept. 1856, buried in the family graveyard near Paulding, Choctaw Co., Miss. He m. Sarah ____ in N. C. before 1800. Sarah b. N.C. 31 Dec. 1780, d. 11 Jan. 1869.
Children: William, Peter, Green, Henry E., Levi, George, Elias, John, Elizabeth, Nancy.

SEYMORE SPENCER

II-5.   Seymore Spencer, son of William and Hannah (Suggs?) Spencer, b. ca. 1778-1782, Montgomery Co., N.C. m. Tabitha Bennett, dau. of Solomon Bennett, Rev. Sol. Seymore d. 1847, Tippah Co., Miss., his son Hiram C. Spencer Administrator of his estate.
Seymore Spencer is the father of Aletha Spencer who married John Allen Godwin, Sr.
Seymore received four land grants in Montgomery Co., N.C. in Dec. 1809, three on Little River and one on Bishop's Creek, a tributary of Little River. He was listed in the 1810 census of Montgomery Co., N.C., but was in Wilson Co., Tenn. by 1820, in Madison Co., Tenn by 1830 and had moved by 1840 to Tippah Co., Miss. where some of his married children lived and where he d. seven years later.
Seymore had bought 300 acres of land for $1,000 in Madison County, Tenn. Nov. 9, 1826 with his sons Mark and Levi signing the deed as witnesses.
Children of Seymore Spencer and Tabitha Bennett:
III-1.   ____ Spencer, son, b. 1794-1800, Montgomery Co., N.C., was 10-15 in 1810 census.
III-2.   Elijah Spencer, b. 1794-1800, Montgomery Co., N.C., in Madison Co., Tenn. census 1830:

1 m. 30-40   1 f. 20-30
1 m. 10-15   1 f.   5-10

Elijah Spencer bought land in Madison Co., Tenn., Apr. 10, 1834, 50 acres for $25.00 from Clark Spencer of Henderson Co., Tenn.
III-3.   Mark Bennett Spencer, b. 1803, Montgomery Co., N.C., d. 24 Dec. 1851, m. Nancy Ann McCollum, bond issued 9 Mar. 1829, Madison Co., Tenn.,

192

li. near Jackson, Tenn. Children: Harriet C.,
John Aron, Duncan, William B., Mary Tabitha, Lydia,
Rebecca Ann, Eliza, all b. Tenn.

III-4. Levi Spencer, b. 1806, li. Madison Co., Tenn. in
1830, in Miss. 1834-37, Clark Co., Ark. by 1849,
in census there 1850 and 1860. He m. (1) Ann ____,
had 9 children: William, Asariah, Martha, _____,
Mary, Jacob, Lotty, John, Rufus. Levi m. (2)
Margaret Sandares 12 Oct. 1865, Clark Co., Ark.

III-5. Lavina Spencer, b. ca. 1808, Montgomery Co., N.C.,
m. Hew McKnight who d. 1877-78.
Children: Rhoda who m. Newton Yewing, li. Ft.
Smith, Ark., at least 2 other daughters.

III-6. Hiram Caldwell Spencer, b. 7 Dec. 1811, d. 20 Nov.
1894, bur. Lone Oak Church Cemetery near Rienzi,
Miss., m. (1) Eliza Buchanan 19 Sept. 1833, dau.
of James M. Buchanan and Mary S. Hall, both of
Scotland. Eliza b. 5 Apr. 1810, d. 30 Oct. 1864
in Tippah Co., Miss.
Children: Matthew, William R., Elizabeth Jane,
Louisa, Levi, Martha Ann, Edmond I., Mark Lafay-
ette, Emarinda (Wt. 3½ lbs. at birth, 12½ lbs. at
12 yrs., grew up normal).
Hiram m. (2) Sarah Jane Wilbanks 1 Jan. 1867.
Children: Alfred Lareus, Hugh Mileous, James
Franklin (d. young), Irenius Newton, Granville
Wise, Albert Gaines (d. young).
Hiram Spencer operated a mill on Muddy River
near Walnut in Tippah Co., Miss. After remarry-
ing he moved to Alcorn County, Miss. He was a
Primitive Baptist Elder, was listed as a Baptist
minister in 1860 census.

III-7. Aletha Spencer, b. 18 Oct. 1814, Montgomery Co.,
N.C., dau. of Seymore Spencer and Tabitha Bennett,
d. 10 Feb. 1899, Mills Co., Tex., m. (1) John
Allen Godwin, son of Allen Godwin and Polly Green
of Cumberland Co., N.C. John Allen b. 1812-15,
N.C., d. 1 June 1853, Clark Co., Ark.
Children: Pleasant Marion, Eli Seymore, Lavina
Jane, Mary Ann, Nancy Elizabeth, Margret Pennah,
Catherine, Ellen, Julia Ann, John Allen, Jr.
Aletha m. (2) J. D. Cain 16 Jan. 1861, Clark
Co., Ark., soon separated.

This family discussed in Chapter 2 on John Allen
Godwin, Sr.

III-8.   William Spencer, son of Seymore Spencer and Tabitha
         Bennett, b. 1815-20, Montgomery Co., N.C. or Wilson
         Co., Tenn.

III-9.   Elizabeth Suggs Spencer, dau. of Seymore Spencer
         and Tabitha Bennett, b. 13 June 1818, m. James M.
         Ingraham who was b. 23 Dec. 1815.   They lived in
         McNairy Co., Tenn. in 1850, ran a store at Myers
         Landing, Ark. in 1878.
           Children: Aletha Jane, Mark Lafayette, Bithea
         Ann, John Spencer, Leander H. (Dr. Lee), Pleasant
         Cisee, Samuel Jefferson, Ada Elizabeth, Toker
         Lorina (Lavina?).

         Joyce Potter Gray of Bonham, Texas, also a descen-
         dant of Seymore Spencer, has supplied much of the
         information on the Spencer family plus material
         from Mr. Rigby's book.

Letter from Hiram C. Spencer to his sister Aletha:

State of Mississippi   April the 8th
Allcorn County   1877

Dear Sister Aletha   I after so long a time try to write
to you in answer to your letter received January the
14th the first time I had heard from you since the war.
I was very glad to hear from you.   I was just in the
act of moving when I received your letter.   I moved
but about one mile and $\frac{1}{2}$ in the same settlement and is
settling a new place as old as I am (66) and my helth
- - - (some gone)
   My oldest son Matthew lives 3 miles west of Ripley,
have six children, 5 boys and one girl.   Richmond my
second son lives in Pontatock County about 50 miles
from me and is doing very well, has six children 3 boys
and 3 girls.   Elizabeth Jane my oldest daughter is
living with me.   Louiza my second daughter lives six
miles from me married Jersey Austin has six children
living two dead.   Martha Ann my third daughter died in
time of the war.   Levi my third son died in time of
the war.   Edmond I my fourth son died in September after the war closed.   Mark Lafayett was living in
Arkansas the last I heard of him in the neighborhood
of James Ingrams.   I have not heard from him in a long
time.   Emarinda that little 7 months child is much the
largest one of my daughters is married to John Beriman
lives in 5 miles of us and has one child five months
old.   These are all of my children by my first wife
Eliza.   She died October the 30, 1864.

194

I was married the first day of January 1867 to Sarah
Jane Willbanks--a young woman by whom I have had four
children all boys. One of them the third one died last
September. My wife and Jane is very good and kind to
me.
I own 240 acres of land hear. Hatchy River runs
through one edge of it. This part of the county has bin
very helthy until last year and so far in this has been
mutch sickness. . .   (Remainder torn away)

The above letter is over 100 years old, written in
ink on small linen tablet paper in very uniform handwriting.

Elizabeth (Spencer) Ingraham to Aletha (Spencer) Godwin

Sebastian County, Ark.   December 7

Dear Sister I reckon you think the time long of hering
from your letter and pickter. I have bin waiting for to
have my pickter taken to send you as I was not abel to
have it taken untel now and I will send it to you. I
can't find language to acpress my joy when I received
yours the people say it so much like me Sister I
would gave any thing to see you If you can travel
come and stay with us awhile. I am not abel to keep
house My youngest daughter that is a living live with
us. She has tow little boyes thay seam all most like
my own children our youngest daughter died 4 years
ago my helth is tourabele I have had a cold for 2
mounth and a sore throat and we have all bin sick with
colds for some time and sverl about has died with
neumonia This is a good country to make a living but
we have some sickness. Our children is all so glad to
her from you and to see your pickture Tha say mother
it so much like you. We have a son that is a dockter
his name is Lee he come to this country and practice
medison five years he maired a widiw that had a large
farm on the river and quit practice for awhile but has
rented his farm and move closer to us and is a going
practice again I am so glad he is a good docter.
--Sister Vina (Lavina) has bin sick this fall--One of
her daughters live in fort Smith and our folks see her
when they go to town roda is her name. it is so pris-
ing to think Sister Vina and you and me has live to
the age we have god has bin very murciful to us and I
hope spared us for a good purpose but your days is all
most gone and I hope your last days may be your best
days and that we may live nearer to god and if faithful to the end we shall soon meet in glory wher parting

will be no more this dus me good for I believ god has
blessed us and will to the end. I read the scriptures
ever day if I am abel and a book by the name of <u>the
Santes</u> <u>rest</u> and it is like preaching to me--
  May god bless you and your children Be sure to anser
this leter do not delay
  Aletha Godwin farwell Elizabeth Ingram
  Dear sister my heaven bless you

FAMILY CENSUS OF SEYMORE SPENCER

Married Tabitha Bennett   Date ca. 1795   Place Montgomery Co., N.C.

Census Year County, State, Pg.	Sex	1810 Montgomery Co., NC p.32	1820 Wilson Co., Tn.	1830 Madison Co., Tn. p.78	1840 Tippah Co., Miss.
Seymore b. 1770-80	M	26-45	26-45	50-60	60-70 d. 1847 Tippah Co., Ms.
Tabitha b. 1780-90	F	26-45	26-45	40-50	50-60
son b. 1794-1800	M	10-16			
Elijah b. 1794-1800	M	10-16		M. 30-40, F. 20-30) M. 10-15, F. 5-10)p.78	
Mark Bennett b. 1803	M	-10	10-16		
Levi b. 1806	M	-10	10-16	M. 20-30, F. 15-20) M. -5)p.78	
Lavina b. 1804-1810	F	-10	10-16		
Hiram C. b. 1811	M		-10	15-20	
Aletha b. 1814	F		-10	15-20	
William b. 1815-20	M		-10	10-15	
Elizabeth S. b. 1818	F		-10	10-15	
		1 slave		2 slaves	

197

FAMILY CENSUS OF HIRAM C. SPENCER

Married(1) Eliza Buchanan 19 Sept. 1833
(2) Sarah Jane Wilbanks 1 Jan. 1867

Census Year County, State	Sex	1840 Tippah Co., MS	1850 Tippah Co., MS	Born	1860 Tippah Co., MS		1870 Tippah Co., MS	Born
Hiram C.	M	20-30	H.C.	30 NC	Hiram C.	48	H.C.	58 NC
Eliza	F	20-30	Eliza	40 SC	Eliza	50	S.J.	32 SC
Matthew	M	5-10	Matthew	16 TN				
Wm. R.	M	- 5	Wm. R.	14 TN				
Elizabeth	F	- 5	Elizabeth	11 MS	Elizabeth J.	22	E.J. Hatley	30 MS
Louisa	F	- 5	Louisa	10 MS				
Levi	M		Levi	10 MS	Levi	19		
Martha	F		Martha A.	8 MS	Martha	17		
Edmond I.	M		Edmond	6 MS	Edmond I.	14		
Mark	M		Mark	3 MS	Mark L.	12		
Emarinda	F				Emmarinda	8	E.	17 MS

198

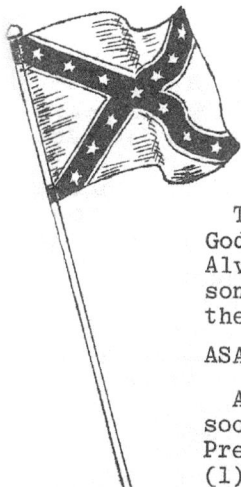

XIV

The Bishops

The mother of Nollie Hill who married Enoch Godwin was Kitty Bell Bishop, daughter of Alvin Bishop and Mary Jane Cox. Alvin was the son of Asa Bishop and Susan Stevens. Asa is the oldest known ancestor in our Bishop line.

ASA BISHOP

Asa Bishop was b. 4 June 1790 in Virginia soon after George Washington was inaugurated President of the new United States. Asa m. (1) Susan Stevens by 1814 and had migrated to North Carolina by the 1820's, then was in Hardeman Co., Tenn. by 1830.

Asa was a farmer and land owner in Hardeman Co. At one very interesting farm sale in 1845 he bought three different lots of hogs, averaging about a dollar apiece. He had 2 slaves in 1830 Tax List.

He m. (2) Elizabeth Stephens 23 May 1850, Hardeman Co., Tenn. Elizabeth was a widow with four children at home. Asa was 60.

Listed near Asa in the 1830 census of Hardeman Co., Tenn. was Fanney Bishop, age 60-70, presumed to be the mother of Asa.

During the Civil War when his sons were away in the service of the Confederacy, Asa passed away and was buried in the family cemetery. His daughters-in-law, Mary Jane and Louisa Bishop, with the help of some faithful slaves and neighbor women dug the grave and buried him not far from the Bishop house. The cemetery is now abandoned among the pines on the old Bishop place some 10-12 miles out of Middleton, Hardeman Co., Tenn. near Porters Creek Baptist Church.

ASA BISHOP

Born June 4, 1790
Died Aug. 30, 1864

Not lost blest thought
but gone before.
There we shall meet
to part no more.

While searching for the children of Asa Bishop, we found marriage records for three Bishop girls who appear to be the first three females on the 1830 census for Asa. One girl is named Susan the same as Asa's wife and the other two married children of Eli Cox as did Alvin Bishop. The Bishop and Cox land joined in Hardeman County. One son on the census is unaccounted for, may have died young.

Children of Asa Bishop and Susan Stevens:

II-1.   Edna Bishop, b. 5 Nov. 1814, d. 16 Jan. 1865, m. Cader Cox 16 Dec. 1835, Hardeman Co., Tenn., buried Bishop Cemetery near Middleton. Cader Cox b. 31 Oct. 1814, d. 7 June 1899, came to Hardeman Co. during early settlement. For many years he kept the stables for the stage line from Memphis to Huntsville.

II-2.   Alvin Bishop, b. 20 Sept. 1821, N.C., d. 14 Sept. 1888, Mills Co., Tex., m. Mary Jane Cox 21 Oct. 1841, Hardeman Co., Tenn.

II-3.   Susan T. Bishop (?), b. 1820-1825, m. W. D. Cooper 20 Jan. 1833, Hardeman Co., Tenn.

II-4.   Sarah Bishop (?), b. 1825-1830, m. Alfred Cox 12 Sept. 1839, Hardeman Co., Tenn.

II-5.   Everett Bishop, b. 1825-1830, d. at 14 of rattlesnake bite, bitten as he was gathering corn, according to Philip Bishop, grandson to David, brother to Everett.

II-6.   Son_____, b. 1825-1830, under 5 in 1830 census, Hardeman Co., Tenn.

II-7.   David Bishop, b. 25 Aug. 1837, Tenn., d. 11 Feb. 1922, Hardeman Co., Tenn., m. Louisa Grantham 1856.

ALVIN BISHOP

Alvin Bishop, son of Asa Bishop and Susan Stevens, b. 20 Sept. 1821, N.C., d. 14 Sept. 1888, Mills Co., Tex., m. Mary Jane Cox 21 Oct. 1841, Hardeman Co., Tenn. Mary Jane, dau. of Eli Cox and Sarah Brown, was b. 13 Sept. 1826, Tenn., d. 8 Jan. 1880 near Comanche, Tex. Both Alvin and Mary Jane Cox are buried at Newberg Cemetery south of Comanche, Tex.

Alvin came with his family at an early age from North Carolina to southern Tennessee settling in Hardeman County several miles out of Middleton near Porters Creek that empties into Hatchie River. The area is rolling sandy land with many pines and much undergrowth, with an average rainfall of 56 inches.

Before the Civil War Alvin farmed with oxen and slave labor. In 1845 he bought a "louse" of oxen at a neighbor's sale for $24.00. He had bought 510 acres of land in 1852

for $700.00 and made several additional purchases after
the war, bringing his total acreage to 1298-1/3 acres.
His place cornered with his wife's father's land, which
he bought from the other heirs when Eli Cox died.

A deed dated 18 Apr. 1876 shows Alvin sold to his
brother David Bishop 510 acres of land for $1600.00, land
in Hardeman Co., Tenn. The deed was signed and attested
at Comanche, Tex. 16 Oct. 1883. David's family lived on
this land for the next 50 years, however in 1968 when we
visited the place, it had been sold, but was still called
the "Bishop Place."

A cousin, Philip Bishop, grandson of David, showed
us the place and family cemetery. No one lived there, but
the house that David's widow had lived in so very indepen-
dently in her last days, was still standing. Philip said
no one wanted to live there now, it was too far out in
the "boondocks."

Alvin Bishop was a staunch Baptist. He is described
by a friend, Oscar Calloway, as a man who could "pray as
good a prayer as any." His grandchildren remember him
with kindness. Once when he was looking at May Carr's
doll, he dropped it on the hearth and broke it. He said,
"Don't cry. I'll get you another one." And he did.

Alvin E. Bishop was a private in the Confederate
Army, Co. A, 13th Tennessee Cavalry. He was taken prisoner of war at Chattanooga, Tennessee on March 22, 1865 and
released three days later on March 25.

The beginning of the War found the people of southern
Tennessee divided in allegiance. Some Northern sympathiz-
ers who lived across the Hatchie River from the Bishops
were carrying out guerrilla tactics. Once Alvin recogniz-
ed a man from the other side of the river on one of his
father's horses. The story goes that the other men with
Alvin wanted to hang the horse thief but Alvin reasoned
with them and told them they had better not do that lest
the other guerrillas burn them out. So they just took
the horse away from the man, removed his clothes, and let
him swim back across the river.

From <u>Tennesseans in the Civil War</u> by the Civil War
Centennial Commission it is found that there were "engage-
ments" at Middleton on Aug. 31 and Sept. 1, 1862. The
Federal Depot, barracks, and stockade were destroyed there
7 Nov. 1863.

Alvin and Mary Jane Bishop had eight children, six
girls and two boys. The four oldest children married in
Tennessee but all moved to Texas in 1878-79 with the exception of Tenny who died shortly before the family came.
Her husband, Jim Collier, and baby daughter came with the
group, including his parents, to Comanche County where
the baby died before her third birthday and was buried in
the Newberg Cemetery.

Godwin-Hill and Related Families

The two oldest daughters and husbands came to Texas first as this letter from Mary Jane to them was written after their arrival.

Tunica, Miss.   August 14: 1878
deare children I will try to wright you once more
we are tolerably well at this time   the children has
had some chills since we bin living heare   Eddy was
Sick yesterday thoe she is peart today   I can kee it
off to morrow we received your letter last evening
was so glad heare from you all thoe sorry to about
Sweet and duke Sufring   So with there eyes I hope
they are better now.   Well Manda I havent much news
to wright I am living in hopes of getting away from
heare Soon   Your papa Says he is agoing to get off
as soon as he can   my prayers to the lord every day is
to spare our lives and helpe us away from hear thoe
my payrs be very weake I trust they are heard the lord
is our helper we must trust in him we must know without his help we cannot do anything So bless the lord
for his goodness.
     . . .(unreadable). . .there was a killing scrape at
___   last week will fretwell and bud owens fell out
went to shooting both got killed instantly fell ded in
2 or 3 feet of eachother   crops is only tolerable we
have Som very good corn Som sorry it is Sufring for
rain now   I heare complaint of rust in cotton goodeal
of it ruined our cows is doing very well   I think Mr.
Auldredg (Will) bye (them) when he comes back from
tennessee he is to bee back the first of September
if he taks them and we can sell our corn in the field
we wanto Start to texes by the first of october we
expect to go in wagons   I want you to write as soon as
you get this tell us what your trip cost and where you
expect to settle   well manda this will do for you and
Sweet both as I have writen to Sweet not long since
I want you both to write often I have writen Some letters to Sweet that she never got dont weight long for
letters before you write I remain your affectionate
mother untel death   M. J. Bishop   Write

Tunica is less than 100 miles from their home near Middleton and about 35 miles south of Memphis. Possibly they had started toward Texas but stopped to make a crop there. By the next fall they were farming south of Comanche, Texas when Mary Jane writes Amanda again, less than two months before she died.

Mercers Gap Comanche Texas   Nov. 25: 1869 (1879)
well amanda I will try to write to you all once more I
hope you will not think harde of me for not writing
Sooner I lost my Specks had none for Sometime I am
ancious to heare from you all we had a letter from
Sweet Som 3 weaks ago the children had hooping cough
She Said it wasnot hurting them much She Said She was
in fine health herself duke was improving of his ris-
ings thoe I fear that She may take the cough yet if She
dose I hope the lord will carry her thrue safe if it
can only bee his good will in all of our troubles and
affliction we must humble our Selves and call on him
to helpe us and he will carry us thrue as the children
often Sings in there Song they lernt at School
Amanda I thought I would have came to See you before
now I want to See you all very bad it seems So verry
long Since I have Seen the little children kiss them
all for me and tell them our little ciller (Cilla) is
goun to heven She said she was going to Stay with herr
mama Mrs. Coliar says no baby you can stay with mee
it Seemed to fret her She (said) no i am going to Stay
with my mama this she talked before she was taken down
duren Sickness She Said mama mama mrs Coliar (said)
what you want She Sayd i want mama. She suffered 12
long days the 13 day god releast her from her pain
and then she went away I often think why dos little
children sufer somuch in death we can only say thats
gods will we must bee Still and know that he is god
well eddy has a chill now her albert and me has bin
havin chills some time they are lite on me not very
hard on them I hope we will ware out after awhile--
times is hard hear corn worth $1.50 per bu. wheat $1.35
meat 12½ cts I will close write Soon fale not I remain
your affection mother until death
                              M. J. Bishop
27 well Neely I will tell you and luther about nel She
pitch in the Sring the other (day) and broke her neck
all up today your papa albert and kitty is off picking
cotton alittle crop they bought from lige alin hill
times is hard with us now corn and meet high and mony
hard to get I hope we will live som way and make a
crop to live on wheat is so high we didnot get any to
sow

     I am indebted to a Bishop cousin Evyonne Eddins
of Brownwood, Tex. for the copies of these letters that
she obtained from another Bishop cousin Nollie Jackson
O'Dell, both great grand-daughters of Aunt Sweet and
Uncle Duke Jackson.

Mary Jane Bishop had not been well in Tennessee and it was hoped that the drier Texas climate would benefit her. The long slow trip and the hardships of setting up a home where none had been before took its toll though and she passed away at 53 years of age on a cold January day in 1880 and was carried about nine miles by wagon to the Newberg Cemetery to be buried beside her granddaughter Cilla Collier. When Alvin passed away eight years later he was buried on the other side of the little granddaughter.

Of the children of this couple, four of the daughters married men named "Jim." Alvin used to say that the devil owed him a grudge and paid him in Jims (gems).

Children of Alvin Bishop and Mary Jane Cox:

III-1.	Amanda Bishop	III-5.	Tennessee Bishop
III-2.	Sarah A. Bishop	III-6.	Elizabeth J. Bishop
III-3.	Thomas J. Bishop	III-7.	Albert S. Bishop
III-4.	Mary E. Bishop	III-8.	Kitty Bell Bishop
	III-9.	Edna P. Bishop	

III-1. Amanda (Mandy) Bishop, b. 24 Mar. 1845, Hardeman Co., Tenn., d. 17 Apr. 1932, Eden, Tex., m. James S. (Jim) Simpson 4 Dec. 1863, Hardeman Co.
Children: Neely, Luther, Lula, Arthur, Walter, lost 3 young children. Arthur and Walter were twins.
Jim was a farmer-stockman in Tenn. They came to Texas about 1877-78, living first at Santa Anna, Coleman Co., then at Democrat north of Mullin, later at Eden.

Mandy and Jim Simpson

204

III-2.   Sarah Ann Bishop, b. 28 Mar. 1851, d. 12 Aug. 1856,
         buried Bishop Cemetery, Hardeman Co., Tenn.

III-3.   Thomas J. Bishop (Tommy), b. 26 July 1853, Harde-
         man Co., Tenn., buried Houston, Tex., m. Mary Ann
         Ammons, license issued 26 Nov. 1873 Hardeman Co.,
         Tenn.
            Tommy was a carpenter and contractor and quite
         an entertaining fellow to be around with his quick
         sense of humor. Ann is described as a "heavenly"
         cook.
            Tommy and Ann lived in Lampasas, Tex. for some
         years before moving to Houston.
            Children: Ellen and Tommy, lost several young.

III-4.   Mary Elizabeth (Sweet) Bishop, b. 28 Aug. 1856,
         Hardeman Co., Tenn., d. 5 Feb. 1932, Eden, Tex.,
         m. Duke Allen Jackson 1 Oct. 1873, Hardeman Co.,
         Tenn.
            Children: Lula, Ophelia, Willoughby, Cora,
         Alma, Mittie, Minnie, Luther, Jeff, Kitty, Alvin,
         and Dot, the last two dying young. Mittie and
         Minnie were twins.
            Two of their children were born in Tennessee
         before they came to Texas in 1877-78. They lived
         in Hood and Coleman Counties, then at Eden. In
         Coleman County Duke Jackson built the first house
         at Santa Anna Mountain located a little west of
         The Gap as it was known in the 1870-80's, accord-
         ing to Beatrice Grady Gay in a history of Coleman
         County called Into the Setting Sun. She also
         states that Mr. Simpson, a relative, built his
         house east of The Gap near a spring. This was
         probably Amanda and Jim Simpson. P. G. Hill and
         Kitty Bishop built their first log home north of
         The Gap, the three sisters living near each other.
            Both Sweet and Duke died of cancer.
            Kitty and Minnie married Robertson brothers and
         Minnie named her only daughter Nollie after our
         mother. Nollie m. Asa O'Dell, but is now a widow
         caring for her mother.
            Ophelia was killed at Bangs in a cyclone 31 Mar.
         1892. Minnie has so graphically described the
         cyclone that it is here included.

                      The Bangs Cyclone

      When Molly and Duke Jackson lived in Bangs a cyclone
   nit one night just as they were going to bed. All the
   family was in bed except Duke, Ophelia, and one of the
   boys. There was a deafening roar but since they lived

near a railroad track they thought at first that it was
a train. When the roaring became even louder, the
father opened the door to see what it was. He closed
the door quickly, but was lifted up, door and all over
the wall with the doorknob still in his hand. His wife
saw him clearly being lifted up and away. He landed
in the orchard little the worse for the flight.

The son had removed one boot and was also lifted up
and blown into the orchard. As soon as he landed a
plow landed right beside him. He had to show the
family his landing tracks beside the plow before they
would believe the plow had landed so close to him.

Ophelia was blown into the yard. When they found her
she was draped over 2 logs and her head was caved in
at the back as if one of the logs had hit her.

As the father landed in the orchard, he could see the
bedclothes flying over and thought it was his children
in their nightclothes being taken away.

The rest of the family were left in their beds on the
floor, but the remainder of the house was completely
gone. Some logs pinned Minnie, Mittie, and another in
their beds, but did them no harm.

III-5. Tennessee (Tennie) Bishop, dau. of Alvin Bishop
and Mary J. Cox, b. 14 Aug. 1858, Hardeman Co.,
Tenn., d. 24 Oct. 1877, buried in Bishop Cemetery,
Hardeman Co., m. J. D. (Jim) Collier 7 Sept. 1875,
Hardeman Co.

Child: Cilla A. Collier, b. 21 Dec. 1876, d.
17 Sept. 1879, buried Newberg Cemetery near
Comanche, Tex.

Of Tennie's short married life to Jim Collier
we have one amusing incident. When the baby Cilla
was small Tennie sent the Grandmother Collier a
clipping of the baby's hair. Husband Jim exchanged some mohair for it before he mailed the letter.
When Mrs. Collier saw the hair, she was terribly
upset for fear the baby was not normal. "Very
strange hair! I never saw hair like that!" she
would say.

III-6. Elizabeth J. (Lyda) Bishop, dau. of Alvin Bishop
and Mary J. Cox, b. 29 Apr. 1861, Hardeman Co.,
Tenn., d. 28 May 1934, m. Jim D. Carr, Jr. 10
Sept. 1884, Comanche, Tex.

IV-1. May Carr m. Luther Crow.
IV-2. Inez Carr m. _____ Wright
IV-3. Susie Carr m. _____ Mayfield
IV-4. James Bishop Carr, teacher-preacher of a band
called "Little Flock of Zion" in Cal.

Lyda Bishop and Jim Carr Family--about 1910
James, _____, May, Inez, Susie (order not certain), Wilma, Lyda, Edith, Jim, J. Earl

IV-5.   J. Earl Carr, a doctor, head of State Mental Hospital, Valdez, Alaska.

IV-6.   Wilma Carr m. ____ Snyder, li. Shreveport, La.

IV-7.   Edith Carr m. ____ Miller, d. at 28, leaving 2 daughters.

     Jim Carr remembered when the Yankee soldiers ramsacked his parents' home during the Civil War. His mother threw what money they had in an unemptied chamber and saved it.

III-7.   Albert Sydney (Bud) Bishop, b. 11 Dec. 1863, Hardeman Co., Tenn., son of Alvin Bishop and Mary Jane Cox, buried Paint Rock, Tex., m. Mattie ___. Bud was sheriff in Paint Rock, Concho Co., Tex. before 1900, then was with the State Highway Dept. for many years.

IV-1.   Gaston Bishop m. Jessie ____, was a rancher in Concho County.

IV-2.   Robert (Rob) Bishop, li. Bronte, killed by a car.

IV-3.   Alda Bishop m. ____ Stewart.

IV-4.   Hugh Bishop m. ____ Skaggs.

IV-5.   Willie Bishop m. Pauline ____.

IV-6.   Jack Bishop m. Nola Arnold, associated with a bank in Paint Rock, Tex.

    V-1.   Alton A. Bishop m. Dorothy Corder, is a medical doctor, Lampasas, Texas.

    V-2.   Jacqueline Bishop m. ____ Hill.

IV-7.   Ollie Bishop m. ____ Waide.

III-8.   Kitty Bell Bishop, b. 11 Mar. 1866, Hardeman Co., Tenn., dau. of Alvin Bishop and Mary Jane Cox. d. 21 June 1889, Ft. Davis, Tex., m. P. G. Hill 16 Aug. 1883, Comanche, Tex.

IV-1.   Nollie Bell Hill m. Enoch Godwin

IV-2.   James Alvin Hill m. Clarissa Houschildt.

IV-3.   Achrol H. Hill m. May Sims.

     This family is further discussed in the James Hill and Enoch Godwin Chapters.

III-9.   Edna P. (Eddie) Bishop, b. 15 Mar. 1868, Hardeman Co., Tenn., m. Jim Townsend.

IV-1.   Nettie Townsend m. ____ Snyder.

IV-2.   Charlie Townsend

     Other children who d. young.

     This family lived at Blanket, Tex. and was one of tragedy. Besides the little ones who died young, both

parents died early in life. Eddie died of creeping paral-
ysis. Her thumbs became numb first, then finger by finger,
limb by limb until it covered her entire body. She became
unable to talk or swallow and the limbs perished away.

Mary Jane Bishop often called her little ones with a
singsong "Tenny, Buddy, Eddie, Kitty."

DAVID BISHOP

David Bishop, son of Asa Bishop and Susan Stevens,
b. 25 Aug. 1837, Tenn., d. 11 Feb. 1922, Hardeman Co.,
Tenn., buried in Bishop Cemetery near Middleton.

He m. Louisa Grantham, dau. of Thomas Grantham and
a Miss Cole in 1856. Louisa b. 11 Jan. 1843, d. 28 July
1942, 99½ years of age, lived on the Bishop place out of
Middleton near Lacy, Tenn.

David was 16 years younger than his brother Alvin.
His mother died when he was young and when he was 13 his
father married a widow with 4 children, so David lived
with Alvin temporarily, was there in 1850 census.

David joined the Confederate Army in 1862, Co. E,
14th Tenn. Cavalry under Nathan Bedford Forrest. He was
attached to Col. White as a currier.

He married at 19; Louisa was 13. David lived to be
84 and she 99, making their years of living together 65.
They farmed with slave help before the war and David worked with lumber for extra cash after the war.

When the slaves were freed they left and followed
the Yankee soldiers around for awhile, but one day a
faithful man, called Jack, came back to David's farm and
said, "Boss, I want to come back and be your nigger. I'm
about to starve to death. This freedom stuff ain't no
good."

Louisa Grantham Bishop was a most unusual woman,
married at 13, had 11 children, at 99 she had a child 84
and a grandchild 64. Her living children's ages totaled
570 years. In her later years she lived on the farm alone
with some help from a Negro couple who worked the farm.
She canned, quilted and read the Bible after she was 99.

Children of David Bishop and Louisa Grantham:

III-1. Susan E. (Sudie) Bishop, b. 2 Sept. 1858, d. 4
        Sept. 1953 at 95, m. Enoch Sain 15 Mar. 1880.
        Enoch b. 31 Oct. 1857, d. 5 Apr. 1925.

III-2. William A. (Billy) Bishop, b. ca. 1860, m. Maria
        Shelton 28 Jan. 1880.

I I-3. Edna F. Bishop, b. ca. 1862, m. J. S. Jackson 31
        Jan. 1877.

III-4. Asa T. Bishop, b. 13 Jul. 1865, d. 1 July 1950,
        m. Etta Macon 9 Jan. 1884. Etta b. 10 Apr. 1857,
        d. 31 Mar. 1956.

III-5. Julius Alvin Bishop, b. 26 Feb. 1867, d. 9 Jan.
        1949, m. Clara Cornelius, bur. Middleton Cemetery.
III-6. Maggie Bishop, b. 27 Apr. 1869, d. 23 Apr. 1893,
        unmarried, bur. Bishop Cemetery, Hardeman Co.,
        Tenn.
III-7. John Bishop, b. ca. 1872.
III-8. David E. (Dunk) Bishop, b. ca. 1876, m. Annie B.
        Cornelius June 1904.
III-9. Walter Lee Bishop, b. 10 Apr. 1878, d. 23 Dec.
        1883, bur. Bishop Cemetery.
III-10. Pitser Miller Bishop, medical doctor, b. ca.
        1881, m. Carrie Tisdale Jan. 1903.
        Children: Tisdale, Philip, Harry M., H. T.
III-11. Chester G. Bishop, b. ca. 1885.

    Many of the descendants of David and Louisa still
live in and around Boliver, Hardeman Co., Tenn. We met
Philip, Harry, and H. T., sons of Dr. P. M. Bishop.
Philip showed us the Bishop place and H. T. furnished
much of the information on the David Bishop family.
    Other Bishop information has come from cemetery and
marriage records of Hardeman County, many of them abstracted by the genealogist Fae J. Owens.

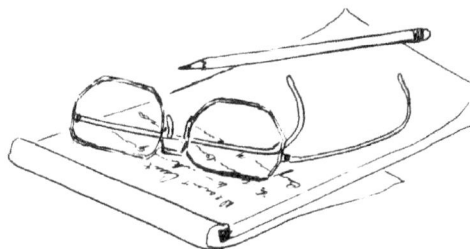

Married (1) Susan Stevens By 1814
(2) Elizabeth Stephens 23 May 1850   Place Hardeman Co., Tenn   Recorded: Bk. II, p. 115, Armour

Census Year County, State, Pg.	Sex	1830 Hardeman, TN p. 341	1840 Hardeman, TN p. 75	1850 Hardeman, TN	1860 Hardeman, TN p. 156
Asa b. 1790	M	40-50	50-60	61 Born Va.	Listed 70 w/David
Susan b. 1790-1800	F	30-40	40-50	Elizabeth 58 N.C.	
Edna b. 1814	F F	15-20			
Alvin b. 1821	M		15-20		
Susan (?) b. 1820-1825	F	5-10			
Sarah (?) b. 1825-1830	F	-5			
Everett b. 1825-1830	M	-5			
son b. 1825-1830	M	-5			
	M	40-50			
David b. 1837	M		-5	Listed w/Alvin 13 Tenn.	
Edward Stephens	M			21 N. C.	
Lewis Stephens	M			12 Tenn.	
Eliza Stephens	F			10 Tenn.	
Jacob Stephens	M			6 Tenn.	

FAMILY CENSUS OF ALVIN BISHOP

Married Mary Jane Cox   Date 21 Oct. 1841   Place Hardeman Co., TN   Recorded b. II, p. 31

Census Year County, State, Pg.	Sex	1850 Hardeman Co., TN		1860 Hardeman Co., TN P.158,1174-1099			1870 Hardeman Co., TN E.D.12-p.16,1-111			1880 Comanche Co., Tex. Pct.2-p.2-15		
			Born			Born			Born			Born
Alvin	M	29	NC	A	38	NC	Alvin	48	NC	Andrew	58	TN
Mary Jane	F	23	TN	Mary	33	TN	M.J.	44	TN			
Amanda	F	5	TN	Amanda S.	14	TN						
David	M	13 bro.	TN									
James	M			James Y.	7	TN	T. J.	16	TN	T. J.	26	Miss.
Mary Elizabeth	F			Mary E.	4	TN	M. E.	13	TN			
Tennessee	F			Infant	2	TN	Tenn	11	TN			
Elizabeth Jane	F						M. J.	9	TN	E. J.	19	Miss.
Albert Sydney	M						A. S.	6	TN			
Kitty Bell	F						K. B.	4	TN	K. B.	14	Miss.
Edna P.	F						E.	2	TN	E. P.	12	Miss.

XV

The Cox Family

Mary Jane Cox who married Alvin Bishop was the daughter of Eli Cox and Sarah Brown of Hardeman Co., Tenn. There is no clear trail back of Eli, but tradition is that three Cox brothers came from England through Virginia and settled in the Albemarle section of North Carolina in what is now Hyde, Beaufort, and Onslow Counties. It is believed that the early settlers in America having the Cox name were Quakers. Many familiar Cox names are mentioned by Henshaw in The Encyclopedia of Quaker Genealogy.

ELI COX

Eli Cox b. 18 Sept. 1786, d. 5 Dec. 1860, buried in the Bishop Family Cemetery in the Lacy-Porter Creek Community in Hardeman Co., Tenn., m. (1) Sarah Brown who was deceased by 1836, m. (2) Virtuous Clarissa Grant 2 Aug. 1836, Hardeman Co., Tenn.

In the 1830 census of Hardeman County Eli is listed as 40-50, wife 40-50, with 9 children. By 1840 his first wife has died, he has remarried a younger woman and has six more children under 10; some may be step-children. He also has 13 slaves in 1840.

Eli Cox made his will 22 Sept. 1858, Hardeman Co., Tenn., it being recorded 8 Jan. 1861. He mentions his wife Clarissa and these heirs:

1.	Susan McDonald (dec'd)	8.	Asa Cox (dec'd)
2.	Franklin M. Cox	9.	Cader Cox
3.	Eliza Rogers	10.	L. D. S. Macon
4.	C. W. Cox	11.	John A. Cox
5.	Mary Bishop	12.	Vashti Mashburn
6.	James A. Cox	13.	Alfred Cox
7.	Sarah Lanier	14.	Bryant Cox

From other records, mostly marriage records of Hardeman County, Tenn., we can enlarge some on the above children, not especially in order of birth, more so in the order of their marriage.

II-1. Vashti Cox m. Moses J. Mashburn 10 Apr. 1828, Hardeman Co., Tenn.

II-2. Asa Cox m. Nancy Harris 22 Dec. 1835, Hardeman Co., Tenn. Asa dec'd by 1858.

II-3. Cader Cox, b. 31 Oct. 1814, d. 7 June 1899, m. (1)
       Edna (Edney) Bishop 16 Dec. 1835, Hardeman Co.,
       Tenn. Edna dau. of Asa Bishop and Susan Stevens
       b. 5 Nov. 1814, d. 16 Jan. 1865. Cader m. (2) Jane
       E. Craig 15 Feb. 1866, Hardeman Co., Tenn.
         Cader Cox is said to have come to Hardeman County
       during its early settlement. He lived in Middleton
       and for many years kept the stables for the stage
       line from Memphis to Huntsville, Ala.
II-4. Alfred Cox m. Sarah Bishop 12 Sept. 1839, Hardeman
       Co., Tenn.
II-5. Susan Cox m. John McDonald 1836, dec'd by 1858,
       Ch.: Serena Isabella, Kitty Ann.
II-6. Elizabeth Cox, b. 1821 N.C., m. John Rogers, Jr.
       29 Oct. 1835, Hardeman Co., Tenn.
II-7. Mary Jane Cox, b. 13 Sept. 1826, d. 8 Jan. 1880,
       m. Alvin Bishop 21 Oct. 1841, Hardeman Co., Tenn.
       (See Bishop Chapter)
II-8. L. D. S. (Eldiss) Cox, b. 28 Jan. 1829, d. 6 May
       1902, Texas, m. Isaiah M. Macon 7 Mar. 1844, Harde-
       man Co., Tenn., 15 children. Isaiah, son of Wil-
       iam and Martha Macon, b. 13 Dec. 1819 N.C., d. 9
       Jan. 1896, Wolf City, Texas.
II-9. John A. Cox m. Martha Horne 17 Dec. 1847, Hardeman
       Co., Tenn.
II-10. Bryant Cox m. (1) Cornelia Bailey 23 Oct. 1851,
       (2) Mary E. Craig 15 May 1866.
II-11. Sarah Cox, b. ca. 1836, Tenn., m. John A. Lanier
       18 Dec. 1856, Hardeman Co., Tenn.
II-12. James A. Cox m. Frances
II-13. Charles W. Cox, m. Lucinda Cochran 6 Dec. 1870,
       Hardeman Co., Tenn.
II-14. Franklin M. Cox, m. L. W. Willis 21 Jan. 1869,
       Hardeman Co., Tenn., Civil War Veteran.

       Four more children listed in census, may have
       d. young.

    Fae Jacobs Owens (Mrs. Robert S. Owens), a descendant
of Eliza Cox Rogers, has contributed generously to the
research on the Cox and Bishop lines. We met in the courthouse in Bolivar, Tenn. in the summer of 1968 and have
shared information since. Her line follows.

I. Eli Cox m. Sarah Brown
    II-6. Eliza Cox, b. 1821, N.C., d. after 1860, m.
           John Rogers, Jr. 29 Oct. 1835, Hardeman Co.,
           Tenn.
             Children: Sarah, Hiram, Mary E., Michael,
           Jane, Jessee, Dolly.

III-1. Sarah Rogers, b. 1837, d. Nov. 1896, buried Harris
        Cemetery, Hardeman Co., Tenn., m. J. W. Rose 18
        Dec. 1856. J. W. b. 1835, son of John Rose and
        Sarah Thompson.
  IV-1. Mary Mollie D. Rose, b. 28 Mar. 1861, d. 6 Dec.
        1932, buried Hebron, m. Samuel Douglas Jacobs
        11 Dec. 1879, Hardeman Co., Tenn. S. Douglas
        Jacobs b. 9 Jan. 1860, d. 22 July 1943, son of
        James Madison Jacobs and Permelia Harris.
          Children: Infant, James Ernest, Grover
        Benoma, Elliot Booker, Wickliffe Wilburn,
        Luther Douglas, Wilton Brooks, Ollie, Dewey
        Wynes.
    V-9. Dewey Wynes Jacobs, b. 13 Nov. 1898, m.
        Nellie Elizabeth Gray 9 Sept. 1923, Hardeman
        Co., Tenn. Nellie E. b. 24 Sept. 1903.
      VI-1. Maggie Fae Jacobs, b. 1931, m. Robert
        Sturgis Owens 1955, Robert b. 1925.
      VII-1. Hugh Keith Owens, b. 26 Aug. 1957.
      VI-2. Euland Norris Jacobs, b. 1934, m. Tommie
        Sue Sain 1957.
        VII-1. Angie Jacobs, b. 1958.
        VII-2. Cindy Jacobs b. 1960.
        VII-3. Chris Jacobs b. 1964.
        VII-4. Amy Jacobs b. 1969.

Eli Cox
Born
Sept. 18, 1786
Died
Dec. 5, 1860
Aged
74 yrs. 2 m. 17.

Dedicated by his
children.

Will of Eli Cox--22 Sept. 1858

State of Tennessee
Hardeman County
    I Eli Cox being of sound mind and in good health
of body, do make and publish this my last will and
testament towit:

    First, that my funeral expenses and all my just
debts be paid out of any money or monies that may be
in my possession at the time of my death or out of the
first money that may come into the hands of my executors belonging to my estate after my decease.

    Second, I give and bequeath six hundred dollars in
cash to be equally divided between the three children
of my daughter Susan McDonald dec'd, wife of John
McDonald to wit: Serena Morgan, Isabella McDonald, and
Kitty Ann McDonald.

    Third, I give and bequeath to my son Franklin M.
Cox a certain Negro slave by the name of Everett, said
boy being about nine years old, also one horse of the
value of one hundred dollars, one feather bed, bed
stead and necessary clothing for said bed and one cow
and calf.

    Fourth, I give and bequeath to my daughter Eliza
Rogers a certain tract of land in said County of Hardeman and lying on Porters Creek on which she now resides
containing about 80 acres, the said tract of land known
as the John Faught place.

    Fifth, I give and bequeath to my son C. W. Cox a
certain Negro slave by the name of Margaret about four
years of age. Also one horse of the value of one hundred dollars, one bed and stead and necessary clothing
for said bed, and one cow and calf.

    Sixth, I give and bequeath to my daughter Mary
Bishop wife of Alvin Bishop a certain Negro slave by
the name of Pinckney about five years of age.

    Seventh, I give and bequeath to my son James A.
Cox, one Negro slave by the name of Lucinda about two
years of age.

    Eighth, I give and bequeath to my daughter Sarah
Lanier one horse of the value of one hundred dollars
and one cow and calf.

    Ninth, I give and bequeath to my wife Clarissa Cox
one third part of the land that I may be in possession
of at my death during her lifetime and after her death
to be equally divided between the heirs of my estate.
Also the best horse I own at the time of my decease,
one bed bedstead and furniture, one cow and calf.

Tenth, It is my will and wish that the remainder of my property and hereafter disposal of shall be equally divided share and share alike between my children mentioned as follows viz: Heirs of Asa Cox decd, Cader Cox, Mary Bishop wife of Alvin Bishop, Eliza Rogers, L. D. S. Macon, wife of Isaiah Macon, John A. Cox, James A. Cox, Charles W. Cox, Sarah Lanier, F. M. Cox and my wife Clarissa Cox and that James A. Cox have the share of Vashti Mashburn he having purchased her claim or right in my estate and also that Alfred Cox and Bryant Cox share equally of the unappropriated portion of my estate with those above mentioned.

And last, it is also my will and wish that the Negroes belonging to me that have not been bequeathed shall remain amongst my children, they dividing the same according to their value.

I do hereby nominate and appoint Cader Cox and James A. Cox my executors to this my last will and testament. This 22 September 1858

Witnesses

W. H. Craddock   Eli Cox   (Seal)
J. K. Harrell

Codicil to the Will of Eli Cox

I Eli Cox being of sound mind do make the following addition to this my last will and testament. It is my will and wish that my wife Clarissa Cox have a certain Negro boy by the name of George during her natural lifetime and after her decease it is my will that my son Franklin M. Cox have the said Negro boy George.

This 5th day of March 1859

W. H. Craddock   Eli Cox
J. K. Harrell

Recorded January 8th 1861.

Godwin-Hill and Related Families

Census of Eli Cox

1830 Hardeman Co., Tenn. p. 341.

Males		Females	
1	5-10	2	- 5
1	10-15	3	10-15
1	15-20	1	40-50
1	20-30		
1	40-50		

1840 Hardeman Co., Tenn. p. 57.

Males		Females	
2	- 5	1	- 5
2	5-10	1	5-10
1	50-60	2	10-15
		1	15-20
		1	30-40

1860 Hardeman Co., Tenn. p. 158, Dist. #12, P.O. Bolivar

1169-1094	Cox,	Eli	71	M	Farmer	Born N.C.
		Clarissa	61	F		N.C.
		Franklin M.	19	M		N.C.

XVI

The Koffman Family

At least four children of the Daniel Koffman family married children of Daniel Hill in east Tennessee in the early 1800's. The Koffmans descended from a line of Swiss Mennonites who were under "severe tribulations" in Switzerland, removed to the Rhine provinces of Germany, then on to Pennsylvania. While religious freedom was permitted in Germany, the thousands of Mennonites who were exiled there from Switzerland made the economic struggle such that constant aid was supplied by the Mennonite congregations in Holland.

In 1683 a few Mennonites came to Pennsylvania and formed Germantown. Others came in 1710, taking up land in Lancaster County. Bright reports were carried back to the Mennonite refugees in Germany and at the conference at Manheim in Feb. 1717, the elders decided to make a mass settlement in Lancaster County, Penn. The Holland congregations helped finance the project and in June 1717 the vessels set sail from Rotterdam, and by way of London, came to Philadelphia, after spending twelve weeks at sea. On Sept. 8, 1717 Captains Eyres, Tower, and Richards appeared before the Council of Pennsylvania with a total list of 363 Palatines brought over in their three vessels. (Vol. 3, Colonel Records, p. 29) Names of ships and passengers are lacking.

But in "Land Warrants and Surveys" on Sept. 27, 1717, a land warrant was issued to Isaac Kaufman with 675 acres surveyed to him in October.

Isaac and Andrew Kaufman were taxed in 1718-1720. From 1727 to 1802 numerous Kaufmans were on ships' passenger lists coming into Pennsylvania.

Above information from A Genealogy and History of the Kaufman-Coffman Families of North America 1584-1937 by Charles Fahs Kaufman.

The Daniel Koffman (1760-1836) line had migrated down the Shenandoah Valley into Virginia, where both Daniel and his wife Elizabeth were born. They were in Greene Co., Tenn. by 1797 when Daniel Coffman bought of John Wilson 43 acres on the north side of Little Chucky along Epperson's Branch to where it enters into Little Chucky River, 13 Feb. 1797, Bk. D., p. 251, Greene Co., Tenn.

John Wilson also sold 52 acres to Adam Coffman on Little Chucky Nov. 10, 1796 and James Wilson and wife Elizabeth sold John Coffman 29 acres on the Mill Fork of Big Limestone 18 Jan. 1797.

Even before these land conveyances, a David Coffman had received a land grant from the state of N.C. for 200 acres 1 Feb. 1785 in Greene Co. on the south side of Lick Creek, later becoming part of Jefferson Co. This David is said to have also come from Pennsylvania through the Shenandoah Valley before settling in Tenn.

Then on 20 Sept. 1787 Andrew Coffman also received 200 acres on Lick Creek from the state of N.C.

Daniel Koffman served on jury duty in Greene Co., Tenn. in 1805, was listed on the Tax List in 1809 on Little Chucky with 130 acres, by 1812 has 473½ acres on Little Chucky with 2 Black polls, slaves, the same for 1813 and in 1814 but with 3 Black polls, slaves, in 1815. Other Koffmans (Coffmans) listed were Nicholas and another Daniel both on Lick Creek.

Lucian R. Koffman of Oak Ridge, Tenn., descendant of Daniel Koffman, tells of Daniel operating a blacksmith shop and grist mill on Lick Creek in conjunction with his farming operations in Greene Co., Tenn.

Daniel Koffman m. (1) Elizabeth (Sherrick?) and had children: (not especially in order of birth)

II-1. Daniel Koffman, Jr.
II-2. Isaiah Koffman, 1793-1838, m. Ellender Hill, 6 Nov. 1817, Jefferson Co., Tenn. Ellender, dau. of Daniel Hill and Ellen (sometimes Ellender) Nodding, b. 17 May 1799, d. 30 Sept. 1838.

    Isaiah and Ellender operated a tavern on the Nolichucky from 1819 to 1827, then moved with the Hill migration to McNairy Co., Tenn. in 1828. They both died of typhoid fever in 1838, leaving several children, including the year-old Narcifia who was raised by John Hill and Anna Koffman.

    Isaiah and Ellender Koffman buried Rose Hill Cemetery, McNairy Co., Tenn.

III-1. Daniel Harrison Koffman, 1818-1845 never married.
III-2. James Carrol Koffman, 1822-1901, born Greene Co., Tenn., m. Abigail Hawkins Atkins who was b. 1818 N.C., d. 1898, Gibson Co., Tenn.
  IV-1. Isiah Jeff. Koffman m. _____ Motley.
  IV-2. John N. Koffman (Dr.) m. Mattie E. Motley 1883.
  IV-3. James H. Koffman, b. 1855, McNairy Co., Tenn., m. (1) Emma B. Phelan 1885, three children, m. (2) Mattie L. Boyd 7 Apr. 1901. Mattie, dau. of Mr. and Mrs. J. T. Boyd of Gibson Co., Tenn., primary school teacher.
    V-1. James H. Koffman Jr. m. _____ Hockaday.
    V-2. Robert H. Koffman m. _____ Bledsoe.

V-3. Frances H. Koffman m. _____ Hamilton.
V-4. Lucian R. Koffman b. 1912, m. Kay Falls,
  li. Oak Ridge, Tenn.
  VI-1. Relma Koffman m. _____ Sharp.
  VI-2. Dan F. Koffman
  VI-3. Larry D. Koffman
  VI-4. M. Keith Koffman
  VI-5. David L. Koffman
IV-4. Elizabeth Koffman m. _____ Morrison.
IV-5. Sarah Koffman m. _____ Bennett.
IV-6. Pricilla Koffman, d. young.
IV-7. Mollie Koffman m. _____ Nicholson.

III-3. Catherine Koffman, dau. of Isaiah Koffman and
  Ellender Hill, m. _____ Walker.
III-4. Scruggs Koffman, d. young, twin to Catherine.
III-5. Mary Elizabeth Koffman, b. 1828, m. _____ Hicks.
III-6. Priscilla Koffman, b. 1830, m. M. G. Hodges.
III-7. Narcifia Koffman, 1837-1929, m. _____ McCollum.

II-3. Elizabeth Koffman, dau. of Daniel Koffman and Eliza-
  beth ____, m. Daniel Hill, Jr., bond 30 Oct. 1819,
  Greene Co., Tenn. Isaiah Koffman signed bond, in
  McNairy Co., Tenn. 1828.

II-4. Anna Koffman, dau. of Daniel Koffman and Elizabeth,
  m.(1)___ Simons, (2) John Hill, bond 30 Oct. 1819,
  Isaiah Koffman signed bond. This was two sisters
  m. two Hill boys at the same time, to McNairy Co.,
  Tenn. in 1828.

II-5. Rebecca Koffman, dau. of Daniel Koffman and Eliza-
  beth, b. 3 July 1793, d. 27 Feb. 1897, age 104, m.
  Elijah Hill 6 Jan. 1820, Greene Co., Tenn. Elijah,
  son of Daniel Hill and Ellen Nodding, b. 1795,
  Jefferson Co., Tenn., d. 1857, McNairy Co., Tenn.
  (See Chapter 7)

II-6. Parthena Koffman, dau. of Daniel Koffman and Elizabeth, m. Martin Denton, d. between 1836-1839.
  III-1. Catherine Elizabeth Denton m. _____ Cathrom.

II-7. Polly Koffman, dau. of Daniel Koffman and Elizabeth,
  m. William McCandery (McCanders).

  There are possibly other children of Daniel and
  Elizabeth Koffman, not traced.

  Daniel Koffman m. (2) Nancy _____ between 1833 and
  1836. It is probable that he died in 1836 in

221

McNairy County, Tenn. In the McNairy Co. Deeds
1823-1838, Bk. A, p. 326, Mrs. Nancy Koffman
gives a Deed of Release to Daniel Koffman and
others.

Know all men by these presents that I, Nancy
Koffman the widow of Daniel Koffman dec'd late
of McNairy County for the sum of $500.00 to me in
hand paid the receipt whereof is hereby acknowledged do hereby release and forever quit claim unto
Daniel Koffman, Isaiah Koffman, Daniel Hill and his
wife Elizabeth and John Hill and his wife Anna,
Martin Denton and his wife Parthena and William
McCandery and his wife Polly all my right title
claim. In witness whereof I have hereunto set
my hand and affixed my seal this August 19th 1836.

Test   Her
Alvan Denny   Nancy   X   Koffman
James Hill   Mark

Lucian R. Koffman of Oak Ridge, Tenn. has furnished
much of the Koffman information. My sister Day
Alva Trainer and I enjoyed visiting with Luke,
his lovely wife Kay, and son David in the summer
of 1977. We researched in Knoxville and explored
Great Smoky National Park with them.

XVII

The Nodding Family

William Nodding, Sr., father of Ellen (Ellender) Nodding who married Daniel Hill, was in the area of Loudoun Co., Va. and just across the Potomac in Montgomery Co., Md. in the 1770's. He witnessed a lease to his son-in-law, Daniel McCray, in Loudoun Co., ca. in 1770, a "lease for lives" of 300 acres about one mile above the Great Falls of the Potomac River, which he signed "William Noddy." The name has many variants: Noding, Nodding, Noddy, Noeding, Nody, Noden.

Daughters of William Nodding married in Montgomery Co., Md. in 1778 and 1780. Then the Noddings were in Washington Co., Tenn. in the 1780's. The will of John Nodding, a son, was proved there in Feb. 1783 and William Nodding, Sr. was granted 300 acres of land there in Nov. 1784. On the Tax List of Washington Co., Tenn., William rendered 300 acres of land and 6 black polls from 1791 to 1795, then 5 black polls for 1796 and 1797, with only 4 black polls the next two years, still with 300 acres of land. He was granted another 300 acres in Washington Co., Tenn. 19 Oct. 1797.

From Montgomery Co., Md. Marriage Records, the William Nodding and John Nodding Wills, and various other records the children of William Nodding, Sr., and his wife Mary are: (Order not known)

II-1. Sarah Nodding	II-5. Alice Nodding
II-2. Mary Nodding	II-6. William Nodding, Jr.
II-3. Elizabeth Nodding	II-7. John Nodding
II-4. Ellen Nodding	

II-1. Sarah Nodding m. Daniel McCray, who was an executor of her father's will. Sarah is dec'd by 1809 when Daniel m. (2) Polly Pretchard (Pritchet) 8 May 1809; Polly dau. of Charles Pritchet.

   III-1. Charles McCray, son of Sarah and Daniel.

II-2. Mary Nodding m. Samuel Bayles (Bayless). Samuel, 1751-1825, Estate Settlement 9 Jan. 1826. Lt. Col. in Tenn. Militia, 1810.

II-3. Elizabeth Nodding m. William Calvert 18 July 1780, Montgomery Co., Md. William, 1757-1834, was a Rev. War Soldier from Maryland.

223

III-1. John Calvert, b. 1781
III-2. Wm. Calvert, b. 1783
III-3. Nancy Calvert, b. 1786
III-4. Leonard Calvert, b. 1787
III-5. Sarah Calvert, b. 1789
III-6. Mary Calvert, b. 1792
III-7. Alice Calvert, b. 1794
III-8. Elizabeth Calvert, b. 1796
III-9. Nodding Calvert, b. 1798
III-10. Johez Calvert, b. 1805

II-4. Ellen Nodding, 1750-1830, m. Daniel Hill, 1757-1846, Rev. War Veteran from Washington Co., N.C. (Chapter Six)

II-5. Alice Nodding m. John Brown 1 Oct. 1778, Montgomery Co., Maryland, d. by Oct. 1804, five children mentioned in her father's will. John Brown, Rev. War Soldier from N.C., m. (2) Martha Elkins.

II-6. William Nodding, Jr., unmarried, will proved May 1793, Washington Co., Tenn.

II-7. John Nodding m. Priscilla ____, no children, wrote will 6 Nov. 1782, proved Feb. 1783, Washington Co., Tenn.

Since both sons of this family died without issue, the name was not carried forward.

The William Nodding will, proved May 1812 in Washington Co., Tenn. demonstrates outstanding kindness in designating ages and dates that the slaves were to be set free.

William Nodding Will
Vol.#1, p. #88, Washington Co., Tenn.

In the name of God Amen
I, William Nodding of Tennessee State, Washington County, (farmer) being frail in body but in perfect mind and memory, thanks be given unto God, calling into mind the mortality of my body and knowing that it is appointed for all men once to die do make and ordain this my last will and testament that is to say-first of all- I give and recommend my soul into the hands of Almighty God that gave it and my body I recommend to the earth to be buried in a decent Christian burial at the descreation of my executors nothing doubting but at the general rescereation I shall receive the same again by the mighty power of God and as touching such worldly estate where with it has pleased

God to bless me with in this life. I give demise and
dispose in the following manner and form. After my
just debts and funeral charges are paid. I give and
bequeath unto my beloved wife Mary Nodding all the
lease that I took from Daniel McCray for that land
where the said McCray now lives which lease is for my
life and Mary Noddings life. I also give and bequeath
unto my daughter Sarah McCray a tract of land as is
supposed two hundred acres which her husband Daniel
McCray has a deed of conveyance from me for together
with one Negro man named Toney in their possession to
be set free in the year one thousand eight hundred and
six on the twenty fourth day of December. I also give
her my smallest still together with my household furniture and moveable effects which negro and effects to
are in their possession.

I also give unto my daughter Mary Bayless sixty two
acres of land which Samuel Bayless her husband hath
taken a deed of conveyance from me for together with
a man of couler named Tom in said Bayless possession
said Tom to be set free on the fourteenth day of February in the year one thousand eight hundred and seven.
I also give to my daughter Elizabeth Calvert seventy
five acres of land now in possession of William Calvert
her husband by deed from me together with the following
persons of color, Bet, Dark, Linn, Peter and George now
in possession of said Calvert and all set free by my
directions at the age of thirty five years except George
who is free at twenty five years by an order of last
County Court of our county at the petition of said
William Calvert to possess the above by paying John
Brown's five orphan children two hundred and fifty dollars
in property the persons decreed to said Calvert are of
following ages. Bet thirty years of age the seventh
day of February last, Dark eleven the sixth day of May
last, Peter six the twentieth of this instant, George
three the fourth of May last. I also give to my daughter Ellinor Hill my girl of Couler named Millie now in
her possession to be free the twenty fifth day of June
one thousand eight hundred and twelve. And as touching
the postirety of any of the slaves or persons of couler
here to fore named in this will I declare and will them
their birth free as white people are by law except the
future children of Bet who are to serve twenty five
years and their children free born. I also give to John
Browns orphan children two hundred and fifty dollars to
be paid by Calvert aforesaid. I also constitute and
ordain Daniel McCray and William Calvert the sole executors of this my last will and testament and I do hereby disallow revoke and disannull all and every other

former testament wills legacies bequeathes or executors
by me in wise before named willed or bequeathed ratifying and confirming this and no other to be my last will
and testament, In witness whereof I here unto set my
hand and seal this twenty fourth day of October in the
year of our Lord one thousand eight hundred and four.
Signed sealed published and declared by the said William
Nodding as his last will and testament in the presence
of us who in his presence and in the presence of each
other have here unto subscribed our names.

His
William X Nodding (Seal)
Mark

William Bayless
Reuben Bayless
Hannah Bayless

The foregoing will was proven in court by the oathes of
William Bayless and Reuben Bayless two of the subscrib-
ing witnesses thereto at May Sessions 1812, and ordered
to be recorded.

Ray York of Corsicana, Texas has supplied much of the
Nodding information plus help on the Hill line.

Name Index

Absher, Emma L., 68
Adams, Rebecca B., 162
Adams, Gordon P., 87
Adams, Scott R., 87,88
Admiro, Carrie, 185
Aldredge, Pearl, 57
Alexander, Barney P., 52, 53, 54, 188
Alexander, Della M., 52, 53, 54
Alexander, Erah, 32
Alexander, Harriet, 52
Alexander, L. Juanita, 52,54
Alexander, Marion L., 52
Alexander, N. Velma, 52
Alexander, Roland Ray, 52
Alexander, Thomas L., 52
Allen, George, 191
Alvis, Lula, 5
Ammons, Mary Ann, 205
Argibright, Eleanor P., 183
Argibright, Mary Alice, 183
Arnold, Nola, 208
Atkins, Abigail H., 220
Attaway, Jack, 31
Anglin, Alice C., 162
Anglin, Angela, 163
Anglin, Kenneth, 163
Anglin, Carol, 163
Auldredg, Mr., 202
Austin, Jersey, 194
Avery, Nancy A., 131

Babyer, Catherine, 150
Babyer, Debbie, 150
Babyer, Paul, 150
Babyer, Steven, 150
Bailey, Anne, 167, 168
Bailey, Cornelia, 214
Bailey, Stephen, Jr., 169
Baker, Hazel, 156
Baker, Susanne, 49
Ballem, Erma Lois, 48
Ballem, James J., 51
Ballem, James Joseph, 51
Ballem, Jimmy, 48
Banta, ___,146
Banta, Brook, 146
Barber, Mary, 10
Barnett, Absolom, 174,175
Barrett, Clara M., 183
Barrington, ___, 31
Bartholomew, Carl, 137
Bartholomew, Dennis R., 137
Bartholomew, Helen, 137
Bartholomew, Vernon A., 137
Barnes, Winnie, 112
Barnes, Bertha, 112
Barnes, Martie, 112
Barton, Alene, 111
Barton, Cora, 111
Barton, Ethel, 111
Barton, Hattie, 111
Barton, John, 111
Barton, Johnnie, 111
Barton, Martha, 111

Batich, Joe, 127
Baum, Shirley, 159
Bayles, Samuel, 223
Bayless, Hannah, 226
Bayless, Mary, 225
Bayless, Reuben, 226
Bayless, Samuel, 225
Bayless, William, 226
Beaman, David, 1
Beard, Rev. Francis, 100
Beard, Par. Franklin, 101
Beard, Jeff, 181
Beaver, J. R., 81
Beckham, Robert L., 180
Beckham, Mrs. R. L., 179
Beckham, Roy, 179
Beckham, Lee Roy, 179
Behoke, Selma M., 161
Belcher, Tex, 162
Bell, Addie Ruth, 156
Bell, Bobby G., 156
Bell, Cleo, 156
Bell, Elon Teresa, 159, 160
Bell, Herbert, 128
Bell, James D., 156
Bell, John, Jr., 156
Bell, John, Sr., 156
Bell, Minnie K., 156
Bell, Paula Ann, 128
Bell, Robert J., 156
Bell, Ruth, 156
Bennett, ___, 221
Bennett, Solomon, 25, 192
Bennett, Tabitha, 25, 192, 193, 194, 197
Beriman, John, 194
Beshears, Earl, 127
Beshears, John C., 127
Beshears, Lois, 127
Beshears, Robert, 127
Beshears, Stephen, 127
Beshears, Vogel, 127
Best, Ninnie, 85
Biggs, Darrell D., 164
Biggs, Virgil, 164
Biggs, Dr. W. D., 60
Bird, Neppie, 32
Birdsong, Charles, 6
Birdsong, Charlie, 6
Birdsong, Jennie, 6
Birdsong, Manning, 6
Birdsong, Margret, 6
Birdsong, Robert, 6
Birdsong, Ruby, 6
Birdsong, Sallie, 6
Birdsong, Wardie, 6
Bishop, Albert, 158
Bishop, Albert S., 204, 208, 209, 212
Bishop, Alda, 208
Bishop, Dr. Alton A., 208
Bishop, Alvin E. 55, 139, 199, 199, 200, 201, 204, 206, 208, 209, 211, 212, 213, 214, 215, 216, 217

Callicutt, Ezekiel T., 4, 5
Callicutt, George T., 5
Callicutt, Haywood, 5
Callicutt, Jane, 4, 24
Callicutt, Jennie, 6
Callicutt, Josephene, 5
Callicutt, Lawrence, 5
Callicutt, Lee, 5
Callicutt, Lura, 5
Callicutt, Martha B., 5
Callicutt, Mary L., 5, 18
Callicutt, Minnie, 4
Callicutt, Mollie, 4
Callicutt, Pennie, 2, 4
Callicutt, Pleasant, 2, 4, 24
Callicutt, Rosa Lee, 5
Callicutt, Sallie C., 6
Callicutt, Sarah, 4, 24
Callicutt, Sarah E., 5
Callicutt, Serena S., 191
Callicutt, Thomas, 4, 24
Callicutt, Thomas A., 5
Callicutt, Thomas J., 5
Callicutt, Vinson, 6
Callicutt, Viola, 5
Callicutt, Willie, 4
Calloway, Oscar, 201
Calvert, Alice, 224
Calvert, Debbie, 86
Calvert, Elizabeth, 224, 225
Calvert, Johez, 224
Calvert, John, 224
Calvert, Leonard, 224
Calvert, Mary, 224
Calvert, Nancy, 224
Calvert, Nodding, 224
Calvert, Sarah, 224
Calvert, William, Jr., 224
Calvert, William, Sr., 223, 225
Carnal, John W., 14
Carnes, Prof., 99
Carr, A. L., 34
Carr, Edith, 207, 208
Carr, Hettie, 33
Carr, Inez, 206, 207
Carr, James B., 206, 207
Carr, J. Earl, 207, 208
Carr, Jim D., 206, 207
Carr, May, 201, 206, 207
Carr, Susie, 206, 207
Carr, Wilma, 207, 208
Carroll, Grace, 182
Carter, Beulah, 185
Carter, Francis I. G., 92, 105
Casbeer, Gladys, 80
Case, Andrew, 111
Case, Charles, 111
Case, Clifton, 111
Case, Dora, 111
Case, James D., 111
Case, John, 108
Case, John A., 111
Case, Johnnie, 111
Case, Jonas, 111
Case, Mary, 108
Case, Mildred, 111

Case, Nettie, 111
Case, Velda, 111
Cathrom, ___, 221
Caudill, Gladys, 134
Cavin, Nathan A., 139
Cavin, Vinnie, 121, 139, 143, 147,
    148, 149, 150
Chambers, Lillie, 165
Chapman, Donald D., Sr., 185
Chapman, Donald J., 185
Chapman, Louise H., 186
Chapman, Quinton D., 185
Cherry, Viola, 186
Cheshier, M. B., 137
Chism, Sallie I., 14
Clark, Jesse, 175
Clement, David, 87, 88
Clement, Don E., Mr. and Mrs., 87
Clemmer, Janie, 13
Clemmer, Samuel E., 17
Cochran, Lucinda, 214
Cockerll, Mary, 35
Cockrell, Jake, 30
Coffman, Adam, 219
Coffman, Andrew, 220
Coffman, David, 220, 222
Coffman, John, 219
Colburn, Alice, 163
Colburn, Eula, 162
Colburn, J. A., Sr., 162
Cole, Karen, 135
Cole, L. D., 135
Cole, Miss, 209
Coleman, Nancy, 97
Coleman, William, 97
Coley, Fannie, 14
Colley, Barbara A., 133
Collier, Allen, 38
Collier, Cilla A., 203, 206
Collier, James H., 38
Collier, Jim, 141, 201, 206
Collier, Louise, 38
Collier, Milton C., 38
Collier, Mrs., 203
Collins, Dolphus F., 14
Conditt, Opal V., 137
Conner, James,
Conradt, Charles, 80
Cook, Billy, 157
Cook, George, 157
Cook, Irene, 181
Cook, Lottie, 10
Cook, Mary, 157
Cook, Tonya, 157
Cooke, Beverly S., 150
Cooke, Ivanell, 148
Cooke, Robert H., 150
Coombs, James E., 14
Coombs, John H., 14
Coontz, Dessie V., 133
Copper, John, 92
Corbin, J. H., 185
Corder, Dorothy, 208
Cornelius, Annie B., 210
Cornelius, Clara, 210
Cornelius, Donna, 157

Godwin, Eli Seamore, 4, 27, 28
Godwin, Eli Seymore, 193
Godwin, Elias, 2
Godwin, Elijah, 4, 20, 32
Godwin, Elijah A., 19
Godwin, Elijah M., 11
Godwin, Elisha, 14, 23, 112
Godwin, Elisha, H., 3, 7, 13, 14
Godwin, Eliza, 14
Godwin, Elizabeth, 2, 40
Godwin, Elizabeth H., 19
Godwin, Ely, 2
Godwin, Enoch, 26, 27, 42, 43, 44,
   45, 46, 47, 55, 56, 58, 60, 61,
   62, 63, 64, 66, 69, 72, 77, 80,
   83, 86, 136, 143, 188, 199, 208
Godwin, Enoch E., 81, 82, 83
Godwin, Essie, 18
Godwin, Essie D., 45, 188
Godwin, Eunice, 10
Godwin, Everee, 11
Godwin, Fannie, 6
Godwin, Fred, 18
Godwin, Gladys, 11
Godwin, Glenna Mae, 44, 47, 55,
   59, 60, 62, 64, 143
Godwin, Gracie, 10
Godwin, Gretchen J., 87, 88
Godwin, Harvey L., 8
Godwin, Hazel, 10
Godwin, Henry M., 11
Godwin, Ina Mae, 5, 18
Godwin, Ira Smith, 47, 56, 59, 62,
   63, 86, 87, 88, 143
Godwin, Iva Mae, 5, 18
Godwin, J. A., 126, 180, 187
Godwin, Jacob, 2, 19, 22
Godwin, Jacob O., 19
Godwin, Jacob G., 10
Godwin, Jacob W., 7, 8, 9
Godwin, James, 1, 2, 20
Godwin, James A., 7, 12, 14, 19
Godwin, James F., 5, 18
Godwin, James T., 5, 18
Godwin, Jeff, 18, 153
Godwin, Jennie R., 8
Godwin, Jessie, 18
Godwin, Joe, 18, 63
Godwin, Joe Ella, 17
Godwin, John, 18
Godwin, John Sr., 56
Godwin, John Allen, Jr., 4, 7, 25,
   26, 27, 28, 34, 36, 39, 40, 41,
   43, 44, 45, 47, 52, 193
Godwin, John Allen, Sr., 3, 4, 6,
   22, 25, 28, 29, 33, 40, 189,
   192, 193
Godwin, John D., 81, 82
Godwin, John D., II, 82
Godwin, John L., 19
Godwin, Joseph E., 12, 13, 14
Godwin, Judy, 63
Godwin, Julia, 8, 9, 18
Godwin, Julia A., 4, 27, 40, 193
Godwin, J. Day Alva, 47, 55, 59,
   62, 69, 70, 143
Godwin, Judith G., 81, 82, 83
Godwin, J. Y., 11

Godwin, Katie, 10
Godwin, Katie Sue, 8
Godwin, Kay, 63
Godwin, Latitia, 23
Godwin, Latitia F., 4, 19, 20
Godwin, Lavina J., 4, 27, 40, 193
Godwin, L. Joseph, 81, 82
Godwin, Leota, 19
Godwin, Liva A., 28, 44
Godwin, Lee, 9
Godwin, Levi, 8, 9, 14
Godwin, Levi S., 3, 7, 22
Godwin, Lillian, 14
Godwin, Lillian M., 47, 56, 62,
   75, 143
Godwin, Lillis V., 10
Godwin, Lottie F., 5, 18
Godwin, Lucinda J., 14
Godwin, L. Parolee, 4, 6, 8, 19,
   23, 55, 59, 112, 115, 116, 117,
   122, 126, 131, 139, 151
Godwin, Lucy C., 10
Godwin, Mabel, 8
Godwin, Maggie A., 14
Godwin, Mamie L., 5, 18
Godwin, Margaret, 40
Godwin, Margaret B., 10
Godwin, Margret L., 12
Godwin, Margret P., 4, 27, 36, 193
Godwin, Marion, 7, 29, 40
Godwin, Marius I., 11
Godwin, Martha, 3, 7, 10, 12, 17,
   19, 20, 22, 115
Godwin, Martha E., 13
Godwin, Martha J., 7, 17, 112
Godwin, Martha L., 19
Godwin, Martha R., 112, 115, 119,
   124
Godwin, Martial, 184
Godwin, Mary, 13
Godwin, Mary Ann, 4, 27, 40, 193
Godwin, Mary E., 17, 19
Godwin, Mary S., 14
Godwin, Mattie B., 5, 18
Godwin, Maud E., 11
Godwin, May Dell, 47, 56, 62, 83,
   143
Godwin, Mets, 11
Godwin, Minerva J., 19
Godwin, M. Alba Tiana, 44, 47, 55,
   62, 66, 143
Godwin, Nancy E., 4, 27, 34, 193
Godwin, Nollie H., 44, 59, 60, 61,
   62, 63, 66, 69, 77, 80, 83, 86,
   136
Godwin, Orilla C., 45, 188
Godwin, Pennie, 2, 3, 4, 22, 192
Godwin, Pleasant M., 4, 27, 28, 193
Godwin, Rena E., 45, 188
Godwin, Riley A., 47, 56, 62, 63,
   80, 81, 82, 143
Godwin, Riley M., 45, 46, 47, 188
Godwin, Robert P., 5, 18
Godwin, Ruby C., 14
Godwin, Rue M., 11
Godwin, Ruth G., 47, 55, 62, 72,
   80, 143
Godwin, Samuel A., 7

Godwin, Samuel H., 13, 17
Godwin, Samuel L., 9, 14
Godwin, Sarah C., 13
Godwin, Sarah D., 12
Godwin, Sarah E., 7, 9, 14
Godwin, Shannon M., 82
Godwin, Silvey, 1
Godwin, Susanne J., 12, 14
Godwin, Thomas, 2
Godwin, Thelma, 8
Godwin, Tim, 18
Godwin, Wilbur T., 10
Godwin, Wilie, 2
Godwin, William, 2
Godwin, William F., 7, 9
Godwin, William J., 8
Godwin, Willie, 14
Godwin, Willie F., 11
Godwin, Willis E., 10
Godwin, Willis L., 11
Godwin, Yvonne, 63, 81, 82
Goering, Susan G., 149
Goolsby, Ben R., 14
Goolsby, Delia, 14
Goolsby, Effie Lee, 14
Goolsby, James T., 14
Goolsby, Josie, 14
Goolsby, Mattie, 14
Goolsby, Modenia, 14
Goolsby, Nando, 14
Goolsby, Ophelia, 14
Goolsby, William D., 14
Goolsby, William H., 14
Goudy, Alice P., 8
Goudy, Bertie, 5
Goudy, Bruce, 5
Goudy, Claud, 5
Goudy, Ernest, 5
Goudy, H. D., 5
Goudy, Joe A., 5
Goudy, Leona, 5
Goudy, Lester, 5
Goudy, Rayburn, 5
Goudy, Roy, 5
Goudy, R. V., 5
Graham, Joseph, 98, 100, 103, 104
Graham, Maude, 182
Graham, Sarah, 103, 104
Grant, Louise, 31
Grantham, Louisa, 209
Grantham, Thomas, 209
Gray, Joyce P., 194
Gray, Maggie A., 165
Gray, Nellie E., 215
Green, Anna Jo, 161
Green, Arola, 18
Green, Edward, 1
Green, Polly, 1, 2, 3, 4, 6, 22,
   25, 193
Greer, Ruby, 67
Gregory, Howard, 149
Gregory, Staci, 149
Gresham, Lutie, 181, 182, 183, 184
Gresham, Harris J., 182
Griffin, Daniel, 101
Griffin, Thomas, 92, 100, 101, 103,
   104, 107

Griffin, Mary, 104
Griffin, William, 94
Grimsley, Herbert K., Jr., 130
Grimsley, Herbert K., Sr., 130
Grimsley, Howard J., 130
Grimsley, William K., 130
Groves, Eddie, 119
Groves, Essie, 121
Groves, Herbert, 119
Groves, Jimmie, 121
Groves, J. Iris, 119, 121
Groves, Luther, 121
Groves, Matt, 121
Groves, Mollie, 119
Groves, Olga, 119
Groves, Sicily, 119
Groves, Willie, 119
Guinn, Elizabeth, 176
Gulley, Valesta H., 136
Gunn, Herman, 18
Gunter, Claburn C., 160
Gunter, Claburn L., 161
Gunter, Claburn S., 161
Gunter, Jo Ann, 162
Gunter, John L., 161
Gunter, Lela M., 162
Gunter, Lisa G., 162
Gunter, Lexie F., 161
Gunter, M. Burdell, 161
Gunter, Minnie, 116, 151, 152, 161,
   162
Gunter, Peggy, 161

Haglestein, Van, 181
Hale, Pearl, 31
Hall, Erma Dean
Hall, Mary S., 193
Hamilton, ___, 11, 221
Hammond, Dee, 38
Hammond, Frances, 38
Hammond, Gary, 38
Hammond, Jean, 38
Hammond, Jo Nell, 38
Hammond, Johnny W., 38
Hampton, Fred, 181
Hampton, Hallie, 182
Hampton, Hazel, 182
Hampton, Herman, 182
Hampton, Jessie, 181
Hampton, Laurene, 182
Hampton, Lucille, 182
Hampton, Luther, 181, 182
Hampton, Maurine, 182
Hampton, Nell, 182
Hampton, Robert, 182
Hampton, Tom, 181
Hamrick, Jackie, 52
Hanes, Ruth, 11
Haralson, Alicia, 86
Haralson, Billy, 86
Haralson, Brian, 86
Haralson, Diana, 86
Hardin, Edwina, 5
Hardwick, Alta B., 38
Hardwick, Noma Lee, 38
Hardwick, Roscoe, 38
Harle, Baldwin, 90, 95, 98, 105

Pitcher, Lee A., 122
Plunk, Drobert P., 108
Polvado, Geraldine, 73
Porter, Lucy, 136
Posey, J. B., 180
Posey, Miles, 180
Posey, Nora, 180
Posey, Penn, 180
Posey, Robert, 180
Powers, Sarah A., 139
Pratt, J. J., 174
Prestien, Clinton L., 133
Prestien, Dolores J., 133
Prestien, Larry H., 133
Prestien, Leo Charles, 133
Prewitt, Don, 148, 149
Prewitt, Edith, 148
Prewitt, James Cal, 150
Prewitt, Jill, 148
Prewitt, Jo Don, 149
Prewitt, Vonda J., 150
Price, Albert R., 53, 54
Price, Bill, 53
Price, Clayton R., 54
Price, Darren D., 54
Price, Gina M., 54
Price, Glen D., 53, 54
Price, Mary, 52
Price, Ricky G., 54
Price, Velma, 53
Price, Willie A., 52
Price, Willie A., Sr., 52
Pritchet, Charles, 223
Pritchet, Polly, 223

Raffi, Mehdi, 76
Rammer, Marjorie, 80
Randles, Ed, 30
Randles, Nola, 30
Randolph, B. R., 108, 113
Ratliff, Chloe J., 129
Ratliff, William P., 129
Ray, Eugene, 8
Reaves, Homer, 18
Reed, Virgil, 32
Reeves, Annie R., 6
Reeves, Harold, 6
Reeves, J. Oscar, 6
Reeves, Mary R., 6
Reeves, Oscar P., 6
Renick, A. E., 14
Renick, Annie R., 14
Rhodes, Catherine, 171, 188
Richardson, Billie H., 39
Richardson, Karen, 39
Richardson, Linda, 39
Richey, Jessie, 166
Rigby, Henry W., 189
Riley, John B., 6
Riley, William R., 6
Ritchie, Sarah E., 31
Roberson, Jessie, 123
Roberts, Alvin E., 49
Roberts, A. R., 49
Roberts, Darla D., 50
Roberts, Debbie L., 51, 52
Roberts, Effie Mae, 47, 48, 49, 51
Roberts, E. H., 188

Roberts, Ely H., 48, 49, 51
Roberts, Erma Lois, 45, 51
Roberts, James A., 52
Roberts, Jeremiah, 31
Roberts, John A., 49, 51
Roberts, Lohn L., 51, 52
Roberts, Kevin H., 52
Roberts, Leonard A., 48, 59, 50
Roberts, Leonard D., 50
Roberts, Mayme O., 48
Roberts, Michael K., 52
Roberts, Patricia A., 51, 52
Roberts, Ruby M., 49
Roberts, Tony H., 52
Robertson, James, 100
Robbins, Freddie, 18
Robbins, Minnie, 18
Robbins, Pearl, 18
Rodgers, George, 104
Rodgers, Siotha P., 10
Rogers, Dolly, 214
Rogers, Eliza, 213, 216, 217
Rogers, Hiram, 214
Rogers, Jane, 214
Rogers, John, Jr., 214
Rogers, Jessie, 214
Rogers, Mary E., 214
Rogers, Michael, 214
Rogers, Sarah, 214, 215
Roman, Gertrude, 147, 149
Roman, Jacob H., 149
Rooker, Henry A., 14
Rose, John, 215
Rose, J. W., 215
Rose, Mary M., 215
Ross, Andra, 65, 66
Ross, Bennie Ray, 64, 65, 66, 76
Ross, Charles L., 158
Ross, Clifton G., 158
Ross, Dan L., 64
Ross, Day Alva, 163, 166
Ross, Edward D., 164
Ross, Glenna Mae, 65, 66
Ross, Joe C., 65, 66
Ross, Lisa A., 66
Ross, Mamie L., 158
Ross, Nancy S., 164
Ross, Rowe A., 164
Ross, Rowe L., 164
Ross, Rufus J., 64, 65
Ross, Shawna A., 158
Ross, Violin, 64
Rowland, Cavinor V., 14
Rugley, Fannie, 56
Rushing, Catherine, 134
Rushing, Mary E., 17
Russel, Nellie, 39
Rust, Crystal A., 160
Rust, Bobby E., 159
Rust, James R., 160
Rust, Willie B., 159

Sain, Enoch, 209
Sain, Tommie S., 215
Salomonsky, Anita L., 76, 77
Salomonsky, Anita Louise, 76
Salomonsky, Benjiman L., 76
Salomonsky, Daniel H., 76

242

Smith, Charlie W., 66
Smith, Christina, 185
Smith, Chronco, 185
Smith, Clarice, 182
Smith, Daniel, 170, 171, 188
Smith, Donald, 182
Smith, Dorcas, 171
Smith, Doris, 185
Smith, Edward, 80
Smith, Edwin J., 181, 183
Smith, Edwin J., Jr., 183
Smith, Edwin J., Sr., 183
Smith, Elias M., 176, 178, 179,
    180, 188
Smith, Elijah, 171
Smith, Elizabeth, 170, 171, 173,
    174, 176, 188
Smith, Elmo, 35
Smith, Eloise, 181
Smith, Enoch, 41, 42, 172, 174,
    176, 177, 178, 180, 184, 186,
    187, 188
Smith, Enoch V., 185
Smith, Erzula M., 135
Smith, Eva N., 184, 185
Smith, E. V., Jr., 185
Smith, Ferrel, 185
Smith, Fleming, 170, 171, 188
Smith, Floreno, 185
Smith, Flossie, 185
Smith, Franklin, 171
Smith, Freda, 185
Smith, Handcock, 170
Smith, Hannah, 188
Smith, Hoyt, 185
Smith, Ida, 181
Smith, Irene, 181, 185
Smith, James, 167, 168, 170, 171,
    172, 173, 174, 175, 176, 188
Smith, James E., 68
Smith, James Elb., 180
Smith, Jane, 42, 176, 177
Smith, J. C., 185
Smith, Jay C., 185
Smith, Jennie, 5
Smith, Jerry R., 67, 68
Smith, Jesse M., 185
Smith, Joe E., 69
Smith, John, 167, 168, 170, 171,
    188
Smith, John F., 42, 171, 174, 176,
    180, 181, 182, 184, 188
Smith, Joy, 185
Smith, Joyce, 185
Smith, J. T., 182, 186, 187
Smith, Julia A., 176, 186, 188
Smith, Junelle, 185
Smith, Lafern, 185
Smith, Lathio, 163
Smith, Laura J., 181
Smith, Laurie A., 74
Smith, Lela B., 185
Smith, Leola, 185
Smith, Lincoln, 73
Smith, Liva A., 39, 41, 42, 43,
    45, 47, 52, 127, 176, 187, 188
Smith, Lloyd D., 73

Smith, Lois, 184
Smith, Lois N., 185
Smith, Lowell, 185
Smith, Mabel C., 181, 182
Smith, Mack, 182
Smith, Madeline, 181, 184
Smith, Manda, 186
Smith, Marguerite, 69
Smith, Marianne, 69
Smith, Mark G., 183
Smith, Marshall H., 185
Smith, Martha, 171, 172, 173, 175
Smith, Martha L., 182
Smith, Mary, 171, 188
Smith, Mary C., 176, 187, 188
Smith, Maude A., 185
Smith, Miles G., 176, 180, 188
Smith, Millie J., 180
Smith, Moses, 171
Smith, Mozello, 185
Smith, Myra W., 35
Smith, Newton E., 176, 184, 185,
    186, 188
Smith, Noreta J., 68, 69
Smith, Norman, 185
Smith, Olive, 7
Smith, Ollie E., 182
Smith, Oscar F., 182
Smith, Patti Sue, 74
Smith, Paul E., 69
Smith, Peggy J., 63, 67, 68
Smith, Peter, Jr., 167, 168, 170,
    171, 188
Smith, Peter, Sr., 167, 168, 169,
    188
Smith, Priscilla, 173, 174, 188
Smith, Rachel A., 171
Smith, Rhoda A., 176, 185, 187, 188
Smith, Richard R., 184
Smith, Robert T., 181, 184
Smith, Rosa E., 180
Smith, Rosa M., 182
Smith, Roy, Jr., 185
Smith, Roy M., 185
Smith, Ruth, 181
Smith, Sadie R., 185
Smith, Samuel, 171
Smith, Samuel L., 184
Smith, Sanford, 171
Smith, Sarah, 171, 188
Smith, Sarah E., 176, 180, 188
Smith, Sidney A., 180
Smith, Steven E., 69
Smith, Susan A., 184
Smith, Susanna, 171
Smith, Talulah A., 181
Smith, Thomas, 167, 168, 169, 170,
    171, 188
Smith, Thomas W., 171
Smith, Tiana, 63, 67
Smith, Vivian, 185
Smith, Walter L., 182
Smith, William, 167, 168, 169, 170,
    171, 172, 188
Smith, Maj. Wm., 173
Smith, William E., 180
Smith, Willis E., 182

245

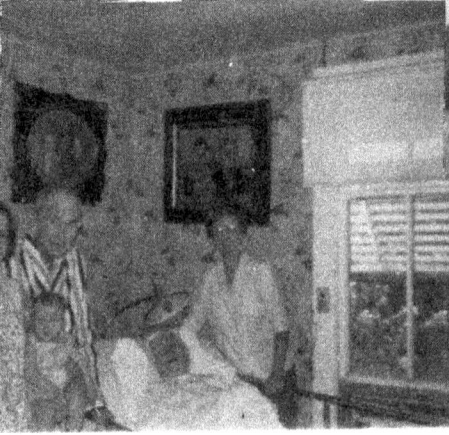

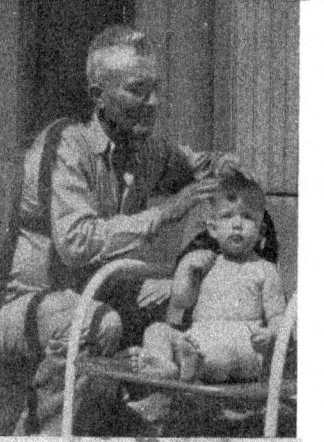

www.ingramcontent.com/pod-product-compliance
Lightning Source LLC
Chambersburg PA
CBHW071956260326
41914CB00004B/817